Wiley Study Guide for 2018 Level I CFA Exam

Volume 5: Fixed Income, Derivatives, & Alternative Investments

Thousands of candidates from more than 100 countries have relied on these Study Guides to pass the CFA® Exam. Covering every Learning Outcome Statement (LOS) on the exam, these review materials are an invaluable tool for anyone who wants a deep-dive review of all the concepts, formulas, and topics required to pass.

Wiley study materials are produced by expert CFA charterholders, CFA Institute members, and investment professionals from around the globe. For more information, contact us at info@efficientlearning.com.

Wiley Study Guide for 2018 Level I CFA Exam

Volume 5: Fixed Income, Derivatives, & Alternative Investments

WILEY

Contents

About the Authors   vii

Study Session 15: Fixed Income: Basic Concepts

Reading 50: Fixed Income Securities: Defining Elements   3
    Lesson 1: Overview of a Fixed-Income Security   3
    Lesson 2: Legal, Regulatory, and Tax Considerations   11
    Lesson 3: Structure of a Bond's Cash Flows   12
    Lesson 4: Bonds with Contingency Provisions   18

Reading 51: Fixed-Income Markets: Issuance, Trading, and Funding   25
    Lesson 1: Overview of Global Fixed-Income Markets   25
    Lesson 2: Primary and Secondary Bond Markets   27
    Lesson 3: Types of Instruments   29
    Lesson 4: Short-Term Funding Alternatives Available to Banks   35

Reading 52: Introduction to Fixed-Income Valuation   39
    Lesson 1: Bond Prices and the Time Value of Money   39
    Lesson 2: Prices and Yields (Part I): Conventions for Quotes and Calculations   45
    Lesson 3: Prices and Yields (Part II): Matrix Pricing and Yield Measures for Bonds   51
    Lesson 4: Prices and Yields (Part III): The Maturity Structure of Interest Rates
        and Calculating Spot Rates and Forward Rates   63
    Lesson 5: Yield Spreads   70

Reading 53: Introduction to Asset-Backed Securities   73
    Lesson 1: Introduction, the Benefits of Securitization, and the Securitization Process   73
    Lesson 2: Residential Mortgage Loans and Residential Mortgage-Backed
        Securities (RMBS)   77
    Lesson 3: Commercial Mortgage-Backed Securities (CMBS) and Non-Mortgage
        Asset-Backed Securities (ABS)   93
    Lesson 4: Collateralized Debt Obligations (CDOs)   96

Study Session 16: Fixed Income: Analysis of Risk

Reading 54: Understanding Fixed-Income Risk and Return   103
    Lesson 1: Sources of Risk   103
    Lesson 2: Interest Rate Risk on Fixed-Rate Bonds   109
    Lesson 3: Yield Volatility, Interest Rate Risk and the Investment Horizon,
        and Credit and Liquidity Risk   130

Reading 55: Fundamentals of Credit Analysis   135
     Lesson 1: Credit Risk, Capital Structure, Seniority Ranking, and Recovery Rates   135
     Lesson 2: Rating Agencies, Credit Ratings, and Their Role in Debt Markets   138
     Lesson 3: Traditional Credit Analysis   140
     Lesson 4: Credit Risk versus Return: Yields and Spreads   147
     Lesson 5: Special Considerations of High-Yield, Sovereign, and Municipal Credit Analysis   149

Study Session 17: Derivatives

Reading 56: Derivative Markets and Instruments   157
     Lesson 1: Dervative Markets, Forward Commitments, and Contingent Claims   157
     Lesson 2: Benefits and Criticisms of Derivatives, and Arbitrage   160

Reading 57: Basics of Derivative Pricing and Valuation   163
     Lesson 1: Fundamental Concepts and Price versus Value   163
     Lesson 2: Forward Contracts   167
     Lesson 3: Futures Contracts   178
     Lesson 4: Swap Contracts   182
     Lesson 5: Option Contracts Part 1: European Option Pricing   187
     Lesson 6: Option Contracts Part 2: Binomial Option Pricing   204
     Lesson 7: Option Contracts Part 3: American Option Pricing   211

Study Session 18 Alternative Investments

Reading 58: Introduction to Alternative Investments   217
     Lesson 1: The Basics of Alternative Investments   217
     Lesson 2: Major Types of Alternative Investments, Part I: Hedge Funds   222
     Lesson 3: Major Types of Alternative Investments, Part II: Private Equity   229
     Lesson 4: Major Types of Alternative Investments, Part III: Real Estate, Infrastructure, and Commodities   235
     Lesson 5: Risk Management   245

ABOUT THE AUTHORS

Wiley's Study Guides are written by a team of highly qualified CFA charterholders and leading CFA instructors from around the globe. Our team of CFA experts work collaboratively to produce the best study materials for CFA candidates available today.

Wiley's expert team of contributing authors and instructors is led by Content Director Basit Shajani, CFA. Basit founded online education start-up Élan Guides in 2009 to help address CFA candidates' need for better study materials. As lead writer, lecturer, and curriculum developer, Basit's unique ability to break down complex topics helped the company grow organically to be a leading global provider of CFA Exam prep materials. In January 2014, Élan Guides was acquired by John Wiley & Sons, Inc., where Basit continues his work as Director of CFA Content. Basit graduated magna cum laude from the Wharton School of Business at the University of Pennsylvania with majors in finance and legal studies. He went on to obtain his CFA charter in 2006, passing all three levels on the first attempt. Prior to Élan Guides, Basit ran his own private wealth management business. He is a past president of the Pakistani CFA Society.

There are many more expert CFA charterholders who contribute to the creation of Wiley materials. We are thankful for their invaluable expertise and diligent work. To learn more about Wiley's team of subject matter experts, please visit: www.efficientlearning.com/cfa/why-wiley/.

READING 50: FIXED-INCOME SECURITIES: DEFINING ELEMENTS

LESSON 1: OVERVIEW OF A FIXED-INCOME SECURITY

Before you get into this reading, you should recognize the following relationships that will facilitate your understanding of the material. These relationships are discussed at great length in later readings:

- The higher (lower) the coupon rate on a bond, the higher (lower) its price.
- An increase (decrease) in interest rates or the required yield on a bond will lead to a decrease (increase) in price (i.e., bond prices and yields are inversely related).
- The more risky the bond, the higher the yield required by investors to purchase the bond, and the lower the bond's price.

LOS 50a: Describe basic features of a fixed-income security. Vol 5, pp 298–304

BASIC FEATURES OF A BOND

The important fixed-income security elements that we describe in this section include:

- The issuer of the bond.
- The maturity of the bond.
- The par value of the bond.
- The coupon rate offered on the bond and coupon payment frequency.
- The currency in which bond payments will be made to investors.

Note that in this section, we focus on "traditional" or nonsecuritized bonds.

Issuer

Bond issuers can be classified based on their characteristics. Major types of issuers include:

- Supranational organizations (e.g., the World Bank and the International Monetary Fund).
- Sovereign (national) governments (e.g., the United States).
- Nonsovereign (local) governments (e.g., the state of Pennsylvania in the United States).
- Quasi-government entities, agencies owned or sponsored by governments (e.g., the postal services in many countries such as La Poste in France).
- Companies or corporate issuers, which include financial issuers (e.g., banks) and nonfinancial issuers (e.g., pharmaceuticals).

Bond issuers can also be classified based on their creditworthiness as judged by credit rating agencies. Bonds can broadly be categorized as investment-grade or noninvestment grade (or high-yield or speculative) bonds.

> Securitized bonds are created by moving some assets (e.g., residential and commercial mortgages, automobile loans, student loans, and credit card loans) into a special legal entity, which then uses those assets to guarantee a bond issue. We discuss such bonds later in the reading.

> We learn more about rating agencies, credit ratings, and classification of issuers based on their credit ratings in a later reading.

Maturity

The maturity date of a bond refers to the date on which the issuer has promised to repay the entire outstanding principal on the bond. A somewhat similar (sounding) concept is the term to maturity or the tenor of the bond, which refers to the period of time remaining until the bond's maturity date.

- Fixed-income securities which, at the time of issuance, are expected to mature in 1 year or less are known as money market securities (e.g., commercial paper and certificates of deposits, CDs).
- Fixed-income securities which, at the time of issuance, are expected to mature in more than 1 year are referred to as capital market securities.
- Fixed-income securities which have no stated maturity are known as perpetual bonds (e.g., consols issued by the U.K. government).

Par Value

The par value (also known as face value, nominal value, redemption value, and maturity value) of a bond refers to the principal amount that the issuer promises to repay bondholders on the maturity date. Bond prices are usually quoted as a percentage of their par value. For example, given that a bond's par value is $1,000, a quote of 90 implies that the bond's current price is $900 (= 90% × $1,000).

- When a bond's price is above 100% of par, it is said to be trading at a premium.
- When a bond's price is at 100% of par, it is said to be trading at par.
- When a bond's price is below 100% of par, it is said to be trading at a discount.

Coupon Rate and Frequency

The coupon rate (also known as the nominal rate) of a bond refers to the annual interest rate that the issuer promises to pay bondholders until the bond matures. The amount of interest paid each year by the issuer is known as the coupon, and is calculated by multiplying the coupon rate by the bond's par value. For example, given a coupon rate of 3% for a bond with a par value of $1,000, the annual interest paid by the issuer will be $30 (= 3% × $1,000). Note that the bond indenture may call for coupon payments annually, semi-annually, quarterly, or monthly. So continuing with the previous example, if it were a semiannual-pay bond, the issuer would make $15 coupon payments every 6 months during the bond's term.

We will describe several other coupon structures, including variable coupon rates, later in the reading.

Note that some bonds do not make any interest payments until maturity. These zero-coupon (or pure discount) bonds are issued at a discount to par value and redeemed at par (the issuer pays the entire par amount to investors at the maturity date). The difference between the (discounted) purchase price and the par value is effectively the interest on the loan.

Currency Denomination

Bonds are issued in many different currencies around the world. Bonds aimed solely at a country's domestic investors are most likely to be issued in the local currency, but if an issue aims to attract global investors, it is likely to be denominated in U.S. dollars or euros to make them more attractive for investors (especially if the local currency is relatively volatile and/or illiquid).

- Dual-currency bonds make coupon payments in one currency and the principal payment at maturity in another currency.
- Currency option bonds give bondholders a choice regarding which of the two currencies they would like to receive interest and principal payments in.

Yield Measures

Market participants use several different yield measures to describe a bond.

- The current yield or running yield equals the bond's annual coupon amount divided by its current price (not par value), expressed as a percentage.
    - For example, the current yield of a $1,000 par bond with a coupon rate of 5% and a current price of $980 equals 5.102% [= (50/980) × 100].
- The yield-to-maturity (YTM) is also known as the yield-to-redemption or the redemption yield. It is calculated as the discount rate that equates the present value of a bond's expected future cash flows until maturity to its current price.
    - Essentially, the YTM represents the internal rate of return on the bond's expected cash flows. Stated differently, the YTM represents the annual return that an investor will earn on a bond if (1) she purchases it today (for its current price), (2) holds it until maturity, and (3) reinvests all interim cash flows at the stated YTM.
    - All else being equal, a bond's yield-to-maturity is inversely related to its price.
        - Given a set of expected future cash flows, the lower (higher) the YTM or discount rate, the higher (lower) the bond's current price.

> The yield-to-maturity and several other important yield measures are discussed at length in a later reading.

LOS 50b: Describe content of a bond indenture. Vol 5, pp 305–313

The Bond Indenture

A bond is a contractual agreement between the issuer and the bondholder. The trust deed is the legal contract that describes the form of the bond, obligations of the issuer, and the rights of bondholders, and it is commonly referred to as the bond indenture. The indenture captures the following information:

- The name of the issuer.
- The principal value of the bond.
- The coupon rate.
- Dates when the interest payments will be made.
- The maturity date.
- Funding sources for the interest payments and principal repayments.
- Collaterals (i.e., assets or financial guarantees underlying the debt obligation above and beyond the issuer's promise to pay).

- Covenants (i.e., actions that the issuer is obligated to perform or prohibited from performing).
- Credit enhancements (i.e., provisions designed to reduce the bond's credit risk).

Since there are (typically) a large number of bondholders, the issuer does not get into a direct agreement with each one of them. Instead, the indenture is held by a trustee who, although appointed by the issuer, owes a fiduciary duty to bondholders. The trustee is primarily responsible for ensuring that the issuer complies with the obligations specified in the bond indenture. Further, in the event of a default, the trustee is responsible for calling meetings of bondholders to determine an appropriate course of action, and may also bring legal action against the issuer on behalf of bondholders.

Before deciding to invest in a particular bond instrument, investors should review the following areas.

Legal Identity of the Bond Issuer and its Legal Form

The bond indenture identifies the party that is obligated to make principal and interest payments by its legal name.

- For sovereign bonds, the legal issuer is typically the institution responsible for managing the national budget (e.g., Her Majesty's Treasury in the U.K.).
  - Note that the legal issuer may be different from the body that actually manages the bond issue process (e.g., the U.K. Debt Management Office, which is an agency of Her Majesty's Treasury).
- Corporate bonds are typically issued by the corporate legal entity (e.g., Volkswagen AG).
  - Note that bonds may be issued by the parent company or a subsidiary.
    - If issued by a subsidiary, investors must focus on the creditworthiness of the subsidiary, unless the bond is guaranteed by the parent. Oftentimes, subsidiaries carry a lower credit rating than the parent.
  - If issued by the parent company, it becomes important to analyze the assets actually held by the parent, as investors may not have recourse to assets held by subsidiaries or operating companies.
    - If bonds are issued by a parent or holding company that has no or very few assets to call in the event of default, investors face higher credit risk than if bonds were issued by one of the operating companies or subsidiaries in the group that actually hold callable assets.
- In case of securitized bonds, a separate legal entity is created (referred to as a Special Purpose Entity or SPE in the United States and Special Purpose Vehicle or SPV in Europe), and it is this entity that is obligated to repay bondholders. What happens is that the originator of the loans (also known as the sponsor or seller of financial assets) sells the assets (loans it has issued) to the SPE, which issues bonds (backed by those assets) to investors to come up with the funds to purchase the assets from the sponsor. The SPE's assets are the **loans** that it has bought from the sponsor, and its liabilities are the **bonds** it has sold to investors. The SPE uses the cash generated from the loans that it holds to service debt obligations owed to investors. This entire process is known as a securitization.

SPEs are bankruptcy-remote vehicles in that once the assets (loans) have been securitized (transferred to the SPE), the sponsor no longer has any ownership rights on them. Therefore, if the sponsor declares bankruptcy, its creditors have no claim on the securitized assets or their proceeds, and the SPE is able to continue to make interest and principal payments to investors using funds generated from the assets.

Source of Repayment Proceeds

The bond indenture also (usually) specifies how the issuer plans to make debt service payments (interest and principal).

- Bonds issued by supranational organizations are usually repaid through (1) proceeds from repayments of previous loans made by the organization or (2) paid-in capital from its members.
  - In some instances, national governments may guarantee certain issues.
  - Supranational organizations can generally also call on members to provide funds to repay loans.
- Sovereign bonds are backed by the "full faith and credit" of the national government.
  - Sovereign bonds issued in local currency are usually considered safer than those issued in a foreign currency, as governments have the power to raise taxes and print local currency to repay local-currency denominated loans. As a result, yields on sovereign bonds are usually lower compared to other local issuers.
- Nonsovereign government debt can usually be repaid through the following sources:
  - The general taxing authority of the issuer.
  - Cash flows from the project that the bonds were issued to finance.
  - Special taxes or fees specifically set up to make interest and principal payments.
- Corporate bond issuers typically rely on their cash flow-generating ability to repay bonds, which in turn depends on their financial strength and integrity.
  - Corporate bonds typically entail a higher level of credit risk than sovereign bonds, and therefore carry a higher yield.
- For securitized bonds, repayment depends on the cash flow generated by the underlying pool of financial assets.
  - Examples of financial assets that are usually securitized include residential and commercial mortgages, automobile loans, student loans, and credit card receivables.

> Printing local currency typically does not help repay foreign currency sovereign debt as the increase in local currency supply leads to depreciation of the local currency.

> Securitized bonds generally differ from corporate bonds in that they are amortizing loans (i.e., the principal amount is gradually repaid during the term of the loan instead of in one lump sum payment at maturity). We will describe amortizing bonds in detail later in the reading.

Asset or Collateral Backing

Assets pledged as collateral and financial guarantees secure a bond issue beyond the issuer's simple promise to pay. While they serve to reduce credit risk, it is important for investors to consider (1) how the specific bonds they own rank in the priority of claims in the event of default and (2) the quality of the collateral backing the bond issue.

- **Seniority ranking:** Secured bonds are backed by assets or financial guarantees to ensure debt repayment in case of default, while unsecured bonds are not protected by a pledge of any specific assets (i.e., they only have a general claim on the issuer's assets and cash flows).
  - In the event of default, unsecured bonds are repaid after secured bonds have been paid off, which makes unsecured bonds more risky, entailing a higher yield.
  - Within the general class of secured bonds, different issues have a different seniority ranking, which dictates the order of payment to secured bondholders in case of bankruptcy.
    - Senior secured debt is paid off before subordinated or junior secured debt.
  - Debentures in the U.S. are an unsecured loan certificate backed by a company's general credit. Elsewhere, debentures typically describe long-term debt securities secured by assets and paying a fixed rate of interest. Investors should review the indenture for specifics.
- **Types of collateral backing:** Bonds can also be classified based on the type of collateral.
  - Collateral trust bonds are secured by securities such as common stock, other bonds, or other financial assets.
  - Equipment trust certificates are secured by specific types of equipment or physical assets (e.g., aircraft, railroad cars, or oil rigs).
    - They are usually issued to take advantage of the tax benefits of leasing.
  - Mortgage-backed securities (MBS) are backed by a pool of mortgage loans. Cash flows generated by the pool are used to make payments on MBS.
  - Covered bonds are backed by a segregated pool of assets (known as the cover pool). One of the things that differentiates them from securitized bonds (such as MBS) is that the assets backing these bonds are still on the sponsor's balance sheet (i.e., they are not transferred to an SPE). As a result, if the sponsor defaults on covered bonds, investors have recourse to both (1) the assets held by the sponsor and (2) the cover pool. (Recall that for securitized bonds, investors only have recourse to the pool of assets, not the assets of the sponsor.) Further, if assets in the cover pool fail to generate adequate cash flow (i.e., they become nonperforming), the issuer is required to replace them with performing assets. As a result, covered bonds entail less risk and therefore offer a lower yield than securitized bonds.

Credit Enhancements

Credit enhancements are provisions that serve to reduce the credit risk of a bond issue, resulting in a lower yield.

- Internal credit enhancement focuses on the structure of the issue regarding priority of payment or the value of collateral. It includes:
  - Subordination: This refers to the allocation of cash flows among the various bond classes or tranches based on their seniority. Basically, the subordinate and junior tranches provide credit protection to the senior tranche, so in the event of default the senior tranche (the one with the highest level of seniority) has the first claim on available cash flows, and only once senior bonds have been paid off do subordinate bonds (and then junior bonds) get repaid. This type of protection is also referred to as a waterfall structure—proceeds from liquidating assets are first allocated to the more senior tranches, while losses are allocated bottom-up with the most senior tranche typically insulated from credit losses unless the total amount of loss exceeds the par amount of subordinated and junior tranches combined.
  - Overcollateralization: This occurs when the value of the collateral posted to secure an issue exceeds the par value of the securities issued. The excess collateral can be used to absorb future losses. For example, a securitized issue with a total par value of $130 million would be overcollateralized by $20m if it is backed by $150 million worth of loans.
  - Excess spread (or excess interest cash flow): A transaction can be structured in a manner such that the cash flows generated from the collateral pool exceed the amount of interest payable to bondholders so that there is a cushion for making interest payments. This excess amount is known as the excess spread, and it is sometimes deposited into a reserve account to protect against future credit losses (by being used to retire principal). This process is known as turboing.
- External credit enhancement refers to guarantees received from a third-party guarantor. Types of external credit enhancement include:
  - Surety bonds (issued by an insurance company) and bank guarantees: In the event of default, both these forms of enhancement reimburse investors for losses (up to a pre-specified maximum amount known as the penal sum).
  - Letters of credit: These are lines of credit provided by a financial institution to the issuer to reimburse any shortfalls in the cash flow generated from the collateral pool.

Note that surety bonds, bank guarantees, and letters of credit all expose investors to third party credit risk (i.e., the risk that the gurantor will not be able to fulfill its obligations). This risk can be mitigated by setting up a cash collateral account, where the issuer immediately borrows the credit-enhancement amount and invests this sum in highly rated instruments. Since the cash is actually in the hands of the issuer, a downgrade of the guarantor will not necessarily affect the rating of the bond issue.

LOS 50c: Compare affirmative and negative covenants and identify examples of each. Vol 5, pp 310–311

Covenants

Covenants are legally enforceable rules agreed upon by the borrower/issuer and lenders/investors at the time of bond issuance.

- Affirmative covenants are **requirements** placed on the issuer. They are typically administrative in nature so they do not lead to additional costs for the issuer, nor do they significantly restrict the issuer's ability to make business decisions. Examples of affirmative covenants include promises to:
  - Make timely payments to bondholders.
  - Comply with all laws and regulations.
  - Maintain the issuer's current lines of business.
  - Insure and maintain assets.
  - Pay taxes.
- Negative covenants are **restrictions** placed on the issuer. While they entail more costs than affirmative covenants and can constrain the issuer in operating the business, they protect bondholders from dilution of their claims, asset withdrawals or substitutions, and inefficient investments by the issuer. Examples of negative covenants include:
  - Restrictions on issuing additional debt so that new debt can only be issued if it can be sustained by the issuer's financial condition.
  - Negative pledges that prevent the issuer from issuing bonds with a higher rank in the priority of claims than those held by existing bondholders.
  - Restrictions on prior claims that protect unsecured bondholders by preventing the issuer from collateralizing previously uncollateralized (or unencumbered) assets.
  - Restrictions on distributions to shareholders (e.g., dividends and share repurchases) to ensure that sufficient cash is available for debt-service going forward.
  - Restrictions on asset disposals that protect bondholders from a breakup of the company.
  - Restrictions on investments that prevent the issuer from making risky or speculative investments.
  - Restrictions on mergers and acquisitions that ensure that if the issuing company is sold, the surviving company or the acquirer takes responsibility for debt service payments.

Note that the aim of negative covenants is to protect bondholders by ensuring that the issuer does not take any action that may hinder its ability to satisfy debt obligations. Bondholders should refrain from being too specific or restrictive when it comes to covenants, as such provisions may force the issuer into default even when it is avoidable.

LESSON 2: LEGAL, REGULATORY, AND TAX CONSIDERATIONS

LOS 50d: Describe how legal, regulatory, and tax considerations affect the issuance and trading of fixed-income securities. Vol 5, pp 313–318

Legal and Regulatory Considerations

There are no unified legal or regulatory requirements that apply to bond investors globally, which makes it important for investors to be aware of where a particular fixed-income security is issued and where it is traded, as they determine which laws and regulations apply.

The global bond market consists of national bond markets and the Eurobond market. A national bond market includes all the bonds that are issued and traded in a particular country and denominated in that country's local currency.

- Bonds issued by entities that are incorporated in that country are known as domestic bonds.
  - For example, bonds issued by Google Inc. in U.S. dollars in the United States would be classified as domestic bonds.
- Bonds issued by entities that are incorporated in another country are known as foreign bonds.
  - For example, bonds issued Toyota Motor Company in U.S. dollars in the United States would be classified as foreign bonds. Foreign bonds often receive nicknames (e.g., these bonds issued by Toyota would be known as "Yankee" bonds [a nickname for foreign bonds in the United States]).

Note that national regulators may subject resident and nonresident issuers to different requirements regarding the issuance process, level of disclosures, or restrictions imposed on the bond issuer and/or the investors who can purchase the bonds.

Eurobonds are issued and traded in the Eurobond market. Eurobonds refer to bonds that are denominated in a currency other than the local currency where they are issued. They may be issued in any country and in any currency (including the issuer's domestic currency) and are named based on the currency in which they are denominated. For example, Eurobonds denominated in U.S. dollars are referred to as Eurodollar bonds, and Eurobonds denominated in Japanese yen are known as Euroyen bonds.

An example of a Eurobond is a U.S. dollars-denominated bond issued by Toyota Motor Company in Australia. This bond would be a Eurodollar bond (since it is denominated in U.S. dollars).

- Eurobonds are usually unsecured and are underwritten by an international syndicate.
- Generally speaking, they are less regulated than domestic and foreign bonds as they do not fall under the jurisdiction of any single country.
- Eurobonds are usually bearer bonds (i.e., no record of bond ownership is kept by the trustee). On the other hand, domestic and foreign bonds are usually registered bonds (the trustee maintains a record of bond ownership).

> Note that Eurodollar bonds cannot be sold to U.S. investors at issuance as they are not registered with the U.S. Securities and Exchange Commission (SEC). Therefore, Toyota can issue a Eurodollar bond in any country, but not in the United States.

Global bonds are bonds that are issued simultaneously (1) in the Eurobond market and (2) in at least one domestic bond market. Simultaneously issuing bonds in different markets ensures that there is sufficient demand for the issue, and that investors are able to participate in the issue regardless of their location.

> Foreign bonds, Eurobonds, and global bonds are often referred to as international bonds.

The differences between domestic bonds, foreign bonds, Eurobonds, and global bonds are important to investors as these different types of bonds are subject to different legal, regulatory, and tax (described in the next section) requirements. There are also differences in terms of frequency of interest payments and how interest payments are calculated, both of which influence the bond's cash flows and price. Bear in mind however, that the currency denomination has a bigger influence on a bond's price than where it is issued or traded. This is because a bond's price is influenced by interest rates, and interest rates are obviously linked to the currency in which the bond is denominated.

Tax Considerations

Interest income is generally taxed at the ordinary income tax rate, which is the same rate that an individual pays tax on her wage or salary. However, municipal bonds in the United Staes are often tax-exempt, in that interest income is often exempt from federal income tax and state income tax in the state of issue. Also note that the tax status of bond income depends on where it is issued and traded. For example, interest paid on some domestic bonds may be net of income tax, while some Eurobonds make gross interest payments.

Aside from interest income, investors in bonds may also generate capital gains from selling a bond prior to maturity. In most jurisdictions, capital gains are taxed at a lower rate than interest income. Further, some countries impose a lower capital gains tax on investments held over a longer time horizon than on those held for a shorter horizon. Some countries do not tax capital gains at all.

An additional tax consideration arises when it comes to bonds issued at a discount. The difference between the par value and the original issue price is known as the original issue discount. In some countries (including the United Staes), a prorated portion of the original issue discount must be included in interest income each year for tax purposes, and taxes must be paid at the rate applicable on interest income. In other countries (such as Japan) the original issue discount is taxed as a capital gain when the bond eventually matures.

Finally, in some jurisdictions, investors who have purchased bonds at a premium can either (1) deduct a prorated portion of the premium paid from taxable income each year until the bond matures, or (2) declare a capital loss when the bond is eventually redeemed at maturity.

LESSON 3: STRUCTURE OF A BOND'S CASH FLOWS

LOS 50e: Describe how cash flows of fixed-income securities are structured. Vol 5, pp 318–329

Principal Repayment Structures

How the bond issuer repays the amount borrowed is important to investors as it affects the level of credit risk faced by them. Credit risk is reduced if there are any provisions that call for periodic retirement of some of the principal amount outstanding during the term of the loan.

- A bullet bond is one that only makes periodic interest payments, with the entire principal amount paid back at maturity.

- An amortizing bond is one that makes periodic interest and principal payments over the term of the bond. A bond may be fully or partially amortized until maturity:
  - A fully amortized bond is one whose outstanding principal amount at maturity is reduced to zero through a fixed periodic payment schedule.
  - A partially amortized bond also makes fixed periodic principal repayments, but the principal is not fully repaid by the maturity date. Therefore, a balloon payment is required at maturity to repay the outstanding principal amount.

Exhibit 3-1 illustrates the payment schedules for a bullet bond, a fully amortized bond, and a partially amortized bond. All the bonds discussed here carry a par value of $1,000 and a coupon rate of 8%. They mature in 5 years and make annual coupon payments. The market interest rate has been assumed to be constant at 8%. Finally, the balloon payment at maturity for the partially amortized bond is assumed to be $200.

Exhibit 3-1: Payment Schedules for Bullet, Fully Amortized, and Partially Amortized Bonds

Bullet Bond

Year	Investor Cash Flows ($)	Interest Payment ($)	Principal Repayment ($)	Outstanding Principal at the End of the Year ($)
0	−1,000.00			1,000.00
1	80.00	80.00	0.00	1,000.00
2	80.00	80.00	0.00	1,000.00
3	80.00	80.00	0.00	1,000.00
4	80.00	80.00	0.00	1,000.00
5	1,080.00	80.00	1,000.00	0.00

- Coupon payment = 0.08 × 1,000 = $80
- Last payment = Coupon + Bullet par repayment = 80 + 1,000 = $1,080

Fully Amortized Bond

Year	Investor Cash Flows ($)	Interest Payment ($)	Principal Repayment ($)	Outstanding Principal at the End of the Year ($)
0	−1,000.00			1,000.00
1	250.46	80.00	170.46	829.54
2	250.46	66.36	184.09	645.45
3	250.46	51.64	198.82	446.63
4	250.46	35.73	214.73	231.90
5	250.46	18.55	231.90	0.00

- The annual payment is constant so it can be viewed as an annuity, and calculated as:
  - N = 5; PV = $1,000; I/Y = 8; FV = 0; CPT PMT; Annual PMT = $250.46
- Interest component of Year 2 payment = 0.08 × 829.54 = $66.36

- Principal repayment component of Year 2 payment = 250.46 – 66.36 = $184.10
- Notice that the annual payment is constant, but over time the interest payment decreases (as the outstanding principal amount decreases each year) and the principal repayment increases.

Partially Amortized Bond

Year	Investor Cash Flows ($)	Interest Payment ($)	Principal Repayment ($)	Outstanding Principal at the End of the Year ($)
0	−1,000.00			1,000.00
1	216.37	80.00	136.37	863.63
2	216.37	69.09	147.27	716.36
3	216.37	57.31	159.06	557.30
4	216.37	44.58	171.78	385.52
5	*416.37	30.84	385.52	0.00

*416.37 = 200 (balloon payment) + 216.37

The examples in this reading were created in Microsoft Excel. Numbers may differ from the results obtained using a calculator because of rounding.

- This bond can be viewed as a combination of (1) a 5-year annuity and (2) a balloon payment at maturity. The sum of the present values of these two elements is equal to the bond price of $1,000.
- The PV of bullet payment is calculated as:
  - N = 5; FV = $200; I/Y = 8; CPT PV; PV = $136.12
- Therefore, PV of 5-year annuity is calculated as:
  - 1,000 – 136.12 = $863.88
- The annuity payment can be calculated as:
  - N = 5; PV = $863.88; I/Y = 8; FV = 0; CPT PMT; Annual PMT = $216.37
- Interest component of Year 2 payment = 0.08 × 863.63 = $69.09
- Principal repayment component of Year 2 payment = 216.37 – 69.09 = $147.27
- Notice that the annual payment is constant, but over time the interest payment decreases and the principal repayment increases.
- Since the principal amount is not fully amortized, interest payments are higher for the partially amortized bond than for the fully amortized bond except for Year 1 (when they are equal).

Sinking Fund Arrangements

A sinking fund arrangement requires the issuer to repay a specified portion of the principal amount every year throughout the bond's life or after a specified date. For example, a $10 million issue with a term of 10 years could require the issuer to redeem bonds worth $2 million par each year starting Year 6 of the issue. Another variation of the sinking fund arrangement operates by requiring the issuer to repay a steadily increasing amount of the bond principal every year.

Callable bonds are discussed in detail later in the reading and in another reading. Reinvestment risk is discussed in detail in a later reading.

Sometimes a call provision may also be added to the bond issue. This call provision usually gives the issuer the option to repurchase bonds before maturity at the lowest of (1) market price, (2) par, and (3) a specified sinking fund price. The issuer is generally allowed to repurchase only a small portion of the bond issue, but it may sometimes make use of a doubling option (if available) to repurchase double the required number of bonds.

From the bondholders' perspective, the advantage of a sinking fund arrangement is that it reduces credit risk (principal is received over the bond's term as opposed to in a bullet payment at maturity). However, it entails two disadvantages. First, it results in reinvestment risk (i.e., the risk that investors will have to reinvest the redeemed principal at an interest rate lower than the current yield to maturity). Second, if the issue has an embedded call option, the issuer may be able to repurchase bonds at a price lower than the current market price, resulting in bondholders losing out.

Coupon Payment Structures

A coupon refers to the interest payment made by the issuer to the bondholder. Various coupon-payment structures are described below:

Floating-Rate Notes (FRN)

The coupon rate of a FRN has two components: a reference rate (such as LIBOR) plus a spread (also known as margin).

- The spread is typically fixed and expressed in basis points (bps). A basis point equals 0.01% so there are 100 bps in 1%. The spread on a FRN is determined at issuance and is based on the issuer's credit rating at issuance. The higher the issuer's creditworthiness, the lower the spread.
- The reference rate resets periodically based on market conditions. As the reference rate changes, the effective coupon rate on the FRN also changes.

Generally speaking, FRNs make coupon payments quarterly. So for example, consider a FRN that makes coupon payments based on 90-day LIBOR plus 20 bps (= LIBOR 90 + 0.20%). Generally speaking, current 3-month LIBOR (LIBOR-90) would be different at each coupon determination date, so this is how the coupon rate on a FRN resets periodically to reflect current market interest rates.

> Occasionally, the spread on a FRN may not be fixed, in which case the bond is known as a variable-rate note.

FRNs have less interest rate risk (i.e., the risk of bond price volatility resulting from changes in market interest rates) than fixed-rate bonds. This is because the coupon rate on a FRN is reset periodically and brought in line with current market interest rates (LIBOR). If market interest rates rise (fall), the periodic coupon on a FRN increases (decreases). Therefore, FRNs are preferred by investors who expect interest rates to increase. However, note that FRN investors still face credit risk. If there is a decline in the perceived credit quality of the issuer (such that the fixed spread no longer adequately compensates investors for credit risk), the price of the FRN will fall below par value.

FRNs may be structured to include a floor or a cap on the periodic coupon rate.

- A floor prevents the periodic coupon rate on the FRN from falling below a pre-specified minimum rate, so it benefits investors (when market interest rates fall).
- A cap prevents the periodic coupon rate on the FRN from rising above a pre-specified maximum rate, so it benefits the issuer (when market interest rates rise).

Note that a FRN may also be structured to have both a cap and a floor, in which, it is known as a collared FRN.

Finally, FRNs may also be structured such that the periodic coupon rate is inversely related to the reference rate (i.e., if the reference rate increases [decreases], the periodic coupon rate decreases [increases]). Such FRNs are known as reverse FRNs or inverse floaters and are preferred by investors who expect interest rates to decline.

Step-Up Coupon Bonds

A step-up coupon bond (which can be fixed or floating) is one where the periodic coupon rate increases by specified margins at specified dates. Typically, the step-up coupon structure is offered with callable bonds to protect bondholders in a rising interest rate environment. If interest rates rise, it becomes increasingly unlikely that the issuer will call the bond, so the step-up feature at least allows investors to benefit from higher coupons. On the other hand, when interest rates are stable or declining, the step-up feature incentivizes issuers to call the bonds before the coupon rate steps up (increases).

> Bear with me here. We will discuss the call feature embedded in callable bonds in detail later in the reading.

However, note that despite the step-up in coupons (and the consequent increase in interest expense), the issuer may not call the bond if refinancing is less advantageous. For example, the issuer would be reluctant to refinance using the proceeds of a new bond issue if its creditworthiness has declined, such that the coupon rate on the new issue would be higher than the stepped-up coupon on the original issue. Also note that although the issuer is not required to call the bond when the coupon rate on a step-up bond increases, there is an implicit expectation from investors that it will. Failure to call the bond may be viewed negatively by market participants.

Credit-Linked Coupon Bonds

The coupon rate on credit-linked coupon bonds changes when the bond's credit rating changes. For example, a bond's coupon rate may be structured to increase (decrease) by a specified margin for every credit rating downgrade (upgrade) below (above) the bond's credit rating at issuance.

Credit-linked coupon bonds protect investors against a decline in the credit quality, and are therefore attractive to investors who are concerned about the future creditworthiness of the issuer. They also provide some protection against poor economic conditions, as credit ratings tend to decline during recessions. Notice that a problem with credit-linked coupon bonds is that since a rating downgrade results in higher interest payments for the issuer, it can contribute to further downgrades or even an eventual default.

Payment-in-Kind (PIK) Coupon Bonds

PIK coupon bonds allow the issuer to pay interest in the form of additional bonds instead of cash. They are preferred by issuers that are financially distressed and fear liquidity and solvency problems in the future. Investors usually demand a higher yield on these bonds to compensate them for the higher credit risk and high leverage of the issuer.

One variation of PIK coupon arrangements allow issuers to make interest payments in the form of common shares worth the amount of coupon due. A PIK toggle note gives the issuer the option to pay interest in cash, in kind, or a combination of the two.

Deferred Coupon Bonds (or Split Coupon Bonds)

These bonds do not pay any coupon for the first few years after issuance, but then pay a higher coupon than they normally would for the remainder of their terms. Deferred coupon bonds are usually preferred by issuers who want to conserve cash in the short run, or for project financing where cash-generation will commence after an initial development phase.

Investors are attracted to deferred coupon bonds as they are usually priced significantly below par. Further, the deferred coupon structure may help investors manage their tax liability by delaying taxes due on interest income. Note that this tax advantage is only available in certain jurisdictions.

A zero-coupon bond can be viewed as an extreme form of a deferred coupon bond. Zero-coupon bonds do not make any interest payments until maturity and are issued at a deep discount to par. Essentially, all interest payments are deferred until maturity.

Index-Linked Bonds

These are bonds whose coupon payments and/or principal repayments are linked to a specified index (such as a commodity or equity index). An example of index-linked bonds are inflation-linked bonds (also known as linkers) whose coupon and/or principal payments are linked to an index of consumer prices (e.g., Treasury Inflation Protection Securities or TIPS issued by the U.S. Government are linked to the Consumer Price Index, CPI, in the United States). Investors are attracted to inflation-linked bonds because they offer a long-term asset with a fixed **real** return that is protected against inflation risk.

National governments issue the largest amounts of inflation-linked bonds (even though they are now increasingly being offered by corporate issuers). Sovereign inflation-linked bond issuers can be grouped into three categories:

1. Countries (such as Brazil and Chile) that issue inflation-linked bonds because they are experiencing high rates of inflation and linking payments to inflation was the only option available to ensure sufficient investor appetite for the issue.
2. Countries (such as Australia and Sweden) that issue inflation-linked bonds to add credibility to the government's commitment to disinflationary policies, and to take advantage of investor demand for securities immune from inflation risk.
3. Countries (such as the United States and Canada) that are concerned about the social welfare benefits of inflation-linked securities.

The cash flows of an index-linked bond may be linked to a specified index via its interest payments, principal payments, or both.

- Zero-coupon-indexed bonds do not pay any coupon so only the principal repayment is linked to a specified index.
- For interest-indexed bonds, only coupon payments are adjusted to changes in the specified index. They repay the fixed nominal principal at maturity.
- Capital-indexed bonds pay a fixed coupon rate, but this rate is applied to a principal amount that is adjusted to reflect changes in the specified index. As a result, both interest payments as well as the principal repayment are adjusted for inflation.
- Indexed-annuity bonds are fully amortized bonds (i.e., annuity payments include both payment of interest and partial repayment of principal). The annual payment on these bonds is linked to the specified index so effectively, both interest and principal payments reflect changes in the index.

> Interest-indexed bonds and capital-indexed bonds are both nonamortizing bonds.

Index-linked bonds may also be linked to an equity index. An example of such a bond is an equity-linked note (ELN), which is a fixed-income security whose final payment is linked to the return on an equity index. ELNs are generally principal-protected (i.e., the investor is guaranteed repayment of 100% of principal at maturity even if the value of the index has fallen since issuance). If the underlying index increases in value, investors receive an amount greater than par upon maturity. However, note that the principal payment is still subject to credit risk of the issuer, so if the issuer defaults, the investor may not receive anything even if the underlying index has increased in value.

LESSON 4: BONDS WITH CONTINGENCY PROVISIONS

LOS 50f: Describe contingency provisions affecting the timing and/or nature of cash flows of fixed-income securities and identify whether such provisions benefit the borrower or the lender. **Vol 5, pp 329–335**

A contingency provision allows for some action given the occurrence of a specified event in the future. Common contingency provisions found in a bond's indenture come under the heading of embedded options.

Callable Bonds

Callable bonds give the **issuer** the right to redeem (or call) all or part of the bond before maturity. This embedded option offers the issuer the ability to take advantage of (1) a decline in market interest rates and/or (2) an improvement in its creditworthiness. If interest rates decline and/or the issuer's credit rating improves, the issuer would call the outstanding issue and replace this old (expensive to pay interest on) issue with a new issue that carries a lower interest rate.

For example, assume that the market interest rate was 6% at the time of issuance and the company issues bonds carrying a coupon rate of 7% with the 100 bps spread reflecting the credit risk of the issuer. Now suppose that the market interest rate falls to 5% and the issuer's credit rating improves such that a spread of only 50 bps is appropriate to compensate investors for credit risk.

- If these bonds were callable, the issuer would call/redeem them and refinance the issue by issuing new bonds carrying a coupon rate of 5% + 0.5% = 5.5% (in line with current market interest rates and the issuer's current credit risk).
- If the bonds were not callable, the company would have continued paying a 7% coupon and would not have been able to take advantage of the decline in market interest rates and the improvement in its own creditworthiness.

While callable bonds benefit the issuer (the call option holds value to the issuer), they expose investors to a higher level of reinvestment risk than noncallable bonds. If bonds are called, bondholders would have to reinvest proceeds at the new (lower) interest rates. To compensate investors for granting the option to call the bond to the issuer and accepting potentially higher reinvestment risk, callable bonds offer a higher yield to investors and sell at lower prices compared to noncallable bonds.

From the perspective of the bondholder, she would pay less for a callable bond than for an otherwise identical noncallable bond. The difference in the value of a noncallable bond and an otherwise identical callable bond is the value of the embedded call option (which the bond holder has effectively written or sold to the issuer).

$$\text{Value of callable bond} = \text{Value of noncallable bond} - \text{Value of embedded call option}$$

$$\text{Value of embedded call option} = \text{Value of noncallable bond} - \text{Value of callable bond}$$

From the perspective of the issuer, it would have to pay more (in the form of a higher coupon or higher yield) to get investors to purchase a callable bond than an otherwise identical noncallable bond. The difference between the yield on a callable bond and the yield on a noncallable bond is the cost of the embedded option to the issuer.

$$\text{Yield on callable bond} = \text{Yield on noncallable bond} + \text{Embedded call option cost in terms of yield}$$

$$\text{Embedded call option cost in terms of yield} = \text{Yield on callable bond} - \text{Yield on noncallable bond}$$

Note that the more heavily the embedded call option favors the issuer, the lower the value of the callable bond to the investor and the higher the yield that must be offered by the issuer.

The bond indenture usually specifies the following details about the call provision:

- Call price, which is the price paid to bondholders when the bond is called.
- Call premium, which is the excess over par paid by the issuer to call the bond.
- Call schedule, which specifies the dates and prices at which the bond may be called.

Some callable bonds are issued with an initial call protection period (also known as lockout period, cushion, or deferment period), during which the issuer is prohibited from calling the bond. The bond can only be called at or after the specified call date.

A make-whole provision in a callable bond usually requires the issuer to pay a relatively high lump-sum amount to call the bonds. This amount is based on the present value of the remaining coupon and principal payments (that are not paid due to the bond's early redemption), based on a discount rate that adds a pre-specified spread to the YTM of an appropriate sovereign bond. The redemption value calculated in this manner generally tends to be much higher than the bond's current market price. The point of including this provision is to make the deal appear more attractive to investors as it allows for them to be handsomely compensated if the bond is called. Practically speaking however, issuers rarely invoke this provision as it is very costly. See Example 4-1.

Example 4-1: Callable bonds

A hypothetical $1,000 par 20-year bond is issued on January 21, 2013 at a price of 98.515. The issuer can call the bond in whole or in part every January 21, from 2019. Call prices at different call dates are listed below:

Year	Call Price ($)
2019	102.000
2020	101.655
2021	101.371
2022	101.095
2023	100.824
2023	100.548
2024	100.273
2025 and thereafter	100.000

1. What is the length of the call protection period?
2. What is the call premium (per bond) for the 2022 call date?
3. What type of exercise style does this callable bond illustrate?

Solution:

1. The bonds were issued in 2013 and are first callable in 2019. Therefore, the call protection period is 2019 − 2013 = 6 years.
2. Call prices are stated as a percentage of par so the call price in 2026 is $1,010.95 (= 101.095% × 1,000). The call premium is the amount paid above par by the issuer. Therefore, the call premium in 2022 is $10.95 (= 1,010.95 − 1,000).
3. The bond is callable every January 21, from 2019 until maturity. Since it is callable on specified dates following the initial call protection period the embedded option is a Bermuda call.

The following exercise styles are available for callable bonds:

- American calls (also known as continuously callable) can be called by the issuer at any time starting on the first call date.
- European calls can only be called by the issuer on the call date.
- Bermuda-style calls can be called by the issuer on specified dates following the call protection period. These dates usually coincide with coupon payment dates.

Putable Bonds

Putable bonds give **bondholders** the right to sell (or put) the bond back to the issuer at a pre-determined price on specified dates. The embedded put option offers bondholders protection against an increase in interest rates (i.e., if interest rates increase [decreasing the value of the bond], they can sell the bond back to the issuer at a pre-specified price and then reinvest the principal at [higher] newer interest rates).

From the perspective of the bondholder, she would pay more for a putable bond than for an otherwise identical nonputable bond. The difference in the value between a putable bond and an otherwise identical nonputable bond is the value of the embedded put option (which the bond holder has effectively purchased from the issuer).

Value of putable bond = Value of nonputable bond + Value of embedded put option

Value of embedded put option = Value of putable bond − Value of nonputable bond

From the perspective of the issuer, it would pay out less (in the form of a lower coupon or lower yield) on a putable bond than it would on an otherwise identical nonputable bond. The difference between the yield on a nonputable bond and the yield on a putable bond is the cost of the embedded option borne by the investor.

Yield on putable bond = Yield on nonputable bond − Embedded put option cost in terms of yield

Embedded put option cost in terms of yield = Yield on nonputable bond − Yield on putable bond

Note that the more heavily the embedded put option favors the investor, the higher the value of the putable bond to the investor and the lower the yield that must be offered by the issuer.

- Details regarding redemption dates and prices at which the bond can be sold back to the issuer are included in the bond's indenture.
- Putable bonds may give investors an opportunity to sell the bond back to the issuer once or multiple times.
  - Putable bonds that only give a single sellback opportunity are called one-time put bonds, while those that give multiple opportunities are called multiple put bonds.
  - Multiple put bonds are generally more expensive (have higher value) than one-time put bonds as they offer bondholders more flexibility.
- The exercise styles used for putable bonds are similar to those used for callable bonds.

Convertible Bonds

A convertible bond gives the bondholder the right to convert the bond into a pre-specified number of common shares of the issuer. Therefore, it can be viewed as a combination of a straight bond and an embedded call option on the issuer's stock. Convertible bonds may also include call or put provisions.

Convertible bonds are attractive to investors as the conversion (to equity) option allows them to benefit from price appreciation of the issuer's stock. On the other hand, if there is a decline in the issuer's share price (which causes a decline in the value of the embedded equity conversion/call option), the price of the convertible bond cannot fall below the price of an otherwise identical straight bond. Because of these attractive features, convertible bonds offer a lower yield and sell at higher prices than similar bonds without the conversion option. Note however, that the coupon rate offered on convertible bonds is usually higher than the dividend yield on the underlying equity.

Convertible bonds hold advantages for the issuer, as yields on convertible bonds are lower than yields on otherwise identical bonds without the conversion option. Further, if the conversion option is exercised, debt is eliminated. Note however, that this comes at the cost of dilution for existing shareholders.

Some terms relevant to the conversion provision are defined below:

- The conversion price is the price per share at which the convertible bond can be converted into shares.
- The conversion ratio refers to the number of common shares that each bond can be converted into. It is calculated as the par value divided by the conversion price.
    - If the par value is $1,000 and the conversion price is $20, then the conversion ratio is 50:1 or 50 (= 1,000/20) common shares per bond.
- The conversion value is calculated as current share price multiplied by the conversion ratio.
    - If the current share price is $25 and the conversion ratio is 50:1, the conversion value is $1,250 (= 25 × 50).
- The conversion premium equals the difference between the convertible bond's price and the conversion value.
    - If the convertible bond's price is $1,300 and the conversion value is $1,250, the conversion premium equals $50.
- Conversion parity occurs if the conversion value equals the convertible bond's price.
    - Continuing with our example, if the stock price were currently $26 (instead of $25), the conversion value would be $1,300 (= 26 × 50), the same as the convertible bond's price. In this case, the conversion premium equals $0. If the common share is trading below $26, the condition is below parity, while if it is trading for more than $26, the condition is above parity.

It is important that you recognize that a callable convertible bond includes (1) an embedded conversion/call option (that favors the investor) on the issuer's stock and (2) an embedded call option (that favors the issuer) on the bond itself.

Although it is common for convertible bonds to reach conversion parity before they mature, bondholders rarely exercise the conversion option, choosing to retain their bonds and receive (higher) coupon payments instead of (lower) dividend payments. As a result, issuers often embed a call option alongside the conversion option in the convertible bond, making them callable convertible bonds. The reason behind this is that the call option may force investors to convert their bonds into common shares when the conversion value is higher than the call price. For this reason, callable convertible bonds sell at a lower price (or offer a higher yield) than noncallable convertible bonds.

Warrants

A warrant is somewhat similar to a conversion option, but it is not embedded in the bond's structure. It offers the holder the right to purchase the issuer's stock at a fixed exercise price until the expiration date. Warrants are attached to bond issues as sweeteners, allowing investors to participate in the upside from an increase in share prices.

Contingent Convertible Bonds ("CoCos")

CoCos are bonds with contingent write-down provisions. They differ from traditional convertible bonds in two ways:

1. Unlike traditional convertible bonds, which are convertible at the **option** of the bondholder, CoCos convert **automatically** upon the occurrence of a pre-specified event.
2. Unlike traditional convertible bonds, in which conversion occurs if the issuer's share price **increases** (i.e., on the upside), contingent write-down provisions are convertible on the **downside**.

To understand the application of CoCos, consider a bank that is required to maintain its core equity capital above a minimum level. To ensure that it continues to adhere to capital requirements in the event of significant losses, the bank could issue CoCos that are structured to automatically convert into equity if it suffers losses that reduce its equity capital below the minimum requirement. Since CoCos are set to convert automatically, they may force holders to take losses, which is why they offer investors a higher yield than otherwise similar bonds.

READING 51: FIXED-INCOME MARKETS: ISSUANCE, TRADING, AND FUNDING

LESSON 1: OVERVIEW OF GLOBAL FIXED-INCOME MARKETS

LOS 51a: Describe classifications of global fixed-income markets.
Vol 5, pp 348–357

CLASSIFICATION OF FIXED-INCOME MARKETS

Fixed-income markets may be classified in the following ways:

Type of Issuer

Bond markets can be classified based on the following three types of issuers:

1. The government and government-related sector, which includes:
   - Supranational (international) organizations (e.g., the World Bank).
   - Sovereign (national) governments (e.g., the United States).
   - Non-sovereign (local) governments (e.g., the state of Pennsylvania).
   - Quasi-government entities (e.g., rail services in many countries).
2. The corporate sector, which includes financial and nonfinancial companies.
3. The structured finance (or securitized) sector, which includes bonds that are created through the securitization process.

> The types of securities associated with these sectors are described in more detail later in this reading and subsequent readings.

Credit Quality

Bond markets can also be classified based on the creditworthiness of the issuer, which is reflected in credit ratings issued by credit rating agencies. Bonds with a credit rating of Baa3 or above by Moody's, or BBB– or above by S&P and Fitch are classified as investment-grade bonds. On the other hand, bonds with ratings below these levels are classified as noninvestment grade (or high-yield, speculative, or junk) bonds. This distinction is helpful for institutional investors, as they may be prohibited from investing in noninvestment-grade bonds.

Maturity

Fixed-income securities may be classified based on their original (at issuance) maturity:

- Money market securities are fixed-income securities that have a maturity of 1 year or less at the time of issuance (e.g., T-bills, commercial paper, and negotiable certificates of deposit).
- Capital market securities are fixed-income securities that have a maturity of more than 1 year at the time of issuance.

Currency Denomination

Fixed-income securities can also be classified based on the currency in which they are issued. The currency in which a bond is issued determines which country's interest rates affect its price.

Geography

Bonds may be classified on the basis of where they are issued and traded.

- Bonds that are issued in a specific country, denominated in the currency of that country, and sold in that country are classified as:
  - Domestic bonds, if they are issued by entities incorporated in that country.
  - Foreign bonds, if the issuer is domiciled in another country.

  Domestic and foreign bonds are subject to the reporting, regulatory, and tax requirements of the country they are issued in.
- A Eurobond is issued internationally (i.e., outside the jurisdiction of the country whose currency it is denominated in). Eurobonds are subject to less reporting, regulatory, and tax constraints than domestic and foreign bonds. Eurobonds are also attractive for issuers as they offer access to a larger number of global investors.

Investors also often distinguish between emerging bond markets and developed bond markets. Although emerging bond markets are much smaller, trading volumes and values have risen sharply in recent years due to increased demand from investors seeking diversification (believing that investment returns across markets are not closely correlated). Generally speaking, emerging market bonds offer higher yields than developed market bonds.

Other Classifications of Fixed-Income Markets

Fixed-income markets may also be classified based on specific characteristics of the securities. For example:

- Inflation-linked bonds offer investors protection against inflation by linking the coupon payment and/or the principal repayment to a consumer price index.
- Tax-exempt bonds, such as municipal bonds (or munis) in the United States are attractive for investors who are subject to income tax because interest income from these bonds is usually exempt from federal income tax and from state income tax (subject to some restrictions). Coupon rates on tax-exempt bonds are typically lower than those on otherwise identical taxable bonds.

Type of Coupon

Bond markets may be classified based on the type of coupon. The coupon rate for a bond (1) may be fixed throughout its term (e.g., plain-vanilla bond), or (2) may change periodically based on some reference rate (e.g., floating-rate notes).

LOS 51b: Describe the use of interbank offered rates as reference rates in floating-rate debt. Vol 5, pp 352–353

Reference Rates

The coupon rate of a floating-rate note (FRN) has two components: (1) a reference rate, plus (2) a spread (or margin).

1. The spread is usually constant and is set at the time of bond issuance. It is based on the issuer's creditworthiness (i.e., the higher the credit quality of the issuer, the lower the spread).

2. The reference rate resets periodically, so the coupon rate is brought in line with market interest rates each time the reference rate is reset. The reference rate is the primary driver of the bond's coupon rate.

The reference rate used for a particular floating-rate bond issue depends on where the bonds are issued and the currency denomination. An example of a reference rate is the London interbank offered rate (Libor), which is the rate at which banks can borrow unsecured funds from each other in the London interbank market for different currencies and different borrowing periods. Libor is used as the reference rate for most floating-rate bonds issued in the Eurobond market. For example, an FRN denominated in GBP that pays coupon semiannualy would typically calculate the coupon as 6-month Libor (or LIBOR-180) plus a spread.

Fixed-Income Indices

Fixed-income indices are generally used by investors (1) to describe a bond market or sector, and (2) to evaluate investment performance. Fixed-income indices usually consist of portfolios of securities reflecting a specific bond market or sector and can be price-or value-weighted.

Investors in Fixed-Income Securities

Investors in fixed-income securities include the following:

- Central banks: Central banks purchase and sell sovereign bonds issued by the national government to conduct open market operations in implementing monetary policy. They may also trade in bonds denominated in foreign currencies to manage the currency's exchange rate and the country's foreign currency reserves.
- Institutional investors: These include pension funds, hedge funds, insurance companies, foundations, endowments, banks, and sovereign wealth funds.
- Retail investors: Retail investors invest in fixed-income securities to take advantage of their relatively stable prices and steady income streams.

> While central banks and institutional investors typically invest directly in fixed-income securities, retail investors tend to invest indirectly through mutual funds and ETFs.

LESSON 2: PRIMARY AND SECONDARY BOND MARKETS

LOS 51c: Describe mechanisms available for issuing bonds in primary markets. Vol 5, pp 359–365

Primary bond markets are those in which issuers sell new bonds to investors to raise capital. On the other hand, secondary bond markets are those in which existing bonds are traded among investors.

Primary Bond Markets

Mechanisms for issuing bonds in primary markets differ based on the type of issuer and the type of bond issued. Bonds may be issued through a public offering or a private placement.

Public Offerings

In a **public offering** (or **public offer**), any member of the public may purchase the bonds. Bond issuers are usually assisted by investment banks, which provide a wide range of financial services. Mechanisms for issuing bonds in the primary market include the following:

Underwritten offerings (also referred to as a firm commitment offering): The bond issuer negotiates an offering price with the investment bank, which then guarantees the sale of the issue at that price. The risk associated with selling the bonds is therefore borne by the investment bank (also known as the underwriter). The underwriting process involves the following phases:

- Determining the funding needs of the issuer.
- Selecting the underwriter (typically an investment bank) to market and sell bonds.
- Structuring the transaction (i.e., determining the maturity date, currency denomination, expected coupon rate, and expected offering price).
- Preparing and submitting required regulatory filings, appointing a trustee, and launching the offering (typically via a press release).
- Assessing market conditions by holding discussions with anchor buyers and analyzing the grey market.
  - Anchor buyers are large institutional investors.
  - The grey market (also known as the when-issued market) is basically a forward market for bonds that are about to be issued. Trading in this market helps underwriters determine the final offer price.
- Pricing the issue accordingly to ensure that it is neither undersubscribed nor significantly oversubscribed.
- Setting the final issue price on the pricing day, which is the last day for investors to commit to purchasing bonds.
- Issuing the bond: The underwriter purchases the bond issue from the issuer, delivers the proceeds to investors, and also starts reselling the bonds through its sales network.

Best efforts offering: The investment bank only acts as a broker and tries its best to sell the bond at the negotiated offering price for a commission. The investment bank bears less risk and has less of an incentive to sell in a best efforts offering compared to an underwritten offering.

> The auction process has been described in detail in the Economics section.

Auctions: Bonds are sold to investors through a bidding process, which helps in price discovery and allocation of securities. U.S. Treasuries are sold via auctions, where primary dealers are the major counterparties to the New York Fed as it conducts monetary policy through open market operations. Individuals account for a very small proportion of direct purchases of Treasury securities.

Shelf registration: Shelf registration allows certain (authorized) issuers to offer additional bonds to the general public without having to prepare a new and separate prospectus for each bond issue. Instead, there is a single prospectus, which can be used for multiple, undefined future offerings over several years. Each issue, however, must be accompanied by an announcement document describing changes to the issuer's financial condition (if any) since the filing of the master prospectus.

Since shelf issuances are subject to lower levels of scrutiny than standard public offerings, only well-established issuers with proven financial strength can make use of this facility. Further, in some jurisdictions, shelf registrations can be purchased only by qualified investors.

Private Placements

In a private placement, only a select group of qualified investors (typically large institutional investors) are allowed to invest in the issue.

- The bonds are neither underwritten nor registered, and can be relatively illiquid as there is usually no secondary market to trade them.
- Investors are usually able to influence the terms of the issue, so privately placed bonds typically have more customized and restrictive covenants compared to publicly issued bonds.

LOS 51d: Describe secondary markets for bonds. Vol 5, pp 365–367

Secondary markets (or aftermarkets) are those in which existing bonds are traded among investors. Secondary markets may be structured in the following two ways:

1. Organized exchanges: These are places where buyers and sellers can meet to arrange their trades. Buyers and sellers may come from anywhere, but transactions must be executed at the exchange in accordance with the rules and regulations of the exchange.
2. Over-the-counter (OTC) markets: In these markets, buyers and sellers submit their orders from various locations through electronic trading platforms. Orders are then matched and executed through a communications network.

The vast majority of bond trading occurs in OTC markets. Dealers quote prices at which they are willing to buy (known as the bid) and sell (known as the ask) from/to customers. The bid-ask spread is a commonly used measure of liquidity in the market. A bid-ask spread of 10 to 12 bps is considered reasonable.

> Liquidity is defined as the ability to make trades quickly at a price close to the security's fair market value.

Settlement for government and quasi-government bonds usually occurs on a T+1 basis (one day after the transaction date), whereas settlement of corporate bonds usually occurs on a T+3 basis (three days after the transaction date). For money market trades, cash settlement (same day settlement) is also common.

LESSON 3: TYPES OF INSTRUMENTS

LOS 51e: Describe securities issued by sovereign governments. Vol 5, pp 367–368

Sovereign Bonds

Sovereign bonds are bonds that are issued by a country's central government (or its treasury). They are issued primarily to cover expenditures when tax revenues are insufficient.

- Sovereign bonds are backed by the taxing authority of the national government.
- Sovereign bonds can be issued in the sovereign's local (domestic) currency or in a foreign currency.
  - Bonds issued in local currency typically carry a higher credit rating than those issued in a foreign currency. While both bonds are backed by the sovereign's taxing power, local currency bonds can also be serviced by printing local currency, whereas foreign currency bonds can only be serviced through foreign currency reserves (which are finite). If the sovereign prints more local currency hoping to exchange it for foreign currency (to service

foreign currency bonds), financial markets would typically be quick to recognize this, resulting in a depreciation of the local currency over time.

Secondary market trading of sovereign bonds is primarily in securities that were most recently issued (known as on-the-run securities). The latest sovereign bond issue for a given maturity is also referred to as a benchmark issue because it serves as a benchmark for otherwise identical bonds (in terms of maturity, coupon type and frequency, and currency denomination) issued by another type of issuer (e.g., non-sovereign, corporate). Generally speaking, as a sovereign issue ages (or becomes more seasoned) it tends to trade less frequently.

There are several types of sovereign bonds issued in the market, including fixed-rate bonds, floating-rate bonds, and inflation-linked bonds.

LOS 51f: Describe securities issued by non-sovereign governments, quasi-government entities, and supranational agencies. Vol 5, pp 371–373

Non-Sovereign Government Bonds

Non-sovereign bonds are those issued by levels of government that lie below the national level (e.g., provinces, regions, states, and cities). They are typically issued to finance public projects, such as schools and bridges. These bonds can be serviced through the following sources of income:

- The taxing authority of the local government.
- The cash flows from the project that is being financed with bond proceeds.
- Special taxes and fees established specifically for making interest payments and principal repayments.

> Non-sovereign bonds are discussed in more detail in a later reading.

Generally speaking, non-sovereign bonds are of high credit quality, but they still trade at higher yields (lower prices) than sovereign bonds. The lower the credit quality and the liquidity of a non-sovereign bond relative to a sovereign bond, the greater the additional yield.

Quasi-Government Bonds

Quasi-government or agency bonds are issued by organizations that perform various functions for the national government, but are not actual governmental entities. These bonds are issued to fund specific financing needs. Examples of quasi-government entities include government-sponsored enterprises (GSEs) in the United States, such as Fannie Mae (that provides mortgage financing) and Sallie Mae (that provides student loans).

- Quasi-government bonds may be guaranteed by the national government, in which case they receive higher ratings and trade at lower yields than similar bonds not carrying the government guarantee.
- Generally speaking, quasi-government entities do not have direct taxing authority, so bonds are serviced with cash flows generated by the entity or from the project that is being financed by the issue.
- In some cases, quasi-government bonds may be backed by collateral.
- Historical default rates on quasi-government bonds have been extremely low.

Supranational Bonds

These bonds are issued by supranational (or multilateral) agencies such as the World Bank (WB) and the International Monetary Fund (IMF). Generally speaking, supranational bonds are issued as plain-vanilla bonds (though floating-rate bonds and callable bonds are also issued). They are typically highly rated and issued in large sizes (so they tend to be very liquid).

LOS 51g: Describe types of debt issued by corporations. Vol 5, pp 373–380

Corporate Debt

Bank Loans: Bilateral and Syndicated Loans

- There are two types of bank loans:
    1. A bilateral loan is a loan from a single bank.
    2. A syndicated loan is a loan from a group of lenders, or syndicate. Syndicated loans are often securitized and then sold in secondary markets to investors. Securitized instruments are discussed in detail in a later reading.
- Most bank loans are floating-rate loans, with Libor, a sovereign rate (e.g., the T-bill rate), or the prime rate serving as the reference rate.
- Bank loans can be customized (with respect to maturity and payment structure) to borrower requirements.
- Access to bank loans depends on (1) the company's financial position, and (2) market conditions and capital availability.
    1. Bank loans are the primary source of debt financing for small and medium-size companies, as well as for large companies in countries where bond markets are underdeveloped.
    2. For highly rated companies in developed markets, bank loans tend to be more expensive than issuing bonds.

Commercial Paper

- Commercial paper is an unsecured debt instrument that is popular among issuers because it is a source of flexible, readily available, and relatively low-cost financing.
- It can be used to meet seasonal demands for cash and is also commonly used to provide bridge financing (i.e., interim financing until long-term financing can be arranged).
- Commercial paper is usually "rolled over" by issuers. This means that companies obtain the funds to pay off maturing paper by issuing more commercial paper. In order to safeguard against rollover risk (the risk that the company will not be able to issue new commercial paper to replace maturing paper), issuers often maintain access to backup lines of credit (also referred to as liquidity enhancement or backup liquidity lines). Rollover risk may arise due to (1) market-wide events (e.g., the "freezing" of debt markets during the 2008 financial crisis) or (2) company-specific events (e.g., significant deterioration in a company's financial position may lead to a sharp increase in the required yield on new paper or to the new issue not being fully subscribed).

> Backup lines of credit typically contain a material adverse change provision which allows the bank to cancel the credit line if the financial position of the issuer deteriorates significantly.

- Terms to maturity can range from overnight to one year.
    - In the United States, because debt securities with terms that do not exceed 270 days are exempt from registration with the SEC, commercial paper is typically issued with a term of 270 days or less.
- Historically, defaults on commercial paper have been relatively rare because commercial paper has a short maturity and tends to be rolled over.
    - Each time an issuer tries to roll over paper, investors can reassess the issuer's financial position, and not subscribe to the issue if they perceive an increase in credit risk.

- Corporate managers are wary of defaulting on issued paper because they do not want to risk losing access to such a flexible source of financing going forward.
- Most investors hold on to commercial paper until maturity, which results in very little secondary market trading in these instruments.
- Yields on commercial paper are higher than yields on short-term sovereign bonds of the same maturity because:
  - Investors in commercial paper face credit risk, while most highly rated sovereign bonds are risk-free.
  - Commercial paper markets are generally less liquid than short-term sovereign bond markets.
- In the United States, yields on commercial paper are higher than yields on municipal bonds because interest income from commercial paper is taxable, while income from municipal bonds is tax exempt.
- U.S. commercial paper (USCP) is issued as a pure discount instrument (the security is issued at a discount to par and pays the par amount at maturity, with the difference between the two being the interest paid). Euro commercial paper (ECP) is quoted on an add-on yield basis, where the interest amount is paid in addition to the par amount at maturity.

Corporate Notes and Bonds

- Corporate bonds can differ based on several characteristics. They can differ based on:
  - Coupon payment structures (e.g., fixed-rate vs. floating-rate).
  - Principal payment structures.
    - Bonds with a serial maturity structure have maturity dates that are spread out over the bond's life. A stated number of bonds mature and are paid off each year until final maturity.
    - Bonds with a term maturity structure are paid off in one lump sum payment at maturity.
    - The difference between (1) bonds with a serial maturity structure and (2) those with a term maturity structure combined with a sinking fund provision is that with a serial maturity structure bondholders know exactly which bonds will be repaid each year, while for issues with a sinking fund arrangement bonds that can be redeemed each year are designated by a random drawing.
  - Terms to maturity. Bonds with terms to maturity less than 5 years are known as short-term bonds, those with terms ranging between 5 and 12 years are known as intermediate-term bonds, and those with terms longer than 12 years are known as long-term bonds.
  - Asset or collateral backing (i.e., secured vs. unsecured).
  - Contingency provisions (e.g., embedded call, put, and conversion options).

Medium-Term Notes (MTNs)

- Medium-term notes (MTNs) are not necessarily intermediate-term securities. They are known as "medium-term" notes because when they were initially issued, they were meant to fill the funding gap between (short-term) commercial paper and long-term bonds. The MTN market can be broken down into three segments:
  1. Short-term securities that may be fixed-rate or floating-rate.
  2. Medium-to long-term securities that generally tend to be fixed-rate.

3. Structured notes, which are essentially notes combined with derivative instruments to create special features desired by certain institutional investors.

- MTNs are unique in that they are offered continuously to investors by the agent of the issuer.
  - First, the issuer provides the agent with an indication of the range of maturities that it wishes to borrow for, and also specifies the yield it is willing to offer on each maturity.
  - Investors then get in touch with the agent and provide details of the amount and maturity that they are interested in.
  - The agent then confirms the issuer's willingness to issue the desired notes and executes the transaction.
- Primary issuers of MTNs tend to be financial institutions, while pension funds, life insurance companies, and banks are among the largest buyers.
- MTNs can be customized/structured to meet investor requirements. While their customized features result in limited liquidity, MTNs offer higher yields than otherwise identical publicly traded bonds.

LOS 51h: Describe structured financial instruments. Vol 5, pp 381–384

Structured Financial Instruments

A wide variety of structured financial instruments exist. A common attribute of all these financial instruments is that they repackage and redistribute risks. In this reading we focus on structured financial instruments apart from asset-backed securities (ABS) and collateralized debt obligations (CDOs).

Generally speaking, structured financial instruments have customized structures that often combine a bond and at least one derivative. The use of derivatives gives the holder of the instrument (which may also be known as a structured product) exposure to one or more underlying assets, such as equities, bonds, and commodities. The redemption value and often the coupons of structured financial instruments are tied to the performance of the underlying asset(s), as opposed to being tied to the issuer's cash flows (as is the case with traditional bonds).

In the sections that follow, we present four broad categories of instruments: capital-protected instruments, yield-enhancement instruments, participation instruments, and leveraged instruments.

Capital-Protected Instruments

Consider the following structured financial instrument (known as a guarantee certificate) that combines an investment in a zero-coupon bond and a call option.

- An investor has $100,000 to invest.
- She purchases a zero-coupon bond with a face value of $100,000 for $99,000, and uses the $1,000 left over to buy a call option on some underlying asset that expires in 1 year.
- The investor will receive $100,000 upon maturity of the zero-coupon bond, so the bond offers the investor capital protection.
- The call option offers the investor participation in any upside on the underlying. Her downside on the option position is limited to the premium paid to acquire the option.

Capital-protected instruments may offer different levels of capital protection. A guaranteed certificate (like the one just described) offers full capital protection, but other structured financial instruments may offer only partial capital protection. It is important to note that the capital protection is only as good as the creditworthiness of the issuer of the instrument. Should the issuer of guaranteed certificates go bankrupt, investors may lose their entire capital.

Yield-Enhancement Instruments

Yield enhancement aims to improve the expected return on an investment by increasing risk exposure. An example of such an instrument is a credit-linked note (CLN), which is basically a bond that pays regular coupons but whose redemption value depends on the occurrence of a well-defined credit event (e.g., a rating downgrade or the default of a reference asset).

- If the specified credit event does not occur, the investor receives the par value of the CLN at maturity.
- However, if the specified credit event occurs, the investor receives the par value of the CLN minus the nominal value of the reference asset to which the CLN is linked.

A CLN allows the issuer to effectively transfer the effect of a particular credit event to investors. The issuer is the protection buyer (as it benefits from having to redeem a lower amount if the credit event occurs), while the investor is the protection seller. In return for taking on credit risk, investors are offered higher coupons on CLNs than on otherwise identical bonds. Additionally, CLNs are usually issued at a discount, which further improves the potential return for investors.

Participation Instruments

Participation instruments allow investors to participate in the return of an underlying asset. Floating-rate bonds (whose coupon rates are reset periodically and brought in line with market interest rates) are examples of such instruments, as they offer investors the opportunity to participate in movements of interest rates.

Most participation instruments are designed to give investors indirect exposure to a particular index or asset price that they are precluded from investing in directly. While both may offer equity exposure, it is important to note that participation instruments differ from capital-protected instruments in that they do not offer capital protection.

Leveraged Instruments

Leveraged instruments are structured financial instruments that aim to magnify returns. An inverse floater is an example of a leveraged instrument, where cash flows move in the opposite direction to changes in the reference rate.

An inverse floater's periodic coupon rate is determined as:

Inverse floater coupon rate = $C - (L \times R)$

C = Maximum coupon rate. (This occurs when the reference rate equals zero.)
L = Coupon leverage.
R = Reference rate on the reset date.

The coupon leverage is the multiple that the coupon rate will change in response to a 100 bps change in the reference rate. For example, if the coupon leverage is 2.5, the inverse floater's coupon rate will *decrease* by 250 bps when the reference rate *increases* by 100 bps.

- Inverse floaters with a coupon leverage greater than zero but lower than 1 are called deleveraged inverse floaters.
- Those with a coupon leverage greater than 1 are called leveraged inverse floaters.
- Inverse floaters often have a floor that specifies a minimum coupon rate (e.g., a floor may be set at zero to avoid the possibility of a negative coupon).

LESSON 4: SHORT-TERM FUNDING ALTERNATIVES AVAILABLE TO BANKS

LOS 51i: Describe short-term funding alternatives available to banks.
Vol 5, pp 384–389

Retail deposits: These include funds deposited at the bank by individual and commercial depositors into their accounts. Retail deposit accounts include:

- Checking accounts, which typically pay no interest but provide customers with transaction services and immediate access to funds.
- Money market accounts, which pay money market rates of return and offer access to funds with little or no notice.
- Savings accounts, which pay interest but are less liquid.

Short-term wholesale funds: These include:

- Central bank funds: Recall (from the Economics section) that banks in many countries are required to place a reserve balance at the central bank. The central bank funds market (the Fed funds market in the United States) is the market for reserves where banks with excess reserves are able to lend them out, and banks short of required reserves are able to borrow them. The interest rate on these borrowings is known as the central bank funds rate (Fed funds rate in the United States), and is influenced by (1) demand and supply for reserves and (2) the central bank's open market operations.
- Interbank funds: The interbank market is the market for loans and deposits between banks. Maturities can range from overnight to one year, and deposits are unsecured. At times of stress (e.g., the 2008 financial crisis), liquidity in the interbank market can dry up significantly.
- Certificates of deposit (CDs): A certificate of deposit (CD) is issued by a bank to a client when she deposits a specified sum of money for a specified maturity and interest rate.
  - A non-negotiable CD is one in which the deposit and interest are paid to the initial depositor at maturity. An early withdrawal penalty is imposed if the depositor withdraws funds before the maturity date.

- A negotiable CD provides the depositor with the option to sell the CD in the open market if she wishes to liquidate it before maturity.
  - Negotiable CDs can be classified as large-denomination CDs and small-denomination CDs. Large-denomination CDs (issued in denominations of $1 million or more in the United States) are an important source of funding for banks, while small-denomination CDs are not as important.
- CDs with long-term maturities are known as term CDs.
- CDs are available in domestic bond markets and in the Eurobond market.
- Yields on CDs are driven by the creditworthiness of the issuing bank and (to a lesser extent) the term to maturity.

LOS 51j: Describe repurchase agreements (repos) the risks associated with them. Vol 5, pp 386–388

Repurchase and Reverse Repurchase Agreements

A repurchase agreement is an arrangement between two parties, where one party sells a security to the other with a commitment to buy it back at a later date for a predetermined higher price. The difference between the (lower) selling price and the (higher) repurchase price is the interest cost of the loan. Effectively, what is happening is that the seller is borrowing funds from the buyer and putting up the security as collateral.

- The annualized interest cost of the loan is called the repo rate.
- A repurchase agreement for one day is known as an overnight repo, and an agreement for a longer period is known as a term repo.
- Repo rates are usually lower than the rates that a broker or bank would charge on a margin loan.

For example, consider a $1,000 par, 4% annual-pay bond that is currently trading at $980. Party A sells this bond to Party B today for $950 with a commitment to repurchase it for $960 (repurchase price) after 60 days (repurchase date).

- The implicit interest rate for the 60-day period is calculated as 960/950 − 1 = 1.053%.
- The repo rate would be 1.053% for 60 days expressed as an effective annual rate.
- The percentage difference between the market value of the security and the amount of the loan is known as the repo margin or haircut. In this example, the margin equals 950/980 − 1 = −3.061%. The margin serves to protect the lender against a decline in the value of the collateral over the term of the repo.
- Note that interest is paid on the repurchase date, which is the date of termination of the agreement.
- Any coupon income received from the bond during the repo term belongs to the seller (borrower).
- Both parties in the repo face counterparty credit risk.
  - Suppose that the buyer (lender) is unable to deliver the collateral on the repurchase date. The seller (borrower) faces the risk that the value of the collateral has risen over the term of the repo. The seller will then be left with an amount of cash that is lower than the current market value of the security.
  - Now suppose that the seller (borrower) is unable to repurchase the collateral on the repurchase date. The buyer (lender) faces the risk that the

value of the collateral (plus any income owed to the seller) has fallen over the term of the repo to a level lower than the unpaid repurchase price.

- When looking at things from the perspective of Party A (the seller or borrower), the transaction would be referred to as a repo.
- When looking at things from the perspective of Party B (the buyer or lender), the transaction would be referred to as a reverse repo.
  - Reverse repos are used to borrow securities to cover short positions. The buyer in the repo transaction immediately sells the security obtained from the seller in the repo on the open market. On the settlement date of the repo, the buyer acquires the relevant security from the open market to deliver it back to the seller. The buyer in the repo (short position on the asset) has positioned herself to profit from a decline in value of the security between the date of inception of the repo and its settlement date.
- Standard practice is to define the transaction based on the perspective of the dealer.
  - If the dealer is borrowing cash and providing collateral, the transaction is termed a repurchase agreement.
  - If the dealer is lending cash and accepting collateral, the transaction is termed a reverse repurchase agreement.

The repo rate depends on the following factors:

- The risk associated with the collateral. Repo rates increase with the level of credit risk in the collateral.
- The term of the repurchase agreement. A longer term typically entails higher repo rates.
- The delivery requirement for the collateral. Repo rates are lower when the collateral must be delivered to the lender.
- The supply and demand conditions of the collateral. The more scarce a particular piece of collateral, the lower the repo rate. This is because the borrower has an asset that lenders of cash may want for specific reasons (perhaps to short the security). Such collateral is said to be "on special" (versus "general collateral").
- The interest rates on alternative sources of financing in the money market. If rates for borrowing from other sources are higher, repo rates will also tend to be higher.

The repo margin is a function of the following factors:

- The length of the repurchase agreement. The longer the term, the higher the repo margin.
- The quality of the collateral. The higher the quality of the collateral, the lower the repo margin.
- The credit quality of the counterparty. The higher the creditworthiness of the counterparty, the lower the repo margin.
- The supply and demand conditions of the collateral. The higher the demand or the lower the supply of the collateral, the lower the repo margin.

READING 52: INTRODUCTION TO FIXED-INCOME VALUATION

LESSON 1: BOND PRICES AND THE TIME VALUE OF MONEY

**LOS 52a: Calculate a bond's price given a market discount rate.
Vol 5, pp 402–406**

**LOS 52b: Identify the relationships among a bond's price, coupon rate,
maturity, and market discount rate (yield-to-maturity). Vol 5, pp 402–411**

Bond Pricing with a Market Discount Rate

The value or price of a bond is computed as the present value of expected future cash flows from the bond. For a plain-vanilla fixed-rate bond, the cash flows are composed of periodic coupon interest payments and principal repayment at maturity. The discount rate used to compute the present value of those cash flows is the market discount rate (also known as the required yield or the required rate of return), which represents the rate of return required by investors to compensate them for the perceived riskiness of the bond.

Let us use an example of a 4-year, 10% annual coupon bond with a par value of $1,000 to illustrate (1) how the value of a bond is computed and (2) some very important relationships regarding bond prices.

Scenario A:

Let's start with assuming that market discount rate for this bond equals the coupon rate offered (10%). The price of the bond can be calculated as:

$$FV = -\$1,000; PMT = -\$100; N = 4; I/Y = 10; CPT\ PV; PV = \$1,000$$

$$\frac{100}{(1+0.1)^1} + \frac{100}{(1+0.1)^2} + \frac{100}{(1+0.1)^3} + \frac{100+1,000}{(1+0.1)^4} = \$1,000$$

Note that the Year 4 payment includes the final coupon payment and principal repayment.

- If the coupon rate offered on the bond equals the rate of return required by investors to compensate them for the risk inherent in the instrument, the bond will sell for its par value.

Scenario B:

Now let's tweak the assumption that the market discount rate equals 10%. Let's assume instead that the bond is less risky so investors only demand a 9% rate of return on the investment. In this case, the price of the bond can be calculated as:

$$FV = -\$1,000; PMT = -\$100; N = 4; I/Y = 9; CPT\ PV; PV = \$1,032.40$$

$$\frac{100}{(1+0.09)^1} + \frac{100}{(1+0.09)^2} + \frac{100}{(1+0.09)^3} + \frac{100+1,000}{(1+0.09)^4} = \$1,032.40$$

- Notice that if the rate of return required by investors is lower (9% versus 10%) due to lower perceived risk, the value or price of the bond is higher ($1,032.40 versus $1,000).
- If the coupon rate offered on the bond is higher than the required yield, the bond will sell for a premium.
- Stated differently, the compensation offered to investors (the coupon) for bearing various risks inherent in the instrument is higher than the compensation required by investors for purchasing the bond (the required yield). Therefore, investors would be willing to purchase the bond at a premium to par.

Scenario C:

Finally, let's assume that the bond is actually more risky (than in Scenario A) so investors demand an 11% rate of return on the investment. In this case, the price of the bond can be calculated as:

$$FV = -\$1,000;\ PMT = -\$100;\ N = 4;\ I/Y = 11;\ CPT\ PV;\ PV = \$968.98$$

$$\frac{100}{(1+0.11)^1} + \frac{100}{(1+0.11)^2} + \frac{100}{(1+0.11)^3} + \frac{100+1,000}{(1+0.11)^4} = \$968.98$$

- Notice that if the rate of return required by investors is higher (11% versus 10%) due to greater perceived risk, the value or price of the bond is lower ($968.98 versus $1,000).
- If the coupon rate offered on the bond is lower than the required yield, the bond will sell for a discount.
- Stated differently, the compensation offered to investors (the coupon) for taking on various risks inherent in the instrument is lower than the compensation required by investors for purchasing the bond (the required yield). Therefore, investors would only be willing to purchase the bond at a discount to par.

The prices calculated under these different interest rate scenarios allow us to reach the following conclusions:

- The higher the discount rate, the lower the present value of each individual cash flow, and the lower the value of the fixed income security.
- The lower the discount rate, the higher the present value of each individual cash flow, and the higher the value of the fixed income security.

Plotting the relationship between the discount rate and value of a fixed-income instrument on a graph will result in a convex curve (see Figure 1-1). This curve is known as the price-yield profile of a fixed income security.

Important: Notice that the *increase* in the price of the bond (from $1,000 to $1,032.40 or 3.24%) if the discount rate *decreases* by 100 basis points (bps) (from 10% to 9% in Scenario B) is *greater* than the *decrease* in the price of the bond (from $1,000 to $968.98 or 3.102%) if the discount rate *increases* by 100 bps (from 10% to 11% in Scenario C). This is a very important takeaway when it comes to bond pricing and is known as the convexity effect.

Figure 1-1: Price-Yield Profile

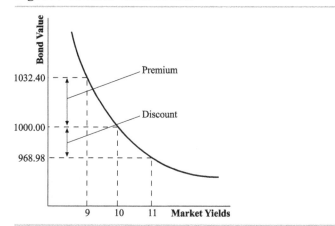

The bond that we have worked with so far (in Scenarios A, B, and C) has paid out coupon annually. While this is the norm in Europe, most Asian and North American bonds make semi-annual coupon payments. To illustrate the valuation of a bond with semi-annual coupon payments, let's start with the assumptions in Scenario B ($1,000 par, 4-year bond with a 10% coupon rate and a yield-to-maturity of 9%) but assume semi-annual instead of annual coupon payments. There will be 8 (= 4 × 2) semi-annual coupon payments on this bond and each coupon payment with be worth $50 (= 10%/2 × $1,000). Given a semiannual yield-to-maturity of 4.5% (= 9% ÷ 2), the value of the bond today can be computed as:

FV = –$1,000; PMT = –$50; N = 8; I/Y = 4.5; CPT PV; PV = $1,032.94

Notice that the value of the bond here is slightly greater than the value of the bond in Scenario B ($1,032.94 versus $1,032.40). Even though the total amount of coupon income is the same ($400), the more frequent coupon payments imply a higher present value for the bond.

Yield-To-Maturity

If the market price of the bond is known, then given the term of the bond, the coupon rate, and coupon payment frequency, we can compute its yield-to-maturity or YTM (also known as redemption yield or yield to redemption). The yield-to-maturity is the (uniform) interest rate that equates the sum of the present values of the bond's expected future cash flows (when discount at that rate) to its current price. It also represents the internal rate of return on the bond's cash flows given three critical assumptions:

1. The investor holds on to the bond until maturity.
2. The issuer makes all promised payments on time in their full amount.
3. The investor is able to reinvest all coupon payments received during the term of the bond at the stated yield-to-maturity until the bond's maturity date. See Examples 1-1 and 1-2.

Example 1-1: Computing the YTM for Semiannual-Pay Coupon Bonds

Compute the YTM of a 10-year, $1,000 par bond with an 8% coupon rate that makes semiannual coupon payments given that its current price is $925.

Solution:

PV = –$925; N = 10 × 2 = 20; PMT = $40; FV = $1,000; CPT I/Y; I/Y = 4.581%

This calculated yield of 4.581% is the yield per semiannual period or semiannual discount rate. By convention, the YTM on a semiannual coupon bond is expressed as an annualized yield by multiplying the semiannual discount rate by two. Therefore, the annualized YTM here is 4.581% × 2 = **9.16%**

> **Important:** When calculating the value of a bond using your financial calculator, make sure that PMT and FV have the same sign, and that PV has the opposite sign. If you invest in a bond you incur an outflow up front, but you get back the coupon and principal. Alternatively, if you issue a bond you have an inflow up front, but you pay out coupon and principal.

Example 1-2: Computing the YTM for Annual-Pay Coupon Bonds

Compute the YTM for a 10-year, $1,000 par bond that pays an 8% annual coupon given that its current price is $925.

Solution:

PV = –$925; N = 10; PMT = $80; FV = $1,000; CPT I/Y; I/Y = 9.178%

This bond's yield-to-maturity equals **9.178%**.

Relationships between the Bond Price and Bond Characteristics

1. A bond's price is inversely related to the market discount rate (the inverse effect). When the discount rate increases (decreases) the price of the bond decreases (increases).
2. Given the same coupon rate and term to maturity, the percentage price change is greater in terms of absolute magnitude when the discount rate decreases than when it increases (the convexity effect).
3. For the same term to maturity, a lower coupon bond is more sensitive to changes in the market discount rate than a higher coupon bond (the coupon effect).
4. Generally speaking, for the same coupon rate, a longer term bond is more sensitive to changes in the market discount rate than a shorter term bond (the maturity effect). Note that while the maturity effect always holds for zero-coupon bonds and for bonds priced at par or premium to par, it does not always hold for long-term low coupon (but not zero-coupon) bonds that are trading at a discount.

Relationship between Price and Maturity

Now let's examine how a bond's value changes as it nears maturity. Let's calculate the values of the $1,000 par, 4-year 10% annual coupon bond as it nears maturity assuming that:

1. It was issued at a premium when market yields were 9%; and
2. It was issued at a discount when market interest rates were 11%.

1. If market interest rates remain at 9% over the term of the bond, the value of the premium bond as it nears maturity is given in the following table:

Time since Issuance (yrs)	Time to Maturity (yrs)	Price (PV of Remaining CF)
0	4	$1,032.40
1	3	$1,025.31
2	2	$1,017.59
3	1	$1,009.17
4	0	$1,000.00

2. If market interest rates remain at 11% over the bond's term, the value of the discount bond as it nears maturity is given in the following table:

Time since Issuance (yrs)	Time to Maturity (yrs)	Price (PV of Remaining CF)
0	4	$968.98
1	3	$975.56
2	2	$982.87
3	1	$991.00
4	0	$1,000.00

From the calculations in the tables above we can conclude that if the yield remains constant:

- A *premium* bond's value *decreases* toward par as it nears maturity.
- A *discount* bond's value *increases* toward par as it nears maturity.
- A *par* bond's value remains *unchanged* as it nears maturity.

At maturity, a bond's value must equal its par value because it is the par value that is returned to investors at maturity. Therefore, over its term, a bond's value is "pulled to par" as illustrated in Figure 1-2.

Figure 1-2: Bond Value Pulled to Par

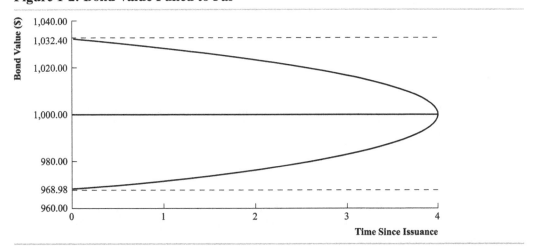

The constant-yield price trajectory shows how the price of a premium/discount code is pulled toward par as it nears maturity.

LOS 52c: Define spot rates and calculate the price of a bond using spot rates. Vol 5, pp 411–413

Pricing Bonds with Spot Rates

Under traditional methods of bond valuation, expected future cash flows are discounted at a uniform rate that reflects the risks inherent in the investment (i.e., the yield-to-maturity). The **arbitrage-free valuation approach** does not use the same rate to discount each cash flow, but uses the relevant spot rate to discount each cash flow that occurs at a different point in time. A **spot rate** (or **zero rate**) is the yield on a zero-coupon bond for a given maturity. For example, the yield on a 5-year zero coupon bond equals the 5-year spot rate and it is the rate that is used under the arbitrage-free valuation approach to discount the cash flow received from a bond at the end of Year 5.

For our purposes, there is no need to get into how spot rates are determined. Just keep in mind that the yield-to-maturity discounts each of the bond's expected cash flows at a uniform rate (i.e., the yield-to-maturity) to determine its price, while under arbitrage-free valuation, the individual discount rate that corresponds to the individual cash flow date (i.e., the spot rate) is used to determine the present value of that particular payment. Generally speaking, long-term spot rates tend to be higher than short-term spot rates as there is more risk associated with cash flows that are expected to be received further out into the future. The general formula for calculating the price of a bond given a series of spot rate is provided below:

$$PV = \frac{PMT}{(1+Z_1)^1} + \frac{PMT}{(1+Z_2)^2} + \ldots + \frac{PMT+FV}{(1+Z_N)^N}$$

where:
z_1 = Spot rate for Period 1
z_2 = Spot rate for Period 2
z_N = Spot rate for Period N

Example 1-3 illustrates how both approaches result in the same value for a particular bond.

Example 1-3: Valuing Bonds Using YTMs and Spot Rates

Suppose a $1,000 par, annual-pay bond matures in 3 years and has a coupon rate of 8%. The bond is currently selling for $1,001.34 with at a yield-to-maturity of 7.948%. The relevant spot rates are given below:

Maturity	Yield on Zero-Coupon Bond (Spot Rate)
1 year	7%
2 years	7.5%
3 years	8%

Verify that the value of the bond computed by discounting each cash flow at the relevant spot rate is the same as the value calculated by discounting all cash flows at the yield-to-maturity.

Solution:

If we discount each cash flow at the relevant spot rate, the value of the bond will equal:

$$\frac{\$80}{(1+0.07)^1} + \frac{\$80}{(1+0.075)^2} + \frac{\$1,080}{(1+0.08)^3}$$
$$= \$74.77 + \$69.23 + \$857.34 = \$1,001.34$$

If we discount every cash flow at the yield-to-maturity, the price of the bond will equal:

N = 3; PMT = –$80; I/Y = 7.948; FV = –$1,000; CPT PV; PV → $1,001.34

LESSON 2: PRICES AND YIELDS (PART I): CONVENTIONS FOR QUOTES AND CALCULATIONS

LOS 52d: Describe and calculate the flat price, accrued interest, and the full price of a bond. Vol 5, pp 413–417

Flat Price, Accrued Interest, and the Full Price

When a coupon bond is sold between coupon payment dates, we must account for the interest or coupon that the seller has earned, but not yet received. The amount that an investor/buyer should pay for a bond equals the present value of future cash flows, but the very next cash flow (the next coupon payment) includes two components:

1. Interest earned by the seller, which has been accrued from the last payment date till the transaction date. This is called accrued interest.
2. Interest earned by the buyer. See Figure 2-1.

Figure 2-1: Valuing a Bond between Coupon-Payment Dates

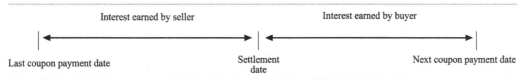

When the price of the bond is determined by calculating the present value of future cash flows as of the settlement date, the computed value is known as the full price (also known as the invoice or dirty price). This price includes accrued interest and reflects the amount that the buyer pays the seller. From this full price, the accrued interest is deducted to determine the flat price (also known as the clean price or quoted price) of the bond.

$$PV^{Full} = PV^{Flat} + AI$$

Dealers usually quote flat prices, and then if a deal is executed the accrued interest is added to the flat price to determine the full price that must be paid by the buyer to the seller on the settlement date. The reason behind quoting flat prices is to avoid misleading investors about the price trend for a bond. Given that the amount of interest accrued on the bond increases each day, full prices rise each day even if the yield-to-maturity remains constant.

Further, full prices suddenly drop at coupon payment dates when coupon is paid and accrued interest falls to zero. Quoting flat prices avoids such misrepresentation.

Also note that it is the flat price that is pulled toward par as the bond nears maturity (as shown earlier in Figure 2). The accrued interest is the part of the full price that does not depend on the yield-to-maturity. Therefore, we can say that it is the flat price that is affected by changes in the market discount rate.

Accrued interest is the seller's proportional share of the next coupon payment. It is calculated as:

$$AI = t/T \times PMT$$

where:
AI = Accrued interest.
t = Number of days from the last coupon payment to the settlement date.
T = Number of days from the last coupon payment date to the next coupon payment date.
PMT = Coupon payment.

The manner in which the number of days between two dates is calculated in the bond market depends on the day-count convention used in the particular sector of the market.

- For government bonds, the actual/actual day-count convention is usually applied. The actual number of days is used including weekends, holidays, and weekdays.
  - For example, if the coupon payment dates for a semiannual-pay bond are May 15 and November 15, the accrued interest for settlement on June 27 would be calculated as 43 (the actual number of days from May 15 to June 27) divided by 184 (the number of days from May 15 to November 15), times the coupon payment.
- For corporate bonds, the 30/360 day-count convention is often used.
  - For example, if the coupon payment dates for a semiannual-pay bond are May 15 and November 15, the accrued interest for settlement on June 27 would be calculated as 42 (= 30 + 12) divided by 180 (= 30 × 6), times the coupon payment.

When it comes to valuing bonds between coupon payment dates, you need to understand that as time passes through the coupon period, the price of the bond increases (as the next coupon payment draws closer) at a rate equal to the discount rate per period. The full price of a fixed-rate bond between coupon payment dates can be computed as its value on the last coupon payment date multiplied by one plus the periodic discount rate (r) compounded over the period of time remaining that has elapsed since the last coupon payment (t/T):

$$PV^{Full} = PV \times (1+r)^{t/T}$$

where:
PV^{Full} = Full price of the bond (value between coupon payments)
PV = Price of bond at last/previous coupon payment date
r = Discount rate per period
t = Number of last coupon payment date to the settlement date
T = Number of days in coupon period
t/T = Fraction of coupon period that has gone by since last payment
(See Example 2-1.)

Example 2-1: Computing Full Price, Accrued Interest, and Flat Price

A 5% U.S. corporate bond is priced for settlement on July 20, 2015. The bond makes semiannual coupon payments on April 21 and October 21 of each year and matures on October 21, 2021. The bond uses the 30/360 day-count convention for accrued interest.

Calculate the full price, the accrued interest, and the flat price per USD100 of par value for three stated annual yields-to-maturity: (A) 4.7%, (B) 5.00%, and (C) 5.30%.

Solution:

Given the 30/360 day-count convention, there are 89 days between the last coupon on April 21, 2015 and the settlement date on July 20, 2015 (9 days between April 21 and April 30, plus 60 days for the full months of May and June, plus 20 days in July). Therefore, the fraction of the coupon period that has gone by equals 89/180. As of the last coupon payment date, there are 6.5 years (and 13 semiannual periods) remaining until maturity.

A. **Stated annual yield-to-maturity of 4.70%, or 2.35% per semiannual period:**

The price as of the last coupon payment date is calculated as:

N = 13; PMT = –$2.50; FV = –$100; I/Y = 2.35%; CPT PV; PV = $101.6636

The full price on July 20 is calculated as:

$PV^{Full} = 101.6636 \times (1.0235)^{89/180} = \$102.838$

The accrued interest is calculated as:

$AI = 89/180 \times 2.50 = \$1.2361$

The flat price is calculated as:

$PV^{Flat} = 102.838 - 1.2361 = \$101.6019$

B. **Stated annual yield-to-maturity of 5.00%, or 2.50% per semiannual period:**

The price as of the last coupon payment date equals the bond's par value, which should be expected, as the coupon rate and the market discount rate are the same.

N = 13; PMT = – $2.50; FV = –$100; I/Y = 2.5%; CPT PV; PV = $100.00

The full price on July 20 is calculated as:

$PV^{Full} = 100.00 \times (1.025)^{89/180} = \$101.2284$

The accrued interest is calculated as:

$AI = 89/180 \times 2.5 = \$1.2361$

The flat price is calculated as:

$PV^{Flat} = 101.2284 - 1.2361 = \$99.9923$

Notice here that the flat price of the bond is lower than its par value, despite the fact that the coupon rate and the yield-to-maturity are equal. The reason for this is that the accrued interest computation does not consider the time value of money. Accrued interest is the interest earned by the seller of the bond for the time between the last coupon payment and the settlement date (in this case 1.2361 per 100 of par value). However, note that this interest income is expected to be received on the next coupon payment date so theoretically, the (true) accrued interest should actually be the present value of 1.2361 as of the settlement date. In practice however, the calculation of accrued interest neglects the time value of money. Therefore reported/computed accrued interest is slightly overstated, which results in a slightly understated flat price. Note that the full price is theoretically accurate as it is calculated as the sum of the present values of the future cash flows as of the settlement date.

C. Stated annual yield-to-maturity of 5.30%, or 2.65% per semiannual period:

The price as of the last coupon payment date is calculated as:

N = 13; PMT = –$2.50; FV = –$100; I/Y = 2.65%; CPT PV → PV = $98.3685

The full price on July 20 is calculated as:

$$PV^{Full} = 99.3685 \times (1.0265)^{89/180} = \$99.6488$$

The accrued interest is calculated as:

$$AI = 89/180 \times 2.5 = \$1.2361$$

The flat price is calculated as:

$$PV^{Flat} = 99.6488 - 1.2361 = \$98.4127$$

Important:
- Notice that the accrued interest is the same in each case because it does not depend on the yield-to-maturity.
- Differences in the flat prices capture the differences in rates of return required by investors.

LOS 52e: Describe matrix pricing. Vol 5, pp 417–420

Matrix Pricing

Matrix pricing is a method used to estimate the market discount rate and price of bonds that are not actively traded. Essentially, prices of comparable (in terms of terms to maturity, coupon rates, and credit quality) are used to interpolate the price of the subject bond.

Example 2-2 illustrates the application of matrix pricing to compute the required yield and price of a bond that is not actively traded.

Example 2-2: Applying Matrix Pricing to Value a Bond

An analyst is trying to estimate the value of a relatively illiquid 6-year, 5% annual-pay coupon bond. She identifies two corporate bonds that have similar credit quality:

- Bond A is a 5-year, 6% annual-pay bond priced at 103.25 per 100 of par value.
- Bond B is an 8-year, 5% annual-pay bond priced at 97.75 per 100 of par value.

Estimate the price of the illiquid bond per 100 of par value.

Solution:

The first step is to determine the yields-to-maturity on the comparable bonds.

The required yield on the 5-year, 6% bond priced at 103.25 is calculated as:

N = 5; PMT = –$6; FV = –$100; PV = $103.25; CPT I/Y; I/Y = 5.244%

The required yield on the 8-year, 5% bond priced at 97.75 is calculated as:

N = 8; PMT = –$5; FV = –$100; PV = $97.75; CPT I/Y; I/Y = 5.353%

The market discount rate for the 6-year bond can be obtained using linear interpolation. The yield on the 6-year bond is estimated as the yield on the 5-year bond plus one-third of the difference between the yields on the 5-year and 8-year bonds.

$$0.05244 + \frac{(3-2)}{(5-2)} \times (0.05353 - 0.05244) = 0.0528$$

Given an estimated yield-to-maturity of 5.28%, the price of the illiquid 6-year, 5% annual-pay bond can be estimated as:

N = 6; PMT = –$5; FV = –$100; I/Y = 5.28%; CPT PV; PV = $98.59

> If more than one bond is provided for a given maturity, then first calculate the average YTM for bonds with that maturity and then apply linear interpolation to estimate the yield for a maturity for which a comparable bond does not exist.

Matrix pricing can also be used when underwriting new bonds to estimate the required yield spread over the benchmark rate on the bonds to be issued.

> Yield spreads and benchmarks are discussed in detail later in the reading.

- The spread refers to the difference between the yield-to-maturity on the new bond and the benchmark bond. It reflects the additional compensation offered by the issuer to compensate investors for the difference in credit risk, liquidity risk, and tax status of the bond relative to the benchmark.
- The benchmark is typically a government bond with a similar term to maturity.

Example 2-3 illustrates the use of matrix pricing to determine the required yield spread on a new bond issue.

Example 2-3: Application of Matrix Pricing to Estimate the Credit Spread on a New Issue

ABC Company is planning to issue a 5-year bond. The only other debt that the company currently has outstanding is a 2.5% annual-pay bond which is currently trading at $102.50 per 100 of par and has 4 full years to maturity (there is zero accrued interest built into its current price).

The following information is provided:

- Currently there are no outstanding government bonds with 4 years to maturity.
- The yield on a 3-year government bond is 0.85%, while the yield on a 5-year government bond is 1.55%.
- The term structure of credit spreads for bonds with the same credit rating as ABC Company suggests that 5-year spreads are around 37 bps higher than 4-year spreads.

Determine the expected market discount rate on the ABC's planned 5-year bond issue.

Solution:

The first step here is to compute the yield-to-maturity on the ABC's outstanding bonds that have 4 years remaining until maturity:

PV = $102.50; PMT = –$2.50; FV = –$100; N = 4; CPT I/Y; I/Y = 1.8459%

Next, we compute the estimated yield-to-maturity on a government bond with 4 years until maturity using the 3-year and 5-year government bond yields. This estimated yield on the 4-year government bond is then used to estimate the credit spread on ABC's 4-year bond.

Estimated 4-year government bond yield = (0.85% + 1.55%) / 2 = 1.20%

Estimated credit spread on ABC's 4-year bond = 1.8459% – 1.20% = 0.6459%

Then, we use the term structure of credit spreads for issues with a similar rating as the one in question to determine the expected spread on the 5-year bond ABC plans to issue:

Expected spread on 5-year bond = Estimated spread on 4-year bond + 0.0037
= 0.006459 + 0.0037 = 0.010159

Finally, we add the expected spread on ABC's planned 5-year issue to the 5-year government bond yield (the benchmark) to determine the expected market discount rate on the issue:

Expected discount rate on new issue = 0.0155 + 0.010159 = 0.025659 or 2.57%

The **term structure of credit spreads** shows the relationship between spreads offered on bonds with a particular credit rating over the "risk-free" yield on government bonds and terms-to-maturity.

LESSON 3: PRICES AND YIELDS (PART II): MATRIX PRICING AND YIELD MEASURES FOR BONDS

LOS 52f: Calculate and interpret yield measures for fixed-rate bonds, floating-rate notes, and money market instruments. Vol 5, pp 420–434

Yield Measures for Fixed-Rate Bonds

The effective annual rate (or effective annual yield) on a fixed-rate bond depends on the assumed number of periods in the year, which is known as the periodicity **of the** stated annual rate or stated annual yield.

> We have already discussed the effective annual rate versus the stated annual rate in detail in the Quantitative Methods section. What we are doing here is using the periodicity (number of compounded periods per year) of the stated annual rate to determine the effective annual rate.

Let's work with four bonds (an annual-pay bond, a semiannual-pay bond, a quarterly-pay bond, and a monthly-pay bond), each with a stated annual yield of 8% to illustrate the concept of periodicity and to highlight the difference between a stated annual yield and the effective annual yield.

An **annual-pay bond** would have a stated annual yield for periodicity of one. The stated annual yield would equal the discount rate per year.

- Effective annual yield = $(1 + 0.08)^1 - 1 = 0.08$ or 8%

A **semiannual-pay bond** would have a stated annual yield for periodicity of two. The rate per semiannual period would be computed as the stated annual yield divided by two.

- Rate per semiannual period = $0.08/2 = 0.04$
- Effective annual yield = $(1 + 0.04)^2 - 1 = 0.0816$ or 8.16%

A **quarterly-pay bond** would have a stated annual yield for periodicity of four. The rate per quarter would be computed as the stated annual yield divided by four.

- Rate per quarter = $0.08/4 = 0.02$
- Effective annual yield = $(1 + 0.02)^4 - 1 = 0.0824$ or 8.24%

A **monthly-pay bond** would have a stated annual yield for periodicity of 12. The rate per month would be computed as the stated annual yield divided by 12.

- Rate per month = $0.08/12 = 0.00667$
- Effective annual yield = $(1 + 0.00667)^{12} - 1 = 0.083$ or 8.3%

Note that:

- The effective annual rate has a periodicity of one as it assumes only one compounding period in the year.
- Given the stated annual rate, as the number of compounding periods (periodicity) increases, the effective annual rate increases.
- Given the effective annual rate, as the number of compounding periods (periodicity) increases, the stated annual rate decreases. (This point will become clear in Example 3-1).

In the United States, most bonds make semiannual coupon payments (periodicity equals two). The stated annual rate that has a periodicity of two is known as a semiannual bond basis yield or semiannual bond equivalent yield. The semiannual bond basis yield is calculated as the yield per semiannual period multiplied by two. To convert a stated annual rate (SAR) for M periods per year, SAR_M, to a stated annual rate for N periods per year, SAR_N, we can use the following formula:

$$\left(1+\frac{SAR_M}{M}\right)^M = \left(1+\frac{SAR_N}{N}\right)^N$$ ... Equation 1

Example 3-1: Computing Stated Annual Yields for Different Compounding Frequencies

A 5-year, 6% semiannual-pay government bond is priced at 98 per 100 of par value. Calculate the annual yield-to-maturity stated on a semiannual bond basis (stated annual yield). Convert this stated annual yield to:

1. A stated annual yield based on annual compounding.
2. A stated annual yield based on quarterly compounding.
3. A stated annual yield based on monthly compounding.

Solution:

We first calculate the yield per semiannual period on the semiannual-pay bond.

N = 10; PMT = \$3; FV = \$100; PV = –\$98; CPT I/Y; I/Y = 3.237%

The calculated yield of 3.237% is the yield per semiannual period. This rate is multiplied by two to determine the stated annual yield or the semiannual bond basis yield:

Semiannual bond basis yield = 3.237% × 2 = 6.47%

1. To determine the stated annual yield based on annual compounding, we need to convert the stated annual yield of 6.47% from a periodicity of two to a periodicity of one.

$$\left(1+\frac{0.0647}{2}\right)^2 = \left(1+\frac{SAY_1}{1}\right)^1$$

SAY_1 = 0.06579 or 6.58%

The stated annual rate of 6.47% based on semiannual compounding compares to a stated annual rate of 6.58% compounded annually. Note that 6.58% (since it represents the yield based on annual compounding) is the effective annual yield on the bond.

---

2. To determine the stated annual yield based on quarterly compounding, we need to convert the stated annual yield of 6.47% from a periodicity of two to a periodicity of four.

$$\left(1+\frac{0.0647}{2}\right)^2 = \left(1+\frac{SAY_4}{4}\right)^4$$

$SAY_4 = 0.06419$ or 6.42%

The stated annual rate of 6.47% based on semiannual compounding compares to a stated annual rate of 6.42% compounded quarterly. Notice that increasing the frequency of compounding has lowered the stated annual rate.

3. To determine the stated annual yield based on monthly compounding, we need to convert the stated annual yield of 6.47% from a periodicity of two to a periodicity of twelve.

$$\left(1+\frac{0.0647}{2}\right)^2 = \left(1+\frac{SAY_{12}}{12}\right)^{12}$$

$SAY_4 = 0.06384$ or 6.38%

The stated annual rate of 6.47% based on semiannual compounding compares to a stated annual rate of 6.38% compounded monthly. Notice again that increasing the frequency of compounding has lowered the stated annual rate.

What we have effectively done in this example is computed the effective annual yield (in Part 1) and the stated annual yields (based on monthly, quarterly, and semiannual compounding) for the same bond. Notice that the effective annual yield of 6.58% (or the yield based on annual compounding) equals:

- 6.47% / 2 = 3.237% (the rate per semiannual period) compounded two times a year.
- 6.42% / 4 = 1.605% (the rate per quarter) compounded four times a year.
- 6.38% / 12 = 0.532% (the rate per month) compounded twelve times a year.

Now notice that given the effective annual rate, an increase in the number of compounding periods (periodicity) results in a lower stated annual rate. Stated differently, compounding more frequently at a lower stated annual rate corresponds to compounding less frequently at a higher stated annual rate.

Bond yields are typically quoted using the street convention, where the yield represents the internal rate of return on the bond's cash flows assuming all payments are made on scheduled dates regardless of whether any scheduled payment dates fall on weekends or holidays. Practically speaking, if a scheduled coupon payment date falls on the weekend or on a holiday, payment is actually made on the next business day. The true yield uses these actual payment dates to compute the IRR. The true yield can never be higher than the street convention yield as weekends and holidays only delay payments.

For corporate bonds, a government equivalent yield is sometimes quoted. This yield basically restates a yield-to-maturity based on a 30/360 day-count convention to one based on an actual/actual day-count convention. The government equivalent yield can be used to compute the spread offered on a corporate bond on top of the yield offered on a government bond (since both are based on the same, actual/actual day-count convention).

Another yield measure that is commonly seen in fixed-income markets is the current yield (also called the income yield or interest yield). It is calculated as the sum of coupon payments received over the year divided by the flat price.

$$\text{Current yield} = \frac{\text{Annual cash coupon payment}}{\text{Bond price}}$$

The current yield is a relatively crude measure of the rate of return to an investor because of the following reasons:

- It neglects the frequency of coupon payments in the numerator.
- It neglects any accrued interest in the denominator.
- It neglects any gains (losses) from purchasing the bond at a discount (premium) and redeeming it for par.

The simple yield on a bond is calculated as the sum of coupon payments received over the year plus (minus) straight line amortization of the gain (loss) from purchasing the bond at a discount (premium), divided by the flat price. See Example 3-2.

Example 3-2: Comparing the Stated YTM on Two Bonds

	Bond A	Bond B
Annual coupon rate	10%	13%
Coupon payment frequency	Semiannually	Quarterly
Years to maturity	3	3
Price (per 100 of par value)	98	105

1. Calculate the current yield and the stated annual yield-to-maturity for each of the two bonds.
2. The analyst believes that Bond B has a little more risk than Bond A. How much additional compensation, in terms of a higher yield-to-maturity, does Bond B offer relative to Bond A as compensation for additional risk?

Solution:

1. Current yield for Bond A:

   $10/98 = 0.10204$ or **10.204%**

   Yield-to-maturity for Bond A:

   N = 6; PMT = –$5; FV = –$100; PV = $98; CPT I/Y; I/Y = 5.399%
   YTM = 5.399% × 2 = **10.798%**

Current yield for Bond B:

13 / 105 = 0.12381 or **12.381%**

Yield-to-maturity for Bond B:

N = 12; PMT = –$3.25; FV = –$100; PV = $105; CPT I/Y → I/Y = 2.755%
YTM = 2.755% × 4 = **11.02%**

2. Bond A's yield-to-maturity is a stated annual rate with a periodicity of 2, while Bond B's yield-maturity is a stated annual rate with a periodicity of 4. Since the two yields are based on different periodicities, we cannot assert that the difference between the two, that is 22.2 bps (= 0.1102 – 0.10798) accurately reflects compensation for additional risk in the bond with the higher yield (Bond B).

Converting the periodicity of Bond A stated annual yield from two to four, we obtain a stated annual yield of 10.656%.

$$(1 + 0.10798/2)^2 = (1 + SAY_4/4)^4$$
$$SAY_4 = 10.656\%$$

This yield can be compared to the calculated yield-to-maturity on Bond B (with a periodicity of 4) of 11.02%. We can then say that the difference between the two, that is 36.4 bps (= 0.1102 – 0.10656) captures the additional compensation offered on Bond B for its greater risk **when yields are annualized for quarterly compounding**.

Converting the periodicity of Bond B's stated annual yield from four to two, we obtain a stated annual yield of 11.172%.

$$(1 + 0.1102/4)^4 = (1 + SAY_2/2)^2$$
$$SAY_2 = 11.172\%$$

This yield can be compared to the calculated yield-to-maturity on Bond A (with a periodicity of 2) 10.798%. We can then say that the difference between the two i.e., 37.4 bps (= 0.11172 – 0.10798) captures the additional compensation offered on Bond B for its greater risk **when yields are stated on a semiannual bond basis**.

For callable bonds, the yield realized by the investor will depend on whether and when (and at what call price) the bond is called. Investors compute the yield-to-call for each call date (based on the call price and the number of periods until the call date) and then determine the yield-to-worst as the worst or lowest yield among the yield-to-maturity and the various yields to call for the bond. See Example 3-3.

Example 3-3: Computing Yields-to-Call and Yield-to-Worst

Consider a 10-year, 8% annual-pay bond that is first callable in 7 years at 114 (per 100 of par value), then callable in 8 years at 105, and at par value on coupon payment dates thereafter. Given that the current price is 121 per 100 of par value, determine the yield-to-worst for the bond.

Solution:

To compute the yield-to-worst, we need to determine all the yields-to-call and the yield-to-maturity.

The yield-to-first-call in 7 years is calculated as:

N = 7; PMT = –$8; FV = –$114; PV = $121; CPT I/Y; I/Y = 5.921%

The yield-to-second-call in 8 years is calculated as:

N = 8; PMT = –$8; FV = –$105; PV = $121; CPT I/Y; I/Y = 5.239%

The yield-to-third-call in 9 years is calculated as:

N = 9; PMT = –$8; FV = –$100; PV = $121; CPT I/Y; I/Y = 5.04%

The yield-to-maturity is calculated as:

N = 10; PMT = –$8; FV = –$100; PV = $121; CPT I/Y; I/Y = 5.248%

Since yield-to-third-call is the lowest among the all the yields-to-call and the yield-to-maturity, it represents the yield-to-worst (5.04%).

While the yield-to-worst is commonly used by bond dealers and investors in fixed-rate callable bonds, a better way to evaluate investments in callable bonds is to use an option pricing model (which requires making an assumption regarding future interest rate volatility) to value the embedded call option. The value of the embedded call option is added to the flat price of the callable bond to determine what is known as the option-adjusted price. Recall that the option embedded in a callable bond favors the issuer, so it reduces the value of the bond from the investor's perspective. Therefore:

Value of callable bond = Value of non-callable bond – Value of embedded call option

Value of non-callable bond (option-adjusted price) = Flat price of callable bond + Value of embedded call option

The option-adjusted price is used to compute the option-adjusted yield. This yield is the required market discount rate where the price is adjusted to include the value of the embedded call option. The option adjusted yield will be lower than the yield-to-maturity on a callable bond because callable bonds offer higher yields than otherwise identical non-callable bonds to compensate investors for effectively selling the embedded call option to the issuer.

Yield Measures for Floating-Rate Notes

Interest payments on a floating-rate note (FRN) are not fixed. They fluctuate from period to period depending on the current level of the reference rate. The idea behind variable interest payments is to offer investors a security that has less market price risk than fixed-rate bonds when interest rates fluctuate. With fixed-rate bonds, changes in interest rates influence the market price as cash flows remain unchanged. On the other hand, with FRNs, future cash flows fluctuate with changes in interest rates.

An important thing to recognize regarding FRNs is that the effective coupon rate for a specified period is determined at the beginning of the period (calculated as the current level of the reference rate plus the quoted margin), but actually paid out at the end of the period. This payment structure is known as "in arrears."

> The most common day-count conventions for FRNs are actual/360 and actual/365.

It is important to understand the mechanics that determine the periodic coupon rate on a FRN. Assume that a FRN offers to pay interest every quarter based on 90-day LIBOR plus a quoted margin of 1%. The reference rate (LIBOR-90) used in calculating the effective coupon rate for the forthcoming 90-day period is prevailing 90-day LIBOR (at the beginning of the period). The actual payment of the coupon occurs at the end of the 90-day period (the next reset date).

For example, if LIBOR-90 on July 1, 2013 stands at 4%, and the quoted margin on a FRN is 100 bps, the issuer will make the coupon payment for the 3-month period from July 1 to September 30 at 5%. The issuer knows the coupon rate for the forthcoming 90 days at the beginning of the period (July 1), but actually makes the payment at the end of the period (September 30).

Important: When working with LIBOR, a lot of candidates forget to unannualize the coupon rate. If the effective coupon rate for a 90-day period on a loan of $1 million is 6%, the coupon payment for the period will be calculated as:

$$0.06 \times 90/360 \times \$1,000,000 = \$15,000$$

The quoted margin is the spread offered to investors on top of the reference rate to compensate them for the greater credit risk of the issuer relative to that implied by the reference rate. However, if the issuer enjoys a credit rating better than that implied by the reference rate, the issuer may be able to obtain a negative quoted margin on a FRN.

The adjustment of the periodic effective coupon rate on a FRN at every reset date in line with market interest rates (the current reference rate) results in the price of the instrument being "pulled toward par" as a reset date approaches. However, a FRN can still trade at a discount/premium if the quoted margin is different from the required margin. The required margin (also known as discount margin) refers to the yield spread above (or below) the reference rate such that the FRN trades at par at every reset rate. If the quoted margin equals the required margin, the FRN will trade at par at each reset date, but if the quoted margin is lower (greater) than the required margin, the FRN will trade at a discount (premium).

Changes in the required margin can be caused by changes in the issue's (1) credit risk, (2) liquidity, and/or (3) tax status. For example, assume that a FRN is issued at par with a coupon rate of LIBOR-90 plus 100 bps. Subsequently, if the issuer suffers a credit rating downgrade such that the required margin rises to 125 bps, the FRN will trade at a discount as the spread offered on top of the reference rate no longer compensates the investor adequately for the credit risk in the instrument.

> At issuance, the required margin typically equals the quoted margin so the FRN is issued at par.

Notice that fixed-rate and floating-rate bonds respond very similarly when it comes to credit risk.

- With fixed-rate bonds, a premium (discount) arises when the fixed coupon rate is greater (lower) than the required yield-to-maturity.
- For floating-rate bonds, a premium (discount) arises when the fixed quoted margin is greater (lower) than the required margin.

However, fixed- and floating-rate bonds respond very differently when it comes to changes in benchmark interest rates.

A simplified FRN pricing model calculates the value of a FRN at a reset date by estimating future cash flows and discounting them to the present.

- Each future coupon payment is assumed to be calculated based on the current level of the reference rate plus the quoted margin on the instrument.
- The discount rate applicable to each future payment is assumed to equal the current reference rate plus the required margin.

Example 3-4 illustrates this method.

Example 3-4: Pricing a FRN on a Reset Date

A $1,000 par quarterly-pay FRN has exactly one year to maturity. The reference rate is 90-day LIBOR and the bond carries a quoted margin of 80 bps. LIBOR-90 today (which happens to be a coupon-reset date) is 2.50%, while the current required margin on the FRN is 94 bps. Assuming a 30/360 day-count convention and evenly spaced periods, determine the current value of the FRN.

Solution:

In the simplified FRN valuation model, all future coupon payments are computed based on the current level of the reference rate (current LIBOR-90 equals 2.50%).

Coupon rate = (2.50% + 0.80%) × (90/360) = 0.825%

Coupon payment = 0.825% × $1,000 = $8.25

We value the bond based on a (constant) quarterly coupon of $8.25. The discount rate is calculated based on the current level of the reference rate (2.50%) plus the required margin (94 bps).

Discount rate per quarter = (2.50% + 0.94%) × (90/360) = 0.86%

Now we can compute the estimated value of the FRN as:

FV = –$1,000; PMT = –$8.25; N = 4; I/Y = 0.86; CPT PV; PV = $998.63

Notice that since the required margin is greater than the quoted margin, this FRN will trade at a discount.

The method illustrated in this example can also be used to estimate the required margin on a FRN given its current coupon rate and its current market price. However, note that this valuation model:

- Computes the flat price of the bond (since it does not account for any accrued interest).
- Applies the same, current level of the reference rate to compute (1) the coupon payment and (2) the discount rate in all future periods. More accurate (but complicated) FRN-pricing models use projected future reference rates to compute coupon payments, and spot rates to compute discount rates.

Yield Measures for Money Market Instruments

Money-market instruments are short-term debt securities with maturities ranging from one day (e.g., repos) to one year (e.g., bank certificates of deposit). Money market yields differ from yields in the bond market in the following three respects:

1. Bond yields-to-maturity are annualized and compounded. Money market yields are annualized but not compounded (they are stated on simple interest basis).
2. Bond yields-to-maturity can usually be calculated by applying standard time value of money analysis and using a financial calculator. Money market yields are often quoted in terms of nonstandard interest rates so users need to work with various pricing equations.
3. Bond yields-to-maturity are typically stated for a common periodicity for all terms-to-maturity. Money market instruments that have different times-to-maturity have different periodicities for the stated annual rate.

Generally speaking, money market yields are expressed on a discount rate basis or on an add-on rate basis, and can be based on a 360-day or 365-day year as you will see in the formulas that follow:

Pricing formula for money market instruments quoted on a discount rate basis:

$$PV = FV \times \left(1 - \frac{\text{Days}}{\text{Year}} \times DR \right)$$ … Equation 2

where:
PV = The PV or current price of the money market instrument.
FV = Future value, or the face value of the instrument at
     maturity.
Days = Number of days from settlement until maturity.
Year = Number of days in the year.
DR = Discount rate expressed as an annual percentage rate.

The equation above can be manipulated and stated in the following form (with DR as the subject):

$$DR = \left(\frac{\text{Year}}{\text{Days}} \right) \times \left(\frac{FV - PV}{FV} \right)$$ … Equation 3

Notice the following:

- The first term (Year/Days) is the periodicity of the annual rate.
- The numerator of the second term is the interest earned on the instrument.
- The interest earned is divided by the FV (which includes all earnings), not the PV (which represents the amount initially invested to purchase the instrument). Theoretically speaking, the discount rate should represent the return earned on the amount invested not on the total return at maturity. Therefore, a money market discount rate understates the rate of return to the investor and understates the cost of borrowing for the issuer (because PV is generally less than FV).

Pricing formula for money market instruments quoted on an add-on rate basis:

$$PV = \frac{FV}{\left(1 + \frac{Days}{Year} \times AOR\right)}$$

... Equation 4

where:

PV = The PV, principal amount or price of the money market instrument.

FV = Future value, or the redemption amount paid at maturity including interest.

Days = Number of days from settlement until maturity.

Year = Number of days in the year.

AOR = Add-on rate, stated as an annual percentage rate.

The equation above can be manipulated and stated in the following form (with AOR as the subject):

$$AOR = \left(\frac{Year}{Days}\right) \times \left(\frac{FV - PV}{PV}\right)$$

... Equation 5

Notice the following:

- The first term (Year/Days) is the periodicity of the annual rate.
- The second term is the interest earned divided by the **PV** of the investment. This makes the add-on rate a reasonable measure for the yield on a money market investment.

While market conventions differ across countries, commercial paper, U.S. T-bills, and bankers' acceptances are often quoted on a discount rate basis, and bank certificates of deposits, repos, LIBOR, and Euribor are quoted on an add-on rate basis. You should be able to notice from the equations above, that in addition to (1) differences in quoted money market rates (discount rate basis versus add-on rate basis), (2) differences in the assumed number of days in a year (360 versus 365), investment analysis for money market securities is made more difficult by the fact that the "amount" of a money market instrument quoted on a discount rate basis is typically the face value at maturity (FV), while the "amount" in an add-on rate quote is the price at issuance (PV). Therefore, in order to make money-market investment decisions, instruments must be compared on a common basis. Typically money-market yields are converted to a rate known as the bond-equivalent yield or investment yield for comparisons. The bond equivalent yield is a money-market rate stated on a **365-day year** on an **add-on rate basis**. See Example 3-5.

Example 3-5: Computing Bond Equivalent Yields

Consider the following quoted rates on four 180-day money market instruments.

Money Market Instrument	Quotation Basis	Assumed Number of Days in the Year	Quoted Rate
A	Discount Rate	360	5.15%
B	Discount Rate	365	5.30%
C	Add-On Rate	360	5.45%
D	Add-On Rate	365	5.50%

Calculate the bond equivalent yield for each instrument. Which instrument offers the investor the highest rate of return if assuming that credit risk is constant across all four?

Solution:

A. Bond A is quoted on a **discount rate** basis. We first use Equation 2 to determine PV, price per 100 of par:

$$PV = FV \times \left(1 - \frac{Days}{Year} \times DR\right)$$

$$PV = 1,000 \times \left(1 - \frac{180}{360} \times 0.0515\right) = 97.425$$

We then insert the PV of Bond A into Equation 5 to determine the add-on rate based on a 365-day year (i.e., the bond equivalent yield):

$$AOR = \left(\frac{Year}{Days}\right) \times \left(\frac{FV - PV}{PV}\right)$$

$$AOR = \left(\frac{365}{180}\right) \times \left(\frac{100 - 97.425}{97.425}\right) = 0.0536$$

Therefore, the bond equivalent yield for Bond A is 5.36%.

B. Bond B is also quoted on a **discount rate** basis (but assuming a 365-day year). We first use Equation 2 to determine PV, price per 100 of par:

$$PV = 100 \times \left(1 - \frac{180}{365} \times 0.053\right) = 97.386$$

We then insert the PV of Bond B into Equation 5 to determine the add-on rate based on a 365 day year (i.e., the bond equivalent yield):

$$AOR = \left(\frac{365}{180}\right) \times \left(\frac{100 - 97.386}{97.386}\right) = 0.0544$$

The bond equivalent yield for Bond B is 5.44%.

C. Bond C is quoted on **add-on rate** basis (assuming a 360-day year). In order to calculate the bond yield equivalent yield we first determine its **future value** (redemption amount) using Equation 4.

$$PV = \frac{FV}{\left(1 + \dfrac{Days}{Year} \times AOR\right)}$$

$$FV = 100 + \left(100 \times \frac{180}{360} \times 0.0545\right) = 102.725$$

We then use Equation 5 to determine the bond equivalent yield (based on a 365-day year).

$$AOR = \left(\frac{365}{180}\right) \times \left(\frac{102.725 - 100}{100}\right) = 0.05526$$

The bond equivalent yield for Bond C is 5.526%.

Another way to compute the bond equivalent yield for Bond C is to start with the AOR of 5.45%, which is based on a 360-day year. Notice that this rate has been computed (using Equation 5) as:

$$AOR = \left(\frac{360}{180}\right) \times \left(\frac{102.725 - 100}{100}\right) = 0.0545$$

The add-on rate based on a 360-day year only needs to be multiplied by a factor of 365/360 to get the 365-day AOR (i.e., the bond equivalent yield).

$$\frac{365}{360} \times 0.0545 = 0.05526$$

D. The quoted rate for Bond D of 5.5% is a bond equivalent yield (an add-on basis yield based on a 365-day year).

Now that we have brought the money market yields for all four instruments on an equal footing (computed their bond equivalent yields) we can make comparisons. If the risk of all four instruments is the same, Bond C offers the highest rate of return, with a bond equivalent yield of 5.526%.

Finally, suppose that an investor wants to convert money market rates to semiannual bond basis yields to compare them to yields on bonds that make semiannual coupon payments. Consider a 90-day money market instrument that offers a bond equivalent yield of 8%. This implies that the periodicity of the instrument is 365/90. We can use Equation 1 to convert a yield based on M = 365/90 to a stated annual yield based on N = 2:

$$\left(1 + \frac{0.08}{365/90}\right)^{365/90} = \left(1 + \frac{SAR_2}{2}\right)^2$$

$$SAR_2 = 0.080811$$

A stated annual rate of 8% for periodicity of 365/90 corresponds to a stated rate of 8.0811% for a periodicity of two. The difference between the two is 8.11 bps. Generally speaking, the lower the level of interest rates, the smaller the difference between the stated annual rates for any two periodicities.

LESSON 4: PRICES AND YIELDS (PART III): THE MATURITY STRUCTURE OF INTEREST RATES AND CALCULATING SPOT RATES AND FORWARD RATES

LOS 52g: Define and compare the spot curve, yield curve on coupon bonds, par curve, and forward curve. Vol 5, pp 433–441

The Maturity Structure of Interest Rates

A yield curve shows the relationship between yields-to-maturity and terms-to-maturity. Theoretically, the yields used to derive the yield curve should be for bonds with identical credit risk, liquidity risk, tax status, and currency denomination. Further, their annual rates should be quoted for the same periodicity and they should offer the same coupon so that they entail the same reinvestment risk. Practically speaking however, these assumptions rarely hold for bonds that are actually used in analyzing the maturity structure or term structure of interest rates (which describes how yields vary with terms to maturity).

The Spot Rate Curve

The ideal data set for analyzing the term structure of interest rates would be yields-to-maturity on zero-coupon government bonds or spot rates for a range of maturities. This data set is known as the spot rate curve. As we learned earlier in the reading, spot rates are yields to maturity on zero-coupon bonds. The distinguishing feature of spot rates is that they are yields that have no element of reinvestment risk. Contrast this with the yield-to-maturity on coupon bonds, which entails a significant element of reinvestment risk (as it assumes that all interim cash flows can be reinvested at the stated YTM until maturity). Because spot rates are free from reinvestment risk, using them best meets the "all other things being equal" assumption in that Treasury zero-coupon bonds or strips (whose yields represent spot rates for different maturities) presumably have the same currency risk, liquidity risk, credit risk, and tax status, and there is no reinvestment risk as there is no coupon. Using spot rates therefore, provides a more accurate relationship between yields and terms to maturity relative to using yields to maturity on coupon-bearing Treasuries.

Yield Curve for Coupon Bonds

A yield curve for coupon bonds shows the yields-to-maturity for coupon-paying bonds of different maturities. To build the Treasury yield curve, analysts use only the most recently issued and actively traded government bonds as they have similar liquidity and tax status. Even though Treasury securities are not available for every single maturity, YTMs for maturities where there are gaps can be estimated through a variety of interpolation methods, the simplest of which is linear interpolation. Linear interpolation evenly distributes the difference in yields over the time period between two maturities. For example, if the yield on the 7-year Treasury is 4% and that on the 10-year Treasury is 5%, linear interpolation would compute the 8-year yield to be 4.33%, and the 9-year yield to be 4.67%.

Par Curve

In addition to the yield curve on coupon bonds and the spot rate curve on zero-coupon bonds, maturity structure can be evaluated using a par curve, which represents a series of yields-to-maturity such that each bond trades at par. The par curve is derived from the spot rate curve, as illustrated in Example 4-1.

Example 4-1: Computing Par Rates from Spot Rates

The spot rates (expressed as effective annual rates) on government bonds are 4.75% for 1 year, and 4.86% for 2 years. Compute the 1-year and 2-year par rates.

Solution:

When trying to calculate the par rate, the aim is to solve for "PMT" which, given the expected payments on a bond and corresponding spot rates, would result in the price of the bond equaling its par value. Recall that for a bond to be trading at par, it's coupon rate must equal the yield-to maturity, so if we compute the coupon (PMT) required to force the bond to trade at par (given a series of spot rates) we can then compute the coupon rate (as PMT/100) and this rate would also represent the par rate for the corresponding horizon.

So let's start with computing the 1-year par rate.

$$100 = \frac{PMT + 100}{(1 + 0.475)^1}; PMT = 4.75$$

The 1-year par rate therefore equals 4.75%.

Next, we compute the 2-year par rate.

$$100 = \frac{PMT + 100}{(1 + 0.475)^1} + \frac{100 + PMT}{(1 + 0.486)^2}; PMT = 4.8578$$

The 2-year par rate therefore equals 4.858%

Forward Curve

A forward market is for future delivery, beyond the settlement horizon of the cash market. A forward rate is the interest rate on a bond or money market instrument traded in the forward market. In more simple terms, the forward rate represents the interest rate on a loan that will be originated at some point in the future. Forward rates are used to construct the forward curve, which represents a series of forward rates, each having the same horizon. Typically the forward curve shows 1-year forward rates stated on a semiannual bond basis.

LOS 52h: Define forward rates and calculate spot rates from forward rates, forward rates from spot rates, and the price of a bond using forward rates. **Vol 5, pp 433–441**

Implied forward rates (also known as forward yields) can be computed from spot rates.

Forward rates can be described as the market's current estimate of future spot rates. We will also use the arbitrage principal in our derivation—two portfolios with identical cash flows and identical risks should have the same value today, all other factors constant.

Consider an investor who has a 1-year investment horizon and is faced with the following alternatives:

- Purchase a 1-year T-bill today. The 1-year spot rate today (yield on the zero-coupon 1-year T-bill) is given as 4.6%.
- Purchase a 6-month T-bill now and upon its expiration, purchase another 6-month T-bill. The 6-month spot rate today (yield on the first 6-month T-bill) is given as 4%.

Notice that in this example we work with 6-month periods. The yields on the bonds have been expressed on a semiannual bond basis yield—the semiannual rate has been multiplied by two.

The investor will be indifferent between these two options if she knows that the return from taking either option with be the same. However, she does not know the return that will be offered after 6 months on the second 6-month T-bill. We can calculate the return required (to make her indifferent between the two options) on a 6-month investment in a T-bill, 6 months from now by using the spot rates available today for the 6-month and the 1-year T-bill:

If she invests $100 today in the 6-month T-bill her return would be:

$$100 \times \left(1 + \frac{0.04}{2}\right)^1 = \$102$$

> 0.04/2 is the effective semiannual discount rate on the 6-month T-Bill. 0.04 is the semiannual bond basis yield.

If she invests in 1-year T-bill, she will end up with:

$$100 \times \left(1 + \frac{0.046}{2}\right)^2 = \$104.65$$

> 0.046/2 is the effective semiannual discount rate on the 1-year T-Bill. 0.046 is the semiannual bond basis yield.

The investor would be indifferent between the two strategies if they offer her an identical return. In order to end up with $104.65 using the rollover strategy, her return on the second 6-month T-bill must equal 5.2% expressed as a semiannual bond basis yield. This figure is calculated as:

$$102 \times \left(1 + \frac{X}{2}\right)^2 = \$104.6529$$

$$\frac{104.6529}{102} - 1 = 5.2\% \text{ expressed as a semiannual bond basis yield.}$$

Forward rates are market estimates of future spot rates.

$_1s_0$ = 1-period spot rate today (t = 0).

$_xs_0$ = x-period spot rate today (t = 0).

$_2f_5$ = 2-period forward rate 5 periods from today.

If the yields presented are semiannual bond basis:

$$\left(1+\frac{\text{6-mth spot rate}}{2}\right)\left(1+\frac{\text{6-mth forward rate 6 mths from now}}{2}\right)=\left(1+\frac{\text{12-mth spot rate}}{2}\right)^2$$

Important: In Examples 12, 13, 14, and 15 we assume that the rates provided are effective annual interest rates.

Example 4-2: Computing Forward Rates

The current 1-year spot rate is 5%, 2-year spot rate is 5.25%, and 3-year spot rate is 5.55%. Calculate the 1-year forward rate 1 year from now and 2 years from now.

Solution:

Calculation of 1-year forward rate 1 year from today:

$$(1+ {_1s_0})(1+ {_1f_1}) = (1+ {_2s_0})^2$$

$$(1+0.05)(1+ {_1f_1}) = (1+0.0525)^2$$

$$_1f_1 = \frac{1.0525^2}{1.05} - 1 = 5.5\%$$

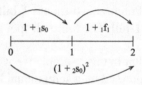

Calculation of 1-year forward rate 2 years from today:

$$(1+ {_1s_0})(1+ {_1f_1})(1+ {_1f_2}) = (1+ {_3s_0})^3$$

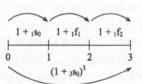

$(1 + {_1s_0})(1 + {_1f_1})$ simply equals the compounding factor for an investment for 2 years at the 2-year spot rate. The equation above can therefore be modified to:

$$(1+ {_2s_0})^2(1+ {_1f_2}) = (1+ {_3s_0})^3$$

$$_1f_2 = \frac{1.0555^3}{1.0525^2} - 1 = 6.15\%$$

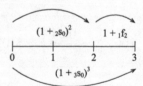

Let's summarize what we have learned so far about the relationship between multi-period spot rates and forward rates:

- $(1+ {_1s_0})(1+ {_1f_1}) = (1+ {_2s_0})^2$
- $(1+ {_2s_0})^2(1+ {_1f_2}) = (1+ {_3s_0})^3$

Therefore we can calculate the 1-period forward rate 7 years from now using the 8-year and the 7-year spot rates:

$$(1+ {_7s_0})^7(1+ {_1f_7}) = (1+ {_8s_0})^8$$

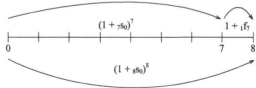

Example 4-3: Calculating Forward Rates

Calculate the 1-year forward rate 6 years from today if the 6-year spot rate is 6.25% and the 7-year spot rate is 6%.

Solution:

$$(1 + {}_6s_0)^6(1 + {}_1f_6) = (1 + {}_7s_0)^7$$

$$(1 + {}_1f_6) = \frac{(1.06)^7}{(1.0625)^6} => {}_1f_6 = 4.51\%$$

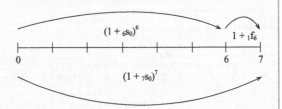

We can also calculate multi-period forward rates using multi-period spot rates. For example, we can use the following equation to calculate the 3-period forward rate 10 periods from now using the 10-year and the 13-year spot rates:

$$(1 + {}_{10}s_0)^{10}(1 + {}_3f_{10})^3 = (1 + {}_{13}s_0)^{13}$$

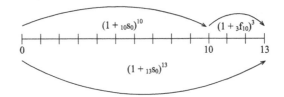

To calculate the x-period forward rate y periods from today, simply remember the following formula:

$$(1 + {}_ys_0)^y(1 + {}_xf_y)^x = (1 + {}_{x+y}s_0)^{x+y}$$

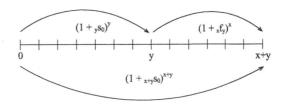

Example 4-4: Calculating Multi-Period Forward Rates

Calculate the 4-year forward rate 12 years from today if the 12-year spot rate is 4.5% and the 16-year spot rate is 4.6%.

Solution:

$$(1 + {}_{12}s_0)^{12}(1 + {}_4f_{12})^4 = (1 + {}_{16}s_0)^{16}$$

$$\left(1 + {}_4f_{12}\right)^4 = \frac{(1.046)^{16}}{(1.045)^{12}} => {}_4f_{12} = 4.9\%$$

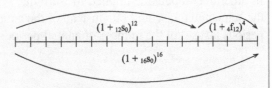

Even though we include the 1-year forward rate today in this example, this rate really is not a forward rate; it is simply the 1-year spot rate today.

Example 4-5: Valuing Bonds Using Forward Rates

The current 1-year forward rate is 4%, the 1-year forward rate 1 year from now is 4.25% and the 1-year forward rate 2 years from today is 4.3%. Calculate the value of a \$1,000 par, annual-pay coupon bond that has a coupon rate of 4% and 3 years remaining to maturity.

Solution:

$$\frac{40}{1+{}_1f_0}+\frac{40}{\left(1+{}_1f_0\right)\left(1+{}_1f_1\right)}+\frac{40}{\left(1+{}_1f_0\right)\left(1+{}_1f_1\right)\left(1+{}_1f_2\right)}$$

$$\frac{40}{1+0.04}+\frac{40}{\left(1+0.04\right)\left(1+0.0425\right)}+\frac{1,040}{\left(1+0.04\right)\left(1+0.0425\right)\left(1+0.043\right)}=\$995.04$$

A forward rate can be looked upon as the marginal or incremental return from expanding the time to maturity by one more year. Assume that an investor with a 3-year investment horizon is deciding between (1) buying a 2-year bond today and reinvesting the proceeds at maturity for another year at the (then-current) 1-year rate and (2) buying a 3-year bond today.

- If the investor believes that the 1-year rate 2 years from now will be greater than the implied forward rate, she would choose the first option.
- If the investor believes that the 1-year rate 2 years from now will be less than the implied forward rate, she would choose the second option.

This example illustrates why the implied forward rate essentially represents the breakeven reinvestment rate. Forward rates are useful to investors in making maturity choice decisions.

Important: Please note that finance authors use different notation when it comes to forward rates. We use $_xf_y$, which refers to the x-period forward rate y years from today, or the interest rate on a loan that has a term of x years, where the loan will be originated y years from today. The CFA Program curriculum uses different notation. In the curriculum, the forward rate 2y5y refers to the 5-year rate 2 years into the future and 3y2y refers to the 2-year rate 3 years from now. We have stuck with our (different) notation because we feel it is easier to work with. You can work with either notation, as it won't affect your answers.

Also note that on the exam, you could be asked to work with annual rates on semiannual-pay bonds. Most of the examples we have worked with so far have used annual-pay bonds. In order to compute the implied forward rate with semiannual, pay bonds, we would use the semiannual discount rate instead of the annual rate, and use the number of semiannual periods instead of the number of annual periods (years). This is illustrated in Example 4-6.

Example 4-6: Computing Implied Forward Rates

Suppose that an investor observes these prices and yields-to-maturity on zero-coupon government bonds.

Maturity	YTM	Price (Per 100 of Par)
1 year	1.833%	$98.19
2 years	2.062%	$95.98
5 years	2.243%	$89.45

The yields-to-maturity are stated on a semiannual bond basis.

1. Compute $_1f_1$ (or 1y1y as the curriculum would put it) implied forward rates, stated on a semiannual bond basis.
2. Compute $_3f_2$ (or 2y3y as the curriculum would put it) implied forward rates, stated on a semiannual bond basis.
3. The investor has a 5-year investment horizon and is choosing between (1) buying the 2-year zero and reinvesting in another 3-year zero in 2 years' time and (2) buying and holding to maturity the 5-year zero. The investor decides to buy the 2-year bond today. Based on his decision, determine the minimum yield-to-maturity she expects on a 3-year zero two years from today.

Solution:

1. $$\left(1+\frac{_1f_0}{2}\right)^2 \times \left(1+\frac{_1f_1}{2}\right)^2 = \left(1+\frac{_2f_0}{2}\right)^4$$

   $$\left(1+\frac{0.01833}{2}\right)^2 \times \left(1+\frac{_1f_1}{2}\right)^2 = \left(1+\frac{0.02062}{2}\right)^4$$

   $$_1f_1 = 0.02291 \text{ or } 2.291\%$$

2. $$\left(1+\frac{_2f_0}{2}\right)^4 \times \left(1+\frac{_3f_2}{2}\right)^6 = \left(1+\frac{_5f_0}{2}\right)^{10}$$

   $$\left(1+\frac{0.02062}{2}\right)^4 \times \left(1+\frac{_3f_2}{2}\right)^6 = \left(1+\frac{0.02243}{2}\right)^{10}$$

   $$_3f_2 = 0.02364 \text{ or } 2.364\%$$

3. The decision to go with the 2-year bond today instead of the 5-year bond suggests that the investor believes that the 3-year forward rate 2 years from now will be greater than or equal to 2.364%.

   The $_3f_2$ implied forward rate of 2.364% is the breakeven reinvestment rate. If the investor expected the 3-year forward rate in 2 years to be less than this implied rate, she would choose to buy the 5-year zero today.

Example 4-6 is different from the earlier examples in this section because the yields presented are on a semiannual bond basis. We first compute the yield for semiannual period and then compound it over two periods to determine the effective annual yield.

LESSON 5: YIELD SPREADS

LOS 52i: Compare, calculate, and interpret yield spread measures.
Vol 5, pp 441–445

Yield Spreads over Benchmark Rates

To understand why bond prices and yields change, it is useful to separate the yield-to-maturity into two components: the benchmark yield and the spread.

> You should note that changes in macroeconomic factors can also cause spreads to narrow or widen across all issuers.

- The benchmark yield is the base rate and is also referred to as the risk-free rate of return. It captures **macroeconomic factors** such as the expected rate of inflation, currency denomination, and the impact of monetary and fiscal policy. Changes in these factors impact all bonds in the market. The benchmark can also be broken down into (1) the expected inflation rate and (2) the expected real rate.
- The spread refers to the difference between the yield-to-maturity on a bond and on the benchmark. It captures all **microeconomic factors** specific to the issuer, such as credit risk of the issuer, changes in the issue's credit rating, liquidity, and tax status of the bond. The spread is also known as the risk premium over the risk-free rate of return.

For example, consider a 5-year corporate bond that offers a yield-to-maturity of 5.50%. The benchmark bond is a 5-year U.S. Treasury, which offers a yield of 4.50%. This means that the corporate bond offers a spread of 100 bps. Now suppose that the yield on the corporate bond increases from 5.50% to 6.00%.

- If the yield on the benchmark has also increased by 50 bps, we can infer that the change in the bond's yield is caused by macroeconomic factors that affect all bond yields.
- However, if the yield on the benchmark has remained the same, we can infer that the change in the bond's yield was caused by firm-specific factors such as changes in the issuer's credit worthiness.

The benchmark varies across financial markets. Fixed-rate bonds often use the yield on a government bond with the same term to maturity as the bond being studied as the benchmark. Typically, the benchmark is the most-recently issued or on-the-run security. On-the-run securities are the most actively traded and have coupon rates closest to the current market yield for a given maturity. Off-the-run securities are more seasoned issues. Generally speaking, on-the-run issues tend to trade at slightly lower yields-to-maturity (higher price) than off-the-run issues because of (1) differences in demand and (2) differences in the cost of financing the securities in the repo market.

In the U.K., United States, and Japan, the benchmark rate for fixed-rate bonds is the government bond yield. The yield spread in basis points over an actual or interpolated government bond yield is known as the G-spread. On the other hand, yield spreads on euro-denominated corporate bonds use the EUR interest rate swap with the same tenor as the bond as the benchmark. The yield spread over the standard swap rate in the same currency and with the same tenor as the subject bond is known as the I-spread or interpolated spread to the swap curve. Note that the government bond yield or the swap rate used as the benchmark for a specific bond will change over time as the remaining term to maturity of the bond changes. For example, when a 5-year bond is issued, the benchmark may be the 5-year government bond yield, but 2 years into the term of this bond, its G-spread will be stated relative to the 3-year government bond yield.

For floating-rate bonds, LIBOR is often used as a benchmark. Note that LIBOR is an interbank rate, not a risk-free rate.

Yield Spreads over the Benchmark Yield Curve

Recall that G-spreads and I-spreads are spreads on top of the Treasury yield curve and swap fixed rates respectively. Let's consider the Treasury yield curve (since you are more familiar with yield curves than swap curves at Level I). Given the term to maturity of a security, the appropriate benchmark yield-to-maturity applies the same discount rate for each cash flow. Theoretically, this method is unappealing because each cash flow received from the bond carries a different amount of risk (typically, cash flows expected to be received further out into the future entail more risk). It makes more sense to use individual spot rate rates to discount each of the bond's expected cash flows as spot rates accurately capture the risk entailed by each corresponding cash flow (i.e., for each time horizon, there is a specific spot rate unless the yield curve is flat). Therefore, practitioners tend to favor use of the z-spread over the G- and I-spreads. The z-spread (or zero-volatility spread or static spread) of a bond is a constant spread over the government (or interest rate swap) spot rate curve.

It is calculated using the following equation:

$$PV = \frac{PMT}{(1+z_1+Z)^1} + \frac{PMT}{(1+z_2+Z)^2} + \ldots + \frac{PMT+FV}{(1+z_N+Z)^N}$$

- The benchmark spot rates z_1, z_2, z_N are derived from the government yield curve (or from fixed rates on interest rate swaps).
- Z refers to the z-spread per period. It is constant for all time periods.

The z-spread is also used to calculate the option-adjusted spread (OAS) on a callable bond. Just like the option-adjusted yield (that we learned about earlier), the OAS is based on an option pricing model and utilizes an assumption about interest rate volatility. The OAS is calculated by subtracting the value of the embedded call option (stated in terms of bps per year) from the z-spread.

$$OAS = z\text{-spread} - \text{Option value (bps per year)}$$

Stated simply, the OAS removes the cost of the option from the z-spread, so the OAS is the spread on top of the spot rate curve that the bond would offer if it were option-free. Since the embedded call option in a callable bond favors the issuer, the OAS (the spread that an otherwise identical option-free bond would offer) is less than the z-spread. An issuer would pay out more (in terms of yield) on a callable bond than on an option-free bond. See Example 5-1.

Example 5-1: Illustrating the G-spread

A 7% annual-pay corporate bond with 2 years remaining to maturity is trading at a price of 107.75. The 2-year, 6% annual-pay government benchmark bond is trading at a price of 106.50. The 1-year and 2-year government spot rates are 1.085% and 2.67%, respectively, stated as effective annual rates.

1. Calculate the G-spread on the corporate bond.
2. Demonstrate that the z-spread is 33.5 bps.

Solution:

1. The yield-to-maturity for the corporate bond is calculated as:

   N = 2; PMT = –$7; FV = –$100; PV = $107.75; CPT I/Y; I/Y = 2.953%

   The yield-to-maturity for the government benchmark bond is calculated as:

   N = 2; PMT = –$6; FV = –$100; PV = $106.5; CPT I/Y; I/Y = 2.622%

   Therefore, the G-spread equals 33.1 bps (= 0.02953 – 0.02622).

2. We solve for the value of the corporate bond using $z_1 = 0.01085$, $z_2 = 0.0267$, and $Z = 0.00335$. The resulting value must equals 107.75 if the z-spread is indeed 33.5 bps.

$$= \frac{7}{(1+0.01085+0.00335)} + \frac{107}{(1+0.0267+0.00335)^2}$$

$$= \frac{7}{1.0142} + \frac{107}{(1.03005)^2}$$

$$= 107.75$$

READING 53: INTRODUCTION TO ASSET-BACKED SECURITIES

LESSON 1: INTRODUCTION, THE BENEFITS OF SECURITIZATION, AND THE SECURITIZATION PROCESS

INTRODUCTION

The focus in this reading is on fixed-income instruments created through a process known as securitization, a process where:

1. Assets (typically loans and receivables) are moved by the owner to a special legal entity.
2. The special legal entity then uses the assets as collateral to issue fixed-income securities (known as asset-backed bonds).
3. Cash flows from the collateral pool are used to make interest and principal payments on those asset-backed bonds.

The assets that are used as collateral to issue asset-backed bonds are called securitized assets and include residential mortgage loans, commercial mortgage loans, automobile loans, student loans, and credit card receivables.

> The securitization process will be described in more detail later in the reading.

LOS 53a: Explain benefits of securitization for economies and financial markets. Vol 5, pp 474–476

BENEFITS OF SECURITIZATION FOR ECONOMIES AND FINANCIAL MARKETS

Before the advent of securitization, financing for most mortgages and other financial assets was provided by financial institutions (e.g., commercial banks). For investors, the only way to participate in such financings was by holding deposits, debt, or equity issued by those financial institutions. Such an arrangement posed the following problems:

- The financial institution represented an additional layer between originating borrowers and ultimate investors.
- Investors were only able to gain exposure to the bank's entire portfolio of assets; that is, they were unable to pick and choose the types of assets they desired exposure to.

Securitization solves these problems, and provides the additional benefits:

- It removes the layer between borrowers and investors. As a result of the reduced role of the financial intermediary (financial institutions, including banks), the cost paid by borrowers is reduced and at the same time the return realized by investors is improved.
- It allows investors to have a stronger legal claim on the collateral pool of assets.
- Investors can pick and choose the types of securities they want to invest in (in terms of interest rate and credit risk).
- Financial intermediaries are able to originate more loans (by using financing provided by outside investors to originate loans) than they would be able to if they were only able to issue loans that they could finance themselves. In other words,

securitization allows banks to originate, monitor, and collect loans beyond what they could do if they were limited to their own deposits and capital. This results in an improvement in their profitability.

- The increase in the total supply of loanable funds benefits organizations (governments and companies) that need to borrow.
- Since securitized bonds are sold in the public market, they enjoy much better liquidity (lower liquidity risk) than the original loans on bank balance sheets. Further, financial markets are made more efficient.
- Securitization encourages innovation in investment products, which can offer investors access to (otherwise directly unavailable) assets that match their risk, return, and maturity profiles. For example, a pension fund looking to invest in long-term assets can invest (directly) in long-term housing loans via residential mortgage-backed securities, as opposed to investing (indirectly) in bonds or stocks issued by banks.
- Even large investors, who may be able to purchase real estate loans, automobile loans, or credit card loans directly, would prefer to invest in asset-backed bonds since they would not be required to originate, monitor, and collect payments from the underlying loans themselves (the securitization process takes care of all this).
- ABS offer companies an alternative means of raising finance that can be considered alongside bond and equity issuance.

Note that along with these benefits, securitization brings many risks. We will describe many of these risks later in the reading.

LOS 53b: Describe securitization, including the parties involved in the process and the roles they play. Vol 5, pp 476–485

THE SECURITIZATION PROCESS

An Example of a Securitized Transaction

Let's work with a hypothetical example to illustrate the securitization process.

Assume that ABC Company is in the business of manufacturing and selling motor vehicles. While some of its sales are made for cash, most sales are made on installment sales contracts where ABC advances loans to customers to finance their purchases. These loans are fixed-rate, full-amortizing loans that have a term of 48 months (four years). ABC receives a monthly payment (that consists of principal and interest) from each loan until it is paid off (fully amortized), while the vehicles serve as collateral against the loans. If a buyer/borrower is unable to make the scheduled monthly payment, ABC can take over ownership of the motor vehicle and sell it to recover the principal amount outstanding.

ABC's credit department decides to whom loans should be advanced and at what terms based on certain criteria (e.g., creditworthiness of purchaser). These criteria are known as underwriting standards. Since ABC is extending the loan, it is referred to as the originator of the loan. ABC's credit department also services the loans that are made. In other words, it collects payments from borrowers, issues notifications to borrowers who have not made scheduled payments, and recovers and disposes of the collateral (vehicles) in case of default. Note that even though this is the case in our example, it is not necessary that the originator of the loan also performs the role of the servicer.

Currently, ABC has 100,000 auto loans worth $1 billion of par value outstanding. These loans are classified as assets (since they are amounts owed to the company) on its balance sheet. ABC wants to raise $1 billion for its expansion program and decides to securitize these loans to raise the funds instead of issuing corporate bonds (due to the potentially lower costs of securitization). The first thing that ABC must do in order to securitize these assets is sell the loans (receivables) to a special purpose vehicle (SPV) or special purpose entity (SPE). The SPV takes legal ownership of the loans and pays ABC $1 billion (the amount it wanted to raise) for them. The SPV obtains these funds by issuing asset-backed securities (ABS) collateralized by the $1 billion pool of loans.

In the prospectus for these asset-backed securities, the SPV is referred to as the issuer or the trust. The seller of the loans, ABC, is referred to as the seller or depositor. It is important for you to understand that each individual loan issued by ABC (the depositor/seller) is collateralized by a motor vehicle, while each ABS issued by the SPV (issuer/trust) is collateralized by cash flows generated from the pool of loans. Figure 1-1 illustrates the securitization described above, while Table 1-1 lists the roles performed by the three primary parties in a securitization.

Figure 1-1: Securitization Illustration for ABC Company

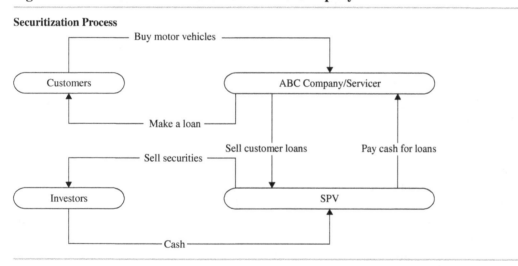

Table 1-1: Parties to the Securitization

Party	Description	Party in Illustration
Seller	Originates the loans and sells loans to the SPV	ABC Company
Issuer/Trust	The SPV that buys the loans from the seller and issues the asset-backed securities	SPV
Servicer	Services the loans	Servicer

Payments received from the collateral (loans) are used to pay servicing fees, other administrative fees, and principal and interest payments to ABS holders. The priority and amount of payments to be distributed to the various classes/tranches of security holders is referred to as the structure's waterfall.

The different types of ABS classes/tranches are described later in the reading.

In addition to the (1) seller/depositor (ABC), (2) the servicer (also ABC in this example), and the (3) issuer/trust (SPV), there are several other parties involved in a securitization:

All parties other than the seller and the issuer, including the servicer when it is different from the seller, are known as third parties to the transaction.

- Attorneys prepare legal documents, including:
  - The purchase agreement between the seller (ABC) and the SPV that includes representations and warranties made by the seller regarding the assets sold.
  - A document that describes the structure's waterfall.
  - The servicing agreement between the SPV and the servicer.
- An independent accounting firm verifies the accuracy of all numerical information in the prospectus and issues a comfort letter for the securitization.
- The trustee or trustee agent (typically a financial institution) holds the assets in a trust, holds the payments due to bondholders until they are paid, and provides remittance reports to bondholders.
- The underwriter markets the securities to investors and handles the logistics of the transaction.
- Rating agencies determine the level of credit enhancement required for each bond class to obtain the credit rating desired by the issuer.
- Guarantors play a very important role for securitized instruments. They are discussed later.

Key Role of the Special Purpose Vehicle

In order for a securitization to serve its purpose, the SPV must be a bankruptcy-remote entity. That is, its obligations remain secure even if the parent company goes bankrupt. We illustrate the key role played by the SPV using our example with ABC and the SPV.

The credit spread that ABC would be required to pay if it were to issue corporate bonds would depend on its perceived credit risk, which would be reflected in the credit rating assigned to it by credit rating agencies (S&P, Moody's, and Fitch). Suppose that the credit rating assigned to ABC is BB, so the credit spread that ABC would be required to pay on any unsecured bonds that it were to issue would be commensurate with the spread required of an entity rated BB. ABC could try to lower its cost of borrowing by collateralizing the bonds with the auto loans it has issued, thereby issuing secured bonds. Practically speaking, however, this exercise (of putting up the auto loans as collateral) will have a negligible impact on the interest rate ABC would have to pay on the proposed bonds. We will shortly illustrate why this is the case.

Now suppose that ABC sells the loans to an SPV in an arm's-length transaction, and the SPV then issues securities to raise the required $1 billion (instead of using the auto loans as collateral for a secured corporate bond issue). Once the auto loans have been sold to the SPV, the SPV takes full legal ownership of the receivables. If ABC were to subsequently go bankrupt, its creditors would have no recourse to those auto loans (as they are legally owned by the SPV). Essentially, when the SPV issues bonds backed by cash flows from the pool of auto loans, the evaluation of credit risk of the issue (and hence its credit rating and required credit spread) is based solely on the collectability of those receivables independent ABC's credit rating. Typically, because of the securitization, the (high) quality of the collateral, and the capital structure of the SPV, a company can raise funds at a lower funding cost by issuing asset-backed bonds than by issuing corporate bonds.

A fair question at this stage would be how bonds issued in a securitization can have a higher credit rating (and a lower funding cost) than secured corporate bonds directly issued by the originator if they are both collateralized by the same assets (pool of auto loans). In order to understand this, we must first become familiar with the rule of absolute priority.

The absolute priority rule refers to the principle that in case of default, senior secured creditors are repaid before subordinated creditors receive anything, and all creditors are repaid before equity holders receive anything. The thing is that the absolute priority rule generally holds in liquidations, but not in a reorganization, where it is possible for the actual outcome regarding distributions to various classes of bondholders and equity holders to be markedly different from the terms stated in the debt agreement. This means that even if there is collateral backing a corporate bond, there is no assurance that the rights of senior secured bondholders will be respected, and this is why collateral backing for a corporate bond does not result in a significant reduction in the credit spread.

However, when it comes to securitization via a bankruptcy-remote SPV, bankruptcy of a company does not affect the SPV, so the rules set forth in the securitization's prospectus regarding how credit losses will be absorbed by each bond class are generally adhered to. Going back to our example, creditors who hold bonds issued by ABC would have no legal claim on the cash flows generated from the securitized pool of auto loans (as they were sold to the SPV). The cash flows from the pool of auto loans are completely and legally independent of anything that happens to ABC. The security holders face credit risk only to the extent that the borrowers of the auto loans that the SPV has purchased from ABC default on those loans.

> The absolute priority rule, the priority of claims, and recovery rates for various classes of bonds in a liquidation and reorganization are discussed in Fixed Income.

Finally, note that not all countries have a legal framework and a concept of trust law that is as well developed as in the United States. Therefore, investors should be wary of legal considerations that apply in countries where they purchase asset-backed bonds.

LESSON 2: RESIDENTIAL MORTGAGE LOANS AND RESIDENTIAL MORTGAGE-BACKED SECURITIES (RMBS)

LOS 53d: Describe types and characteristics of residential mortgage loans that are typically securitized. Vol 5, pp 485–489

Please note: Throughout this reading, the term "mortgage-backed securities," or MBS, refers to securities backed by high-quality real estate mortgages, and the term "asset-backed securities," or ABS, refers to securities backed by other types of assets.

RESIDENTIAL MORTGAGE LOANS

A mortgage loan is a borrowing that is secured by some form of real estate. In case the borrower (usually someone wishing to buy a home) fails to make her mortgage payments, the lender (usually a bank or mortgage company) has the right to seize the property (foreclose on the loan) and recover the amount due by selling it.

Typically, the amount of the loan is less than the property's purchase price. The difference between the purchase price and the amount borrowed equals the down payment made by the borrower. Upon initiation of the mortgage loan, the borrower's equity equals the down payment, but over time, the borrower's equity changes as a result of (1) changes in the market value of the property and (2) payment of periodic mortgage payments (that include a principal component).

The ratio of the purchase price to the amount of the mortgage loan is known as the loan-to-value (LTV) ratio. The lower (higher) the LTV ratio, the higher (lower) the borrower's equity, the less (more) likely the borrower is to default, and the more (less) protection the lender has for recovering the amount loaned in case the borrower defaults.

In the sections that follow, we discuss the five primary specifications of mortgage design.

Maturity

The term of a mortgage loan refers to the number of years to maturity. In the United States, the term of mortgage loans typically varies between 15 and 30 years, while in Europe the term varies between 20 and 40 years. In Japan, terms can extend to as many as 100 years.

Interest Rate Denomination

The interest rate on a mortgage loan is called the mortgage rate or contract rate. Typically, mortgage rates are specified in one of the following forms:

Fixed-rate: The mortgage rate is fixed over the term of the loan.

Adjustable-rate mortgage (ARM) or variable-rate mortgage: The mortgage rate is reset periodically (daily, weekly, monthly, or annually).

- In an index-referenced adjustable-rate mortgage, the reset rate may be based on some reference rate or index.
- In a reviewable ARM, the mortgage rate is determined at the lender's discretion.

Note that ARMs typically have clauses placing caps on (1) the maximum interest rate change at any reset date and (2) the maximum interest rate that can be charged at any point during the mortgage's entire term.

Initial period fixed rate: The mortgage rate is fixed initially for a specified period and is then adjusted to either (1) a new fixed rate, in which case it is known as a rollover or renegotiable mortgage, or (2) a variable rate, in which case it is known as a hybrid mortgage.

Convertible: The mortgage rate is initially either fixed or adjustable, with the borrower having an option to convert the mortgage into a fixed rate or adjustable rate for the remaining term of the mortgage.

Amortization Schedule

Most mortgages around the world are structured as amortizing loans, where the principal amount outstanding declines over time as monthly payments (that consist of both an interest component and a principal repayment component) come in. Mortgage loans can be structured as fully amortizing loans or partially amortizing loans (where the last payment is referred to as a balloon payment).

In certain countries, mortgages are structured as interest-only mortgages, where no principal repayment is specified for a number of years. Other types of mortgage loans call for no principal repayment through the entire term of the mortgage, so the balloon payment at maturity equals the original loan amount. These mortgages are known as interest-only lifetime mortgages or bullet mortgages.

Prepayments and Prepayment Penalties

A mortgage loan may allow the borrower to prepay (make a principal repayment that exceeds the scheduled repayment for the month) a portion, or the entire amount, of the outstanding mortgage principal at any point during the term of the mortgage. This option is known as a prepayment option or early retirement option. Certain mortgages (known as prepayment penalty mortgages) may stipulate that the borrower pay some sort of penalty if she prepays within a certain time period following inception or the mortgage (this time period can also extend through the entire term of the mortgage). Since borrowers can accelerate payments on the mortgage loan, the cash flows from the loan cannot be known with certainty, and this risk faced by lenders is known as prepayment risk. Homeowners usually prepay their mortgages by refinancing their loans when interest rates fall. The owner of the mortgage loan receives her principal ahead of schedule and can reinvest the proceeds at current (lower) rates. The prepayment penalty is meant to compensate the lender for this loss.

> Prepayment risk affects all mortgage loans, not just level-payment, fixed-rate, fully amortized mortgage loans.

Rights of the Lender in a Foreclosure

In the United States, residential mortgages are typically structured as nonrecourse loans, while in Europe they are primarily structured as recourse loans. If the borrower defaults, resulting in foreclosure:

- In a recourse loan, the lender has a claim against the borrower if the proceeds from sale of the property fall short of the mortgage balance outstanding.
- In a nonrecourse loan, the lender does not have such a claim against the borrower if the proceeds from sale of the property fall short of the mortgage balance outstanding.

Whether a lender has recourse to the borrower in case of default is an important determinant of the probability of default on a mortgage loan. With a nonrecourse loan, if the market value of the property declines below the mortgage amount outstanding, the borrower has an incentive not to repay the loan even if she has the funds available (as she would end up paying more than the current value of the property). This is known as a strategic default. In the case of a recourse loan, the borrower will be less likely to strategically default because the lender can come after her other income/assets to recover the shortfall.

LOS 53c: Describe typical structures of securitizations, including credit tranching and time tranching. Vol 5, pp 481–482

LOS 53e: Describe types and characteristics of residential mortgage-backed securities, including mortgage pass-through securities and collateralized mortgage obligations, and explain the cash flows and risks for each type. Vol 5, pp 491–496

LOS 53f: Define prepayment risk and describe the prepayment risk of mortgage-backed securities. Vol 5, pg 488

RESIDENTIAL MORTGAGE-BACKED SECURITIES

In the United States, residential mortgage-backed securities are divided into two sectors:

- Agency RMBS, which are issued by (1) federal agencies (e.g., Ginnie Mae, which is a federally related institution) and (2) quasi-government entities (e.g.,

Freddie Mac and Fannie Mae, which are government-sponsored enterprises, or GSEs).

- ○ There is no credit risk for agency RMBS issued by Ginnie Mae as they are backed by the full faith and credit of the U.S. government.
- ○ There is minimal credit risk for agency RMBS issued by GSEs as they are guaranteed by the GSEs themselves.
- ○ Note that mortgage loans issued by GSEs must satisfy specific underwriting standards established by various government agencies to qualify for the collateral pool backing agency RMBS issued by GSEs.
- Nonagency MBS, which are issued by private entities.
  - ○ They typically come with credit enhancements (described later) to reduce credit risk.
  - ○ Note that there are no restrictions on the types on nonagency mortgage loans that can be used to back nonagency RMBS.

Mortgage Pass-Through Securities

A mortgage pass-through security is created when shares or participation certificates in a pool of mortgage loans are sold to investors.

Cash Flow Characteristics

The cash flow collected from the collateral pool includes scheduled principal and interest payments, and prepayments. However, the amount and timing of cash flows paid to investors in the pass-through securities are different from those of the cash flows collected from the collateral pool of mortgages.

Payments made by borrowers pass through the government agency (and on to investors) net of servicing and guaranteeing fees. Therefore, the pass-through rate (coupon rate on the pass-through security, which is net interest/net coupon) is lower than the mortgage rate on the underlying pool of mortgages.

Note that the mortgage loans that are securitized to create pass-through securities do not all carry the same mortgage rate and maturity. Therefore, a weighted average coupon (WAC) rate and weighted average maturity (WAM) are calculated to describe the pool of mortgages that serves as collateral for the pass-through securities.

- The weighted average coupon (WAC) rate is calculated by weighting the mortgage rate of each loan in the pool by its percentage of mortgage balance outstanding relative to the total mortgage balance outstanding for all mortgages in the pool.
- The weighted average maturity (WAM) is calculated by weighting the number of months to maturity of each loan in the pool by its percentage of mortgage balance outstanding relative to the total mortgage balance outstanding for all mortgages in the pool.

Conforming versus Nonconforming Loans

The underlying loans for agency RMBS must be conforming mortgages. That is, they must meet specified underwriting standards relating to (1) the maximum loan-to-value (LTV) ratio, (2) the loan documentation required, (3) whether insurance is required, and (4) the maximum loan amount.

If a loan is a nonconforming mortgage (i.e., it does not satisfy the underwriting standards mentioned earlier), it can only be used as collateral for privately issued mortgage pass-through securities. These nonagency RMBS are issued by thrift institutions, commercial banks, and private conduits.

Measures of Prepayment Rate

Since the mortgage loans that are securitized to create pass-through securities entail prepayment risk, the pass-through securities themselves also expose investors to prepayment risk. In describing prepayments, market participants refer to a prepayment rate or prepayment speed in terms of a monthly measure known as the single monthly mortality (SMM) rate or its corresponding annualized rate, the conditional prepayment rate (CPR).

The SMM equals the amount of prepayment for a month as a percentage of the mortgage balance that was available to be prepaid that month. Note that the mortgage balance available to be prepaid during a particular month equals the mortgage balance available to be repaid that month (mortgage balance outstanding at the beginning of the month) adjusted for the scheduled principal payment. The SMM for month t is calculated as:

$$SMM_t = \frac{\text{Prepayment in month } t}{\text{Beginning mortgage balance for month } t - \text{Scheduled principal payment in month } t}$$

Market participants prefer to define prepayment rates in terms of the annualized CPR. A CPR of 6% means that, ignoring scheduled principal repayments, approximately 6% of the mortgage balance outstanding at the beginning of the year will be prepaid by the end of the year.

In the United States, prepayment rates over the term of mortgage securities are described in terms of a prepayment pattern or benchmark introduced by the Public Securities Association (PSA). The PSA prepayment benchmark is defined in terms of a monthly series of CPRs. The benchmark assumes that prepayment rates are relatively low during the early years of the term of a mortgage, but gradually increase and eventually level off at higher rates (once the loans are seasoned). The 100 PSA benchmark assumes the following:

- A CPR of 0.2% in Month 1.
- The CPR increases by 0.2% per year every month for the next 30 months until it reaches 6% per year.
- A CPR of 6% for the remaining term.

100 PSA
- If $t < 30$, then CPR = 6% – (t/30).
- If $t \geq 30$, then CPR = 6%.
- t = Number of months that have passed since mortgage origination.

Note: If the mortgage pool consists of loans that had an original term of 360 months (30 years) and if the weighted average maturity of the pool is currently 357 months, the mortgage pool is seasoned three months. Therefore, in determining prepayments for the next month, the CPR (and corresponding SMM) for Month 4 (NOT Month 1) is applicable.

Slower or faster prepayment speeds are described in terms of percentages of 100 PSA. For example, 75 PSA implies three quarters of the CPR of the 100 PSA benchmark, while 250 PSA implies 2.5 times the CPR of the 100 PSA benchmark.

Cash Flow Construction

Table 2-1 shows the cash flows to bondholders for selected months on a hypothetical pass-through security with the following assumed features:

- The par value of the collateral pool of mortgages is $400 million.
- All the mortgages are fixed-rate, level-payment, fully amortizing loans.
- The WAC rate for the pool is 8.125%.
- The WAM for the pool is 357 months.
- The pass-through rate (net of servicing and other fees) is 7.5%.
- The prepayment rate is 165 PSA.

Table 2-1: Monthly Cash Flows for Hypothetical Mortgage Pass-Through Security

Month	Outstanding Balance	Total Principal	Net Interest	Cash Flow
1	400,000,000	709,923	2,500,000	3,209,923
2	399,290,077	821,896	2,495,563	3,317,459
3	398,468,181	933,560	2,490,426	3,423,986
4	397,534,621	1,044,822	2,484,591	3,529,413
5	396,489,799	1,155,586	2,478,061	3,633,647
80	207,862,347	2,050,422	1,299,140	3,349,562
81	205,811,925	2,032,197	1,286,325	3,318,522
82	203,779,729	2,014,130	1,273,623	3,287,753
98	173,617,879	1,745,550	1,085,112	2,830,662
99	171,872,329	1,729,979	1,074,202	2,804,181
100	170,142,350	1,714,544	1,063,390	2,777,934
101	168,427,806	1,699,243	1,052,674	2,751,917

Table 2-1: *(continued)*

Month	Outstanding Balance	Total Principal	Net Interest	Cash Flow
176	75,390,685	861,673	471,192	1,332,865
177	74,529,012	853,813	465,806	1,319,619
178	73,675,199	846,023	460,470	1,306,493
179	72,829,176	838,300	455,182	1,293,482
356	299,191	150,389	1,870	152,259
357	148,802	148,802	930	149,732

Note: You do not need to know how to derive the cash flows in the table above (it is a fairly complicated exercise). We have inserted this table here as the values it contains will be used to derive Table 2-3 in Example 2-1.

Weighted Average Life

For nonamortizing bonds (or bullet bonds) we know that, for a given coupon rate, the longer the maturity of the bond, the greater its interest rate risk (duration). For mortgage-backed securities, principal payments (scheduled payments and prepayments) are made over the term of the security. When evaluating the interest rate risk of an MBS, using its legal maturity (the date at which the last payment is due) is inappropriate, as it does not reflect the actual pattern of principal payments. For example, it would be incorrect to assume that a 30-year corporate bond and a 30-year MBS with the same coupon rate carry the same interest rate risk.

Therefore, market participants use average life (the weighted average time it will take for all the principal payments [i.e., scheduled repayments and projected prepayments] to be received) as a measure of the interest rate risk of a mortgage-backed security. The average life of an MBS depends on the assumed prepayment speed: the higher the prepayment speed assumed, the shorter the average life of the mortgage-backed security.

Contraction Risk and Extension Risk

An investor in a mortgage pass-through faces uncertainty regarding the amount and timing of payments, as they depend on the speed at which prepayments actually come in. This uncertainty is referred to as prepayment risk, which encompasses contraction risk and extension risk.

Contraction risk occurs when interest rates fall. There are two adverse consequences of lower interest rates for pass-through investors.

- Option-free bond prices increase when interest rates fall. However, for mortgage loans, the issuer (homeowner) has the right to prepay and can easily do so by refinancing her mortgage. This option to prepay is similar to the call option granted to the issuer of a callable bond. When interest rates fall, it becomes feasible for the mortgage issuer/borrower to prepay (just like it becomes feasible for an issuer

Duration can also be used to evaluate the interest rate risk of an MBS.

The response of callable bond prices to a decline in interest rates has been discussed in "Fixed-Income Securities: Defining Elements" and is revisited later in "Understanding Fixed-Income Risk and Return."

to call a callable bond), so the upside potential of the pass-through security is limited. It experiences price compression at low interest rates and exhibits negative convexity.

- To make things worse, when interest rates fall, refinancing activity typically increases and leads to an increase in prepayments, reducing or shortening the average life of the pass-through. The (higher-than-expected) cash flows from the pass-through must then be reinvested at current (lower) rates.

Extension risk occurs when interest rates rise.

- The price of a pass-through (just like the price of any bond) will decline when interest rates increase.
- To make things worse, refinancing activity and prepayment rates slow down when interest rates rise, increasing or lengthening the average expected life of the pass-through. Consequently, a greater-than-anticipated amount remains invested in the pass-through at the coupon rate of the instrument, which is lower than current interest rates.

COLLATERALIZED MORTGAGE OBLIGATIONS

The fact that mortgage pass-through securities entail significant uncertainty regarding the amount and timing of their cash flows (contraction and extension risk) makes them undesirable for institutional investors interested in matching the cash flows from their investment portfolios with the expected maturity of their liabilities and obligations. Collateralized mortgage obligations (CMOs) redistribute the cash flows from mortgage pass-through securities into packages/classes/tranches with different risk exposures to prepayment risk. The risk/return characteristics and exposures to prepayment risk of the various CMO tranches are different from those of the underlying mortgage pass-through securities, which makes them attractive as investments to different types of investors.

An important thing to bear in mind is that for CMOs, the mortgage-related products from which cash flows are obtained are considered the collateral (i.e., a pool of mortgage pass-through security serves as the collateral). Recall that for mortgage pass-through securities, a pool of mortgage loans serves as collateral.

The major varieties of CMO structures are described next.

Sequential-Pay Tranches

In this CMO structure, each class/tranche of bonds is retired sequentially in a predetermined order. An example of the rules for monthly distribution of principal payments (scheduled payments plus prepayments) would be:

- Distribute all principal payments to Tranche A until it is fully paid off.
- Once Tranche A is paid off, distribute all principal payments to Tranche B until it is fully paid off.
- Once Tranche B is paid off, distribute all principal payments to Tranche C until it is fully paid off.
- And so on.

Note that the rules for distributing coupon interest are different from the rules for distributing principal payments (scheduled amortization and prepayments). Each tranche is paid coupon interest each month at its stated coupon rate based on its principal amount outstanding at the beginning of the month. The principal payment pattern for each of the tranches is not known, as it depends on the actual prepayment rate of the collateral. Therefore, PSA rate assumptions are made to project cash flows for each tranche. Example 2-1 provides an illustration of a sequential-pay CMO structure with four tranches. This comprehensive example will serve to clarify all the features of sequential-pay CMOs that have been described.

Example 2-1: Monthly Cash Flows on Sequential-Pay CMO

A sequential-pay CMO structure is backed by $400m worth of mortgage pass-through securities. The pass-through coupon rate is 7.5%, the weighted average coupon is 8.125%, and the weighted average maturity is 357 months. Table 2-2 provides par values, coupon rates, and payment rules for the sequential-pay tranches.

Note that the total par value of the four tranches equals the par value of the collateral pass-through securities ($400m). The cash flows on the collateral for selected months were provided in Table 2-1. Further note that in our example, the coupon rate on the tranches equals the pass-through coupon rate (7.5%). Typically, however, a different coupon rate is offered on each tranche.

Table 2-2: Four-Tranche Sequential Pay Structure

Tranche	Par Amount ($)	Coupon Rate (%)
A	194,500,000	7.5
B	36,000,000	7.5
C	96,500,000	7.5
D	73,000,000	7.5
Total	400,000,000	

Payment Rules

- For payment of monthly coupon interest: Disburse monthly coupon interest to each tranche on the basis of the amount of principal outstanding for the tranche at the beginning of the month.
- For disbursement of principal payments: Disburse principal payments to Tranche A until it is fully paid off. After Tranche A is fully paid off, distribute principal payments to Tranche B until it is fully paid off. After Tranche B is fully paid off, distribute principal payments to Tranche C until it is fully paid off. After Tranche C is completely paid off, disburse principal payments to Tranche D until it is fully paid off.

Demonstrate the distribution of monthly cash flows from the pool of pass-through securities to the four tranches of the CMO assuming that prepayments come in at 165 PSA.

Solution:

Table 2-3 lists monthly cash flows for selected months for all four tranches **assuming 165 PSA**.

Table 2-3: Selected Monthly Cash Flows for Sequential-Pay CMO in Example 2-1 (Assuming 165 PSA)

Month	Tranche A Balance ($)	Principal ($)	Interest ($)	Tranche B Balance ($)	Principal ($)	Interest ($)	Tranche C Balance ($)	Principal ($)	Interest ($)	Tranche D Balance ($)	Principal ($)	Interest ($)
1	194,500,000	709,923	1,215,625	36,000,000		225,000	96,500,000		603,125	73,000,000		456,250
2	193,790,077	821,896	1,211,188	36,000,000		225,000	96,500,000		603,125	73,000,000		456,250
3	192,968,181	933,560	1,206,051	36,000,000		225,000	96,500,000		603,125	73,000,000		456,250
4	192,034,621	1,044,822	1,200,216	36,000,000		225,000	96,500,000		603,125	73,000,000		456,250
5	190,989,799	1,155,586	1,193,686	36,000,000		225,000	96,500,000		603,125	73,000,000		456,250
80	2,362,347	2,050,422	14,765	36,000,000		225,000	96,500,000		603,125	73,000,000		456,250
81	311,925	311,926	1,950	36,000,000	1,720,271	225,000	96,500,000		603,125	73,000,000		456,250
82				34,279,729	2,014,130	214,248	96,500,000		603,125	73,000,000		456,250
98				4,117,879	1,745,550	25,737	96,500,000		603,125	73,000,000		456,250
99				2,372,329	1,729,979	14,827	96,500,000		603,125	73,000,000		456,250
100				642,350	642,350	4,015	96,500,000	1,072,194	603,125	73,000,000		456,250
101							95,427,806	1,699,243	596,424	73,000,000		456,250
176							2,390,685	861,673	14,942	73,000,000		456,250
177							1,529,012	853,813	9,556	73,000,000		456,250
178							675,199	675,199	4,220	73,000,000	170,824	456,250
179										72,829,176	838,300	455,182
356										299,191	150,389	1,870
357										148,802	148,802	930

Each tranche receives interest each month (coupon rate × balance outstanding at the beginning of the month). The aggregate amount of interest paid out to the tranches for any particular month equals the total amount of interest collected from the collateral pool during that month (since the pass through rate equals the coupon rate). For example, total interest collected from the collateral in Month 5 equals $2,478,061 (see Table 2-3), and the total amount of interest paid out to the four tranches during Month 5 also equals $2,478,061 ($1,193,686 + $225,000 + $603,125 + $456,250; see Table 2-3).

Step 1: Initially all principal payments (scheduled amortization + prepayments) received from the pass-through securities are forwarded to Tranche A. For example, the entire principal payment received from the collateral pool in Month 1 (i.e., $709,923; see Table 2-1) goes to Tranche A.

Step 2: Tranche A is fully paid off in Month 81. The remaining principal payments received during Month 81 ($1,720,271) are forwarded to Tranche B. All principal payments going forward are distributed to Tranche B until it is fully paid off.

Step 3: Tranche B is fully paid off in Month 100. The remaining principal payments received during Month 100 ($1,072,194) are forwarded to Tranche C. All principal payments going forward are distributed to Tranche C until it is fully paid off.

Step 4: Tranche C is fully paid off in Month 178. The remaining principal payments received during Month 178 ($170,824) are forwarded to Tranche D. All principal payments going forward are distributed to Tranche D until it is fully paid off.

Step 5: Tranche D is fully paid off in Month 357.

Notice how:

- Tranche B receives only interest payments (no principal payments) until Tranche A is paid off.
- Tranche C receives only interest payments (no principal payments) until Tranche B is paid off.
- Tranche D receives only interest payments (no principal payments) until Tranche C is paid off.

The principal pay-down window or principal window for a tranche is the time period between the first and last principal payments to that tranche. The principal pay-down windows for the four sequential-pay tranches are listed in Table 2-4. Note that the figures in this table are based on the 165 PSA prepayment assumption.

Table 2-4: Principal Pay-Down Windows for Sequential-Pay CMO Tranches Assuming 165 PSA

Tranche	Principal Paid During	Principal Pay-Down Window
A	Month 1 to Month 81	81 months
B	Month 81 to Month 100	20 months
C	Month 100 to Month 178	79 months
D	Month 178 to Month 357	180 months

Note that although the payment rules for distribution of cash flows from the collateral pass-through securities are known, the actual amount of cash flows that will come in is uncertain (it depends on the actual speed of prepayments). The 165 PSA assumption only allows us to project expected, not actual, cash flows.

Now let's describe what we have accomplished by "repackaging" the mortgage pass-through securities into sequential-pay CMO tranches. Table 2-5 lists the average lives of the pass-through and the four sequential-pay CMO tranches that we created from the pass-through securities under a variety of prepayment speed assumptions.

Table 2-5: Average Life for Collateral and CMO Tranches under Different Prepayment Assumptions

(PSA)	Average Life (in Years)				
	Collateral	Tranche A	Tranche B	Tranche C	Tranche D
50	15.11	7.48	15.98	21.02	27.24
100	11.66	4.90	10.86	15.78	24.58
165	8.76	3.48	7.49	11.19	20.27
200	7.68	3.05	6.42	9.60	18.11
300	5.63	2.32	4.64	6.81	13.36
400	4.44	1.94	3.70	5.31	10.34
500	3.68	1.69	3.12	4.38	8.35
600	3.16	1.51	2.74	3.75	6.96
700	2.78	1.38	2.47	3.30	5.95

Notice that:

We have not illustrated the derivation of the numbers used to calculate these average lives, nor have we performed these calculations, as this is not required. We are just using the average life numbers for illustrative purposes.

- The four sequential-pay tranches have average lives that are both longer and shorter than the collateral pass-through securities. The average life of the collateral pool assuming 165 PSA is 8.76 years.
- Tranche A is given priority in the distribution of principal payments (has the shortest average life) and therefore offers the most protection against extension risk. This protection comes from the other three tranches in the CMO structure (Tranches B, C, and D) that consequently have higher extension risk.
- Tranche D has the longest average life and offers the most protection against contraction risk. This protection comes from the other three tranches in the structure (Tranches A, B, and C) that face higher contraction risk.
- This exercise of redistributing prepayment risk by creating different bond classes with differing exposures to prepayment risk is known as time tranching. More formally, time tranching occurs when prepayment risk (or the timing of distribution of cash flows) is redistributed among the various classes of ABS.
- Notice how the securities created come closer to satisfying the asset/liability needs of institutional investors. Short-term investors would be drawn toward Tranche A, while longer-term investors would find Tranche D most attractive.
- There is still considerable variation in the average lives of the tranches depending on prepayment speeds. This variation is mitigated in the PAC structure described next.

Planned Amortization Class (PAC) Tranches

PAC bonds were introduced in the bond market to improve upon sequential-pay structures (that entail significant variation in average lives depending on realized prepayment patterns) and to offer investors greater protection from prepayment risk (both contraction and extension risk). PAC bonds bring increased predictability of cash flows, as they specify a repayment schedule that will be satisfied as long as actual prepayments realized from the collateral fall within a predefined band.

We illustrate the characteristics of a PAC bond through a CMO structure that has one PAC tranche and one support tranche. First, a lower and upper PSA prepayment rate assumption is made for the PAC tranche. This is known as the initial PAC collar or initial PAC band. Principal payments are calculated for each month under the lower PSA prepayment assumption and the upper PSA prepayment assumption, and investors in the PAC tranche are promised a minimum monthly principal payment equal to the **lower** of the principal payments under the two PSA assumptions. The greater certainty in payments for the PAC tranche comes at the expense of greater uncertainty for the support or companion tranche, which absorbs the prepayment risk. Note that the support tranche provides **two-sided protection** (i.e., protection against extension **and** contraction risk) to the PAC tranche.

Example 2-2: PAC Tranches

In this example, $400m worth of mortgage pass-through securities carrying a coupon rate of 7.5% (that are backed by a pool of mortgage loans with a weighted average coupon of 8.125% and a weighted average maturity of 357 months) serve as collateral for a planned amortization class (PAC) CMO structure with one PAC tranche and one support tranche. The PAC tranche has an initial PAC collar of 90 PSA and 300 PSA.

Tranche	Par Amount ($)	Coupon Rate (%)
PAC	243,800,000	7.5
Support	156,200,000	7.5
Total	400,000,000	

Payment Rules
- For payment of monthly coupon interest: Disburse monthly coupon interest to each tranche on the basis of the amount of principal outstanding for the tranche at the beginning of the month.
- For disbursement of principal payments: Disburse principal payments to the PAC tranche based on its schedule of principal repayments. The PAC tranche has priority with respect to current and future principal payments to satisfy the schedule. Any excess principal payments in a month over the amount necessary to satisfy the schedule for the PAC tranche are paid to the support tranche. When the support tranche is completely paid off, all principal payments are to be made to the PAC tranche regardless of the schedule.

Table 2-6 lists the average lives of the PAC and support tranches under a variety of prepayment rate assumptions.

Table 2-6: Average Lives for PAC and Support Tranches under Various Prepayment Speeds

Prepayment Rate (PSA)	PAC Bond (P)	Support Bond (S)
0	15.97	27.26
50	9.44	24
90	7.26	20.06
100	7.26	18.56
150	7.26	12.57
165	7.26	11.16
200	7.26	8.38
250	7.26	5.37
300	7.26	3.13
350	6.56	2.51
400	5.92	2.17
450	5.38	1.94
500	4.93	1.77
700	3.7	1.37

Notice the following:

- Over the collateral's life, if prepayments occur at any rate that falls within the initial PAC collar (90300 PSA), the average life of the PAC tranche will be known with certainty (7.26 years).
- Over the collateral's life, if actual prepayments occur at a rate that is slower than the lower PSA band (90 PSA), the average life of the PAC tranche extends, but that of the support tranche extends more substantially (as it carries more extension risk). The PAC tranche has a priority claim against principal payments, so principal payments to the support tranche are deferred until the PAC tranche receives its scheduled principal payments. This reduces extension risk for the PAC tranche.
- Over the collateral's life, if actual prepayments occur at a rate that is faster than the upper PSA band (300 PSA), the average life of the PAC tranche contracts, but that of the support tranche contracts more substantially (as it carries more contraction risk as well). All excess principal payments are absorbed by the support tranche until it is fully paid off. Once this occurs, all principal payments will be distributed to the PAC tranche, which would then be referred to as a broken or busted PAC.
- The average life of the support tranche fluctuates more wildly than that of the PAC tranche. Therefore, support tranches entail the greatest prepayment risk.
- The greater the par value of the support tranche relative to that of the PAC tranche, the greater the prepayment protection for the PAC, the lower the PAC's average life variability, and the greater the support tranche's average life variability.

CMO structures can also be created with more than one PAC tranche. Each PAC tranche has its own schedule of payments, with each tranche being paid off in sequence.

Floating-Rate Tranches

There is often demand for tranches that carry a floating rate. Even though the collateral for CMOs carries a fixed rate, it is possible to create a floating-rate tranche (along with an inverse-floater tranche) from any of the fixed-rate tranches in a CMO structure. Since the floater varies positively with interest rates, and the inverse floater varies negatively with interest rates, they offset each other.

NONAGENCY RESIDENTIAL MORTGAGE-BACKED SECURITIES

As mentioned earlier, nonagency RMBS are not guaranteed by the government or a GSE, which makes the evaluation of credit risk an important consideration when investing in them. Within the nonagency RMBS sphere, market participants identify two types of transactions based on whether the mortgage loans in the collateral pool are prime or subprime loans. Prime loans are those advanced to borrowers with high credit quality and substantial equity in the underlying property, whereas subprime loans refer to loans advanced to borrowers with lower credit quality or loans that do not have first lien on the underlying property (i.e., the current potential lender has a subordinate claim on the underlying property).

While nonagency RMBS share many similarities with agency RMBS in terms of features and structures, the following two complementary mechanisms are typically required in structuring nonagency RMBS:

1. Cash flows are distributed according to a set of rules that determines the distribution of interest and principal payments to tranches with varying levels of priority/seniority.
2. There are also rules for allocating realized losses, with senior tranches having a priority claim over payments and subordinated tranches absorbing losses.

When it comes to forecasting cash flows on nonagency MBS, investors must make assumptions regarding (1) the default rate for the collateral and (2) the recovery rate (in case of default, repossession and subsequent sale of a recovered property typically generate cash flows for payments to bondholders).

In order to obtain favorable credit ratings, nonagency RMBS (as well as other types of asset-backed bonds that are discussed later in this reading) are credit enhanced. The amount of credit enhancement built into an issue depends on the credit rating desired by the issuer.

Internal Credit Enhancements

Internal credit enhancements include:

- Reserve funds:
  - Cash reserve funds: The entity seeking to raise the funds deposits some of the proceeds of sale of the loan pool with the SPV. This cash can be used to pay for potential future losses.
  - Excess spread accounts: The excess spread or cash that remains after the payment of net coupon, servicing fees, and all other expenses is kept in reserve to pay for future credit losses on the collateral. For example, if the

interest rate paid by borrowers in the loan pool is 5.75%, and 0.75% is paid for servicing fees while 4.75% is the interest rate paid to bond classes, the excess spread equals 5.75% (0.75% + 4.75%) = 0.25% or 25 bps.

Note that if any funds remain in the reserve account after paying off the last bond class in the securitization, the cash is returned to the residual owner of the SPV.

- Overcollateralization: This refers to a situation where the value of the collateral exceeds the par value of the securities issued by the SPV. The amount of overcollateralization (excess collateral) can be used to absorb future losses. For example, a securitization backed by $350m worth of loans against which securities with a total par value of $325m are issued is overcollateralized by $25m. Note that the amount of overcollateralization for an issue changes over time due to (1) defaults, (2) amortization, and (3) prepayments.

- Senior/subordinate structure: This type of structure has senior bond classes and subordinate bond classes (also known as non-senior/junior bond classes). The structure basically provides credit tranching as the subordinate bond classes provide credit protection to the senior classes. More formally, credit tranching occurs when credit risk (or risk of loss from default) is redistributed among the various classes of ABS. To understand how the senior-subordinate structure works, consider the following ABS structure:

Bond Class	Par Value ($ millions)	Initial Pass-Through Rate (%)
A (Senior)	250	3
B (Subordinate)	60	3.5
C (Subordinate)	15	4.2
Total	325	

The first $15m of losses are absorbed by Class C. Losses in excess of $15m are absorbed by Class B until total losses exceed $75m. Class C provides credit enhancement not only to Class A (the senior bond class), but also to Class B (the other subordinate bond class). Class A only suffers from credit losses once the total amount of credit losses exceeds $75m.

The issue with the senior-subordinate structure is that the level of credit protection provided by subordinate classes changes over time due to voluntary prepayments and defaults. To protect investors in the senior bond classes, a shifting interest mechanism is added to the structure. This mechanism locks out subordinated classes from receiving payments for a period of time if the collateral performs poorly, thereby ensuring that the level of credit protection enjoyed by the senior classes does not deteriorate over time.

External Credit Enhancements

External credit enhancements are third-party guarantees for payments to security holders should the issuer not be able to meet payment requirements. Monoline insurers are the most common third-party financial guarantors. Their business is restricted to providing guarantees for financial products (such as municipal securities and ABS). However, the popularity of monoline insurers has declined in recent years following the financial difficulties and downgrades of major monoline insurers in the aftermath of the financial crisis of 2007 to 2009.

LESSON 3: COMMERCIAL MORTGAGE-BACKED SECURITIES (CMBS) AND NON-MORTGAGE ASSET-BACKED SECURITIES (ABS)

LOS 53g: Describe the characteristics and risks of commercial mortgage-backed securities. Vol 5, pp 503–508

COMMERCIAL MORTGAGE-BACKED SECURITIES (CMBS)

Credit Risk

CMBS are backed by a pool of commercial mortgage loans on income-generating properties (e.g., apartments, warehouses, shopping centers, etc.). In the United States (and many other countries), commercial mortgage loans are nonrecourse loans (i.e., if there is a default and proceeds from sale of the property are insufficient for repayment, the lender has no recourse to the borrower for the unpaid amount). As a result, evaluation of credit risk for commercial mortgage loans requires examining the income-generating capacity and value of each property on a stand-alone basis.

Two measures are commonly used to evaluate the potential credit performance of a commercial property:

- The debt-service coverage (DSC) ratio is used to evaluate the adequacy of income generated from the property to service the loan. It is calculated as net operating income (NOI) divided by debt service. NOI is calculated as rental income minus cash operating expenses and a noncash replacement reserve that reflects depreciation of the property over time.
    - A ratio greater than 1 means that cash flow from the property covers debt servicing costs adequately.
    - The higher the ratio, the lower the credit risk.
- The loan-to-value ratio equals the loan amount divided by the appraised value of the property.
    - The lower the ratio, the lower the credit risk.

Basic CMBS Structure
- A credit-rating agency determines the level of credit enhancement required for the issuer to attain the credit rating desired by the issuer. For example, if the DSC and LTV ratios are unable to warrant the desired credit rating, the issuer may use subordination to attain the desired credit rating.
- Different bond classes are created, with each class having a different priority on cash flows. The various bond classes are retired sequentially with all principal repayments, prepayments, and proceeds from default (from selling repossessed properties) being used to repay the highest-rated tranche first.
- Losses from loan defaults are charged against the lowest-rated tranche first. If this tranche is not rated by credit-rating agencies, it is known as the first-loss piece, residual tranche, or equity tranche. The equity tranche typically has no specific interest rate (as it is the residual tranche). Investors price it based on the expected residual rate of return. Actual returns can be better or worse than expected depending on actual future interest rate movements and actual defaults.
- Interest payments are made to all tranches.

Two characteristics that are usually specific to CMBS are call protection and balloon maturity provisions.

1. Call protection

Typically, CMBS investors have significant call protection, which actually results in these securities trading more like corporate bonds than like RMBS. Call protection can come at (1) the loan level or (2) the structural level.

Call protection at the loan level can come in the following forms:

- Prepayment lockouts, which prohibit any prepayments during a specified period of time.
- Defeasance, which occurs when the borrower, instead of prepaying the loan, provides funds to the servicer to invest in a portfolio of Treasuries whose cash flows replicate those of the loan assuming no prepayments. Upon completion of the defeasance period, these securities are liquidated to pay off the loans. Note that there is no cash distribution to bondholders when the loan is defeased. Further, the credit quality of the deal improves as cash flows from Treasuries replace expected cash flows from the commercial loan pool as collateral. The cost of creating such a portfolio is the cost of defeasing the loan that must be paid by the issuer.
- Prepayment penalties are levied upon borrowers if they wish to refinance their loans.
- Yield maintenance charges are intended to compensate the lender for interest lost due to prepayments. These charges make lenders indifferent to the timing of prepayments, as they are always "made whole."

Call protection at the structure level comes from credit tranching. Senior tranches are given priority on principal payments, while principal losses from defaults impact the lowest-rated tranches first.

2. Balloon maturity provisions

Most commercial loans that back CMBS have balloon maturity provisions—that is, they require a significant amount of principal to be repaid at maturity (as opposed to during the term of the loan). This exposes investors to balloon risk, as there will be a "default event" if the borrower is unable to generate the entire (significant) amount of funds required to retire the balloon balance by either (1) refinancing the loan or (2) selling the property. In the context of CMBS transactions, balloon risk is more like extension risk, as there is usually a workout period during which the borrower and lender try to modify the original terms of the loan to ensure eventual repayment. Note that the interest rate charged over the workout period (known as default interest rate) may be higher than the interest rate on the original loan.

LOS 53h: Describe types and characteristics of non-mortgage asset-backed securities, including the cash flows and credit risk of each type.
Vol 5, pp 508–512

NON-MORTGAGE ASSET-BACKED SECURITIES

Non-mortgage assets that have been used as collateral in securitizations include auto loan and lease receivables, credit card receivables, personal loans, and commercial loans.

Generally speaking, the collateral backing asset-backed securities can be classified as either amortizing or nonamortizing assets.

Amortizing loans

- The periodic cash flows include interest payments, principal repayments (in accordance with an amortization schedule), and (if allowed) prepayments.
- Examples include residential mortgage loans and automobile loans.

Nonamortizing loans

- These only require a monthly minimum payment with no scheduled principal payment.
- If the payment received is less than the interest amount due, the shortfall is added to the outstanding loan balance.
- If the payment is greater than the interest amount due, the excess serves to reduce the outstanding loan balance.
- Since there is no scheduled principal payment amount, the concept of prepayment does not apply to nonamortizing assets.
- Examples include credit card receivables.

The type of collateral (amortizing versus nonamortizing assets) has a significant effect on the structure of the securitization.

- When amortizing assets are securitized, the total face value (total amount outstanding) declines over time due to scheduled repayments and prepayments, and the number of outstanding loans (composition of the collateral) declines as a result of (1) defaults and (2) full principal repayments or full amortizations.
- On the other hand, securitizations of nonamortizing loans usually take the form of a revolving structure, where the composition of the collateral can change over the term of the securities. This is because principal repayments can be either (1) reinvested by purchasing additional loans or (2) passed on to security holders.
  - During an initial lockout or revolving period (which immediately follows the origination of the transaction), all principal repayments are reinvested in additional loans with a principal amount equal to the total principal amount received. While this can result in a smaller total number of individual loans comprising the collateral, the total face value outstanding remains the same.
  - During the principal amortization period (which follows the lockout period) principal repayments are not used to purchase additional loans, but are distributed to security holders.

We now describe the securitization of the two most popular non-mortgage assets: (1) auto loan receivables (that are amortizing loans) and (2) credit card receivables (that are nonamortizing loans).

Auto Loan Receivable–Backed Securities

These securities are backed by auto loan and lease receivables. Cash flows for auto loan–backed securities consist of regularly scheduled monthly interest and principal payments and prepayments. Prepayments result from the following:

- Sales and trade-ins requiring full payoff of the loan.
- Repossession and subsequent resale of the automobile.
- Proceeds from insurance claims arising from loss or destruction of the vehicle.
- Cash payments to save interest costs.
- Refinancing of the loan at lower interest rates.

Generally speaking, auto loan–backed securitizations come with some form of credit enhancement. Typically, the securitizations involve a senior/subordinate structure (to provide credit protection to the senior tranches). Further, some securitizations also involve reserve accounts, overcollateralization, and excess interest on the receivables.

Credit Card Receivable–Backed Securities

Credit cards may be issued by banks, retailers, and travel and entertainment companies. When a purchase is made on a credit card, the credit card company (the credit card issuer or lender) effectively extends a loan to the card holder (borrower) equal to the cost of purchase. In return, the card holder agrees to repay the amount borrowed along with any applicable finance charges. These receivables for the credit card company are used as collateral for credit card receivable–backed securities.

- The cash flow from a pool of credit card receivables includes (1) finance charges collected (interest charges on the unpaid balance after the grace period), (2) fees (for late payments and membership), and (3) principal repayment.
- Interest payments are made to security holders periodically (monthly, quarterly, or semiannually). The interest rate may be fixed or floating (typically with no cap).

As mentioned earlier, credit card receivable–backed securities are nonamortizing securities. During the revolving period (also known as the lockout period) any principal repayments from the pool of receivables are used to purchase additional receivables to maintain the size of the pool. During this period, the cash flow passed on to security holders consists only of (1) finance charges and (2) fees collected from the pool of receivables. Principal repayments are passed on to security holders only once the principal-amortizing period sets in.

Even though receivables in a revolving structure may not be prepaid (since there is no concept of prepayment here), all the bonds may be retired early if an early or rapid amortization provision is triggered. An example of a trigger for early amortization is poor performance of the collateral. In such a situation, principal repayments received from the collateral pool during the lockout period would be passed on to security holders to pay down principal, not to purchase additional loans.

LESSON 4: COLLATERALIZED DEBT OBLIGATIONS (CDOs)

LOS 53i: Describe collateralized debt obligations, including their cash flows and risks. Vol 5, pp 512–515

A collateralized debt obligation (CDO) is a security that is backed by a diversified pool of securities that may include:

- Corporate bonds and emerging market bonds (collateralized bond obligations or CBOs).
- ABS, RMBS, and CMBS (structured finance CDOs).
- Leveraged bank loans (collateralized loan obligations or CLOs).
- Credit default swaps and other structured securities (synthetic CDOs).

Structure of a CDO Transaction

- Like an ABS, a CDO also involves the creation of an SPV.
- A CDO manager (also known as collateral manager) is responsible for managing the collateral portfolio of assets (consisting of debt obligations).
- The funds used to purchase the collateral assets are raised from the issuance of bonds to investors. Bond classes may include senior bonds, mezzanine bonds (with credit ratings between senior and subordinated bonds), and subordinated bonds (also known as the residual or equity class).
- Restrictive covenants are placed on the manager to ensure that the credit ratings assigned to the various tranches at issuance are maintained during the term of the CDO.
- Cash flows from the underlying portfolio of assets include (1) coupon interest payments, (2) proceeds from maturing assets, and (3) proceeds from sale of assets. These cash flows are used to make interest and principal payments to the various bond classes.
- From the asset manager/issuer's perspective, the aim is to earn a rate of return on the collateral pool of assets that is higher than the interest costs of bonds issued. This excess return accrues to the equity holders and the CDO manager. Effectively, issuing a CDO is like undertaking a leveraged transaction where the idea is to use borrowed funds (raised from bonds issued) to generate a return that exceeds the funding cost.
- From the investors perspective, each class of bonds entails a different level of risk. Senior/mezzanine bond investors may be able to earn a potentially higher return than on a comparably rated corporate bond by gaining exposure to debt products that they may not otherwise be able to purchase. Equity investors can earn an equity-type return by taking the (higher) risk associated with the subordinated class.
- Certain restrictions are placed on the manager (via various tests and limits) to ensure that the senior bond classes are adequately protected and the ratings issued to the bond classes are maintained. Failure to meet these tests may trigger an immediate payoff to the senior bond classes until the tests are satisfied. This payoff would have the effect of deleveraging the CDO (as the asset manager's reliance on its cheapest source of funding [i.e., senior bonds] would be reduced).

The example in the next section will make the cash flows and credit risks of a CDO clearer.

Illustration of a CDO Transaction

Example 4-1: A Hypothetical CDO Transaction

Consider a $50 million CDO with the following structure:

Tranche	Par Value ($)	Coupon Rate
Senior	40,000,000	LIBOR + 50 basis points
Mezzanine	5,000,000	5-year Treasury rate plus 100 basis points
Subordinate/Equity	5,000,000	

The collateral backing the CDO is composed of corporate bonds with a par value of $50million. They mature in five years and offer a coupon rate equal to the 5-year Treasury rate plus 200 basis points (bps).

Notice that the senior tranche (which comprises the largest portion of the total issue) is variable-rate, while the collateral consists of fixed-rate assets. In order to eliminate

An interest rate swap is simply an agreement between two parties to exchange periodic interest payments based on a certain notional amount.

this mismatch, the asset manager enters into an interest rate swap with the following characteristics:

- A notional principal of $40 million.
  - The notional principal on the swap is $40m (not $50m) because the floating-rate exposure of the issuer is limited to the par value of the senior tranche.
- The fixed-rate payer (the asset manager) will make payments at a rate equal to the 5-year Treasury rate plus 50 basis points.
- The floating-rate payer (the swap counterparty) will make payments at LIBOR.

Assume that the 5-year Treasury rate at the time when the CDO is issued equals 5%. In this case:

Interest received by the asset manager on the collateral is calculated as:

$50,000,000 × (0.05 + 0.02) = $3,500,000

Interest paid to the senior CDO tranche is calculated as:

$40,000,000 × (LIBOR + 50 bps)

Interest paid to the mezzanine tranche is calculated as:

$5,000,000 × (0.05 + 0.01) = $300,000

Interest paid by the asset manager on the interest rate swap as the fixed-rate payer is calculated as:

$40,000,000 × (0.05 + 0.005) = $2,200,000

Interest received by the asset manager on the interest rate swap as the floating-rate receiver is calculated as:

$40,000,000 × (LIBOR)

Total interest payments received by the asset manager are calculated as the sum of floating-rate receipts from the swap and the interest received on the collateral:

Interest from collateral + Interest from swap counterparty
= $3,500,000 + $40,000,000 × (LIBOR)

Total interest paid out by the asset manager is calculated as the sum of payments to the senior and mezzanine CDO tranches and the fixed-rate payments on the swap:

Interest to senior tranche + Interest to mezzanine tranche + Fixed-rate interest on swap
= $40,000,000 × (LIBOR + 50 bps) + $300,000 + $2,200,000
= $2,500,000 + $40,000,000 × (LIBOR + 50 bps)

Netting the interest payments coming in and going out, we have:

$3,500,000 + $40,000,000 × (LIBOR) − [$2,500,000 + $40,000,000 × (LIBOR + 50 bps)]
= $1,000,000 − ($40,000,000 × 50 bps)
= $800,000

Asset management fees and other charges are deducted from the net interest earned by the CDO to determine the amount earned by the equity tranche. For example, if these charges amount to $100,000, then the annual return on the equity tranche equals:

$$\frac{\$800,000 - \$100,000}{\$5,000,000} \times 100 = 14\%$$

Do note, however, that we have made several simplifying assumptions in this example, including:

- There are no defaults. If there were defaults, there would be a risk that the manager may not be able to pay off the senior and/or mezzanine tranches, resulting in a loss. Investors in the equity tranche risk the loss of their entire investment.
- The collateral is composed of bonds that are all noncallable. Therefore, the coupon rate does not decline from securities being called.
- Practically speaking, the asset manager must start returning principal to the senior and mezzanine tranches once the reinvestment period is over (i.e., the securities issued do not have bullet maturities like the example assumed). Therefore, the interest rate swap must be structured in a manner that accounts for the amortization of principal over time.

The major difference between an ABS and a CDO is that in an ABS the cash flows from the collateral pool are used to pay off bondholders without the active management of collateral. In a CDO, the manager buys and sells debt obligations (assets) to (1) generate the cash flow required to repay bondholders and to (2) earn a competitive return for the equity tranche.

READING 54: UNDERSTANDING FIXED-INCOME RISK AND RETURN

LESSON 1: SOURCES OF RISK

LOS 54a: Calculate and interpret the sources of return from investing in a fixed-rate bond. Vol 5, pp 530–536

SOURCES OF RETURN

There are three sources of return on a fixed-rate bond:

1. Receipt of promised coupon and principal payments.
2. Reinvestment of coupon payments.
3. Potential capital gains/losses if the bond is sold prior to maturity.

In this reading, we will assume that issuers always make promised coupon and principal payments, so our focus here is not on credit risk. Instead, we focus on the impact of a change in interest rates, which affects (1) income from reinvestment of coupon payments and (2) the market price of the bond if sold prior to maturity.

If a bond is purchased at a premium/discount, it adds another dimension to the total rate of return:

- A discount bond offers a coupon rate that is *lower* than the required rate of return, so amortization of the discount (as the bond's carrying value is pulled **up** to par as it nears maturity) serves to enhance the return to bring it in line with the market discount rate.
- A premium bond offers a coupon rate that is *higher* than the required rate of return, so amortization of the premium (as the bond's carrying value is pulled **down** to par as it nears maturity) serves to lower the return to bring it in line with the market discount rate.

We will now go through a series of examples to demonstrate the effects of changes in interest rates on total rates of return realized by two investors:

- Investor A is a buy-and-hold investor who holds on to the bond until maturity.
- Investor B is a short-term investor who sells the bond prior to maturity.

In Examples 1-1 and 1-2, interest rates are unchanged, but the investors have different investment horizons.

Example 1-1

Investor A (the buy-and-hold investor) purchases a 10-year, 8% annual-pay bond at a price of 85.503075 (per 100 of par). The investor holds the bond until maturity and is able to reinvest all coupon payments received during the term of the bond at the YTM at issuance.

1. Compute the total amount of reinvestment income earned by Investor A.
2. Determine her realized rate of return on the investment.

Solution:

1. In order to calculate the amount of reinvestment income earned over the bond's term, we first need to calculate the YTM at issuance (which is the rate at which coupon payments are reinvested):

   N = 10; PMT = $8; PV = −$85.503075; FV = $100; CPTI / Y; I / Y = 10.40%

   Next, we must compute the future value of the ten $8 coupon payments that are received over the bond's term if they are invested until maturity at the bond's YTM (10.40%):

   I / Y = 10.40; PMT = $8; N = 10; PV = 0; CPT FV; FV = $129.970678

   We can now compute total reinvestment income as the difference between the FV of this annuity (calculated as $129.970678) and the total amount of coupon income (10 × $8 = $80) received from the bond.

   Reinvestment income = $129.970678 − $80 = $49.970678

   The investor's total return equals the sum of the reinvestment income, coupon payments and principal redemption at maturity.

   Total return = $49.970678 + $80 + $100 = $229.970678

2. The realized rate of return is calculated as:

$$\$85.503075 = \frac{\$229.970678}{(1+r)^{10}} = \$1,000$$

   r = 0.1040 or 10.40%

Think of this reinvestment income as the "interest-on-interest" income from compounding.

Takeaway: This example illustrates that the YTM represents the investor's realized rate of return on a bond if the following three conditions hold:

1. The bond is held till maturity.
2. The issuer does not default.
3. All coupon payments can be reinvested through the term of the bond at a rate that equals the bond's YTM at issuance.

Example 1-2

Investor B (the short-term investor) purchases a 10-year, 8% annual-pay bond at a price of 85.503075 (per 100 of par) implying a YTM of 10.40%. The investor holds the bond for 4 years, after which she sells the bond at a price that entails a YTM of 10.40% (the YTM at date of sale is the same as the YTM at issuance). She is also able to reinvest the coupons at 10.40%.

1. Compute the total amount of reinvestment income earned by Investor B.
2. Determine her realized rate of return on the investment.

Solution:

1. The future value of the four $8 coupon payments that are received over the investment horizon if they are invested until maturity at 10.40% (YTM at issuance) is calculated as:

   I/Y = 10.40; PMT = $8; N = 4; CPT FV; FV = $37.347111

   Total reinvestment income is calculated as:

   Reinvestment income = $37.347111 − ($8 × 4) = $5.347111

   The bond's selling price at the end of Year 4 is calculated as the PV of expected future payments:

   N = 6; I/Y = 10.40; PMT = $8; FV = $100; CPT PV; PV = $89.66877

   The investor's total return is calculated as the sum of the selling price, coupon receipts and reinvestment income:

   Total return = $89.66877 + $32 + $5.347111 = $127.015881

2. The realized rate of return is calculated as:

$$\$85.503075 = \frac{\$127.015881}{(1+r)^4}$$

   r = 0.1040 or 10.40%

Investor B's horizon yield (or annualized holding period rate of return) in this example is 10.40%.

Takeaway: This example illustrates that the horizon yield equals the YTM at issuance if the following two conditions hold:

1. The bond is sold at its carrying value (i.e., at a price that lies on its constant-yield price trajectory).
2. All coupon payments can be reinvested at a rate that equals the bond's YTM at issuance until date of sale.

Carrying value refers to the value of a bond (at any time between the purchase date and maturity date) that entails the same YTM as when the bond was purchased. The carrying value reflects amortization of any premium/discount since the time of purchase. To facilitate your understanding of carrying value of a bond, think back to the FRA section where we described the effective interest method of determining the carrying value of a liability.

Going back to Example 1-2, the carrying value of the bond at the end of Year 1 equals $86.395394 (N = 9; I/Y = 10.40; PMT = $8; FV = $100; CPT PV), which means that discount amortization for Year 1 equals $0.892319 (= 86.395394 − 85.503075). By the end of Year 4 (time of sale) the carrying value of the bond has risen to $89.66877. This increase in the value of the bond is a movement along the constant-yield price trajectory (YTM = 10.40%).

Capital gains/losses arise if a bond is sold at a price different from its carrying value. In Example 1-2, at the end of Year 4, the bond is sold at a price that equals its carrying value ($89.66877, priced to yield 10.40%), so there is no capital gain/loss.

In Examples 1-3 and 1-4, we illustrate the impact on our investors' horizon yields if interest rates rise by 100 bps (i.e., the market discount rate increases from 10.40% to 11.40%).

Example 1-3

Investor A (the buy-and-hold investor) purchases a 10-year, 8% annual-pay bond at a price of 85.503075 (per 100 of par). After she purchases the bond, but before she receives the first coupon payment, interest rates rise to 11.40%.

1. Compute the future value (FV) of reinvested coupons (coupon receipts plus reinvestment income).
2. Determine her realized rate of return on the investment.

Solution:

1. The future value of the ten $8 coupon payments that are received over the investment horizon if they are invested until maturity at 11.40% is calculated as:

$$I / Y = 11.40; \ PMT = \$8; \ N = 10; \ PV = 0; \ CPT \ FV; \ FV = \$136.380195$$

2. The realized rate of return is calculated as:

$$\$85.503075 = \frac{\$136.380195 + \$100}{(1+r)^{10}}$$

$$r = 0.1070 \ or \ 10.70\%$$

The buy-and-hold investor benefits from the higher coupon reinvestment rate as her realized rate of return *rises* by 30 bps from 10.40% (in Example 1-1) to 10.70%. Note that there is no capital gain or loss since the investor holds the bond until maturity.

Example 1-4

Investor B (the short-term investor) purchases a 10-year, 8% annual-pay bond at a price of 85.503075 (per 100 of par). After she purchases the bond, but before she receives the first coupon payment, interest rates rise to 11.40%. The investor sells the bond at the end of Year 4 (when it is priced to yield 11.40%).

1. Compute the future value (FV) of reinvested coupons (coupon receipts plus reinvestment income).
2. Determine her realized rate of return on the investment.

Solution:

1. The future value of the four $8 coupon payments that are received over the investment horizon if they are invested until the end of Year 4 at 11.40% is calculated as:

    I / Y = 11.40; PMT = $8; PV = 0; N = 4; CPT FV; FV = $37.89972

    The selling price of the bond (at the end of Year 4) is calculated as the present value of remaining payments:

    N = 6; I / Y11.40; PMT = $8; FV = $100; CPT PV; PV = $85.780408

2. The realized rate of return is calculated as:

$$\$85.503075 = \frac{37.899724 + \$85.780408}{(1+r)^4}$$

r = 0.0967 or 9.67%

The short-term investor (Example 1-4) has a *lower* rate of return now that interest rates have gone up compared to her return if interest rates were to remain unchanged (Example 1-2) –9.67% vs. 10.40%. Even though the FV of reinvested coupons goes up ($37.899724 here vs. 37.347111 in Example 1-2) with the increase in interest rates, this benefit is more than offset by the resulting capital loss of $3.888362 (= $89.66877 – $85.780408) as the bond is sold for less than its carrying value.

Examples 1-5 and 1-6 assume that interest rates fall by 100 bps from 10.40% to 9.40%.

Example 1-5

Investor A (the buy-and-hold investor) purchases a 10-year, 8% annual-pay bond at a price of 85.503075 (per 100 of par). After she purchases the bond, but before she receives the first coupon payment, interest rates decline to 9.40%.

1. Compute the future value (FV) of reinvested coupons (coupon receipts plus reinvestment income).
2. Determine her realized rate of return on the investment.

Solution:

1. The future value of the ten $8 coupon payments that are received over the investment horizon if they are invested until maturity at 9.40% is calculated as:

    I / Y = 9.40; PMT = $8; PV = 0; N = 10; CPT FV; FV = $123.888356

2. The realized rate of return is calculated as:

$$\$85.503075 = \frac{\$123.888356 + \$100}{(1+r)^{10}}$$

r = 0.1010 or 10.10%

The buy-and-hold investor suffers from the lower coupon reinvestment rate as her realized rate of return *falls* by 30 bps from 10.40% to 10.10%. Note that there is no capital gain or loss since the investor holds the bond until maturity.

Example 1-6

Investor B (the short-term investor) purchases a 10-year, 8% annual-pay bond at a price of 85.503075 (per 100 of par). After she purchases the bond, but before she receives the first coupon payment, interest rates fall to 9.40%. The investor sells the bond at the end of Year 4 (when it is priced to yield 9.40%).

1. Compute the future value (FV) of reinvested coupons (coupon receipts plus reinvestment income).
2. Determine her realized rate of return on the investment.

Solution:

1. The future value of the four $8 coupon payments that are received over the investment horizon if they are invested until the end of Year 4 at 9.40% is calculated as:

   I / Y = 9.40; PMT = $8; N = 4; CPT FV; FV = $36.801397

   The selling price of the bond (at the end of Year 4) is calculated as:

   N = 6; I / Y = 9.40; PMT = $8; FV = $100; CPT PV; PV = $93.793912

2. The realized rate of return is calculated as:

$$\$85.503075 = \frac{\$36.801397 + \$93.793912}{(1+r)^4}$$

   r = 0.1117 or 11.17%

The short-term investor has a higher rate of return, now that interest rates have gone down compared to her return; if interest rates were to remain unchanged – 11.17% here vs. 10.40% in Example 1-2. Even though the FV of coupon payments goes down ($36.801397 here vs. 37.347111 in Example 1-2) with the decrease in interest rates, this loss is more than offset by the resulting capital gain of $4.125142 (= $93.793912 – $89.66877) as the bond is sold for more than its carrying value.

It is very important that you understand the following:

- In all our examples:
  - Interest income for the investor is the return associated with the passage of time. It includes (1) coupon receipts, (2) reinvestment income, and (3) amortization of any discount (premium) from purchasing the bond at a price less (greater) than its par value.
  - A capital gain (loss) to the investor is associated with a change in value of the security caused by a change in the yield-to-maturity (market discount rate).

- In practice, the calculation of interest income and capital gains/losses reported in financial statements depends on financial and tax accounting rules.
- The investment horizon is an important factor in determining fixed-income risk and return. There are two types of interest rate risk, which offset each other:
  - Reinvestment risk. The future value of any interim cash flows received from a bond (these could be coupon payments as well as principal repayments on amortizing bonds) increases when interest rates rise and decreases when interest rates decline.
  - Market price risk. The selling price of a bond (at any point during its term or before maturity) decreases when interest rates rise and increases when interest rates decline.

Reinvestment risk matters more to a long-term investors (such as the buy-and-hold investor in our examples), while market price risk matters more to short-term investors. Therefore, two investors who are holding the same bond can have different exposures to interest rate risk depending on their individual investment horizons.

LESSON 2: INTEREST RATE RISK ON FIXED-RATE BONDS

LOS 54b: Define, calculate, and interpret Macaulay, modified, and effective durations. Vol 5, pp 538–548

LOS 54c: Explain why effective duration is the most appropriate measure of interest rate risk for bonds with embedded options. Vol 5, pp 545–548

Duration

Duration measures the sensitivity or responsiveness of a bond's **full price** (including accrued interest) to changes in **its yield-to-maturity** (or market discount rate). When measuring duration, we assume that all other variables that influence a bond's price, including its time to maturity, remain constant. There are several types of duration. Broadly speaking, duration can be classified as:

- Yield duration, which measures the responsiveness of a bond's price with respect to **its own yield-to-maturity**. Yield duration statistics include Macaulay duration, modified duration, money duration, and the price value of a basis point.
- Curve duration, which measures the responsiveness of a bond's price with respect to **a benchmark yield curve** (e.g., government yield curve, forward curve, or government par curve). Coupon duration statistics include effective duration.

Macaulay Duration

Macaulay duration represents the weighted average of the time it would take to receive all the bond's promised cash flows, where the weights are calculated as the present value of each cash flow divided by the bond's **full price**. See Examples 2-1 and 2-2.

Example 2-1: Calculating Macaulay Duration (for Annual-Pay Bond)

Consider a newly-issued 10-year, 8% annual-pay bond priced at 85.503075 per 100 of par value to yield 10.40%. Calculate the bond's Macaulay duration.

Solution:

Period (1)	Cash Flow (2)	Present Value (3)	Weight (4)	Period × Weight (5)
1	8	7.24638	0.08475	0.08475
2	8	6.56375	0.07677	0.15353
3	8	5.94542	0.06953	0.20860
4	8	5.38535	0.06298	0.25194
5	8	4.87803	0.05705	0.28525
6	8	4.41851	0.05168	0.31006
7	8	4.00227	0.04681	0.32766
8	8	3.62525	0.04240	0.33919
9	8	3.28374	0.03840	0.34564
10	108	40.15439	0.46963	4.69625
		85.50307	**1.00000**	**7.00288**

Calculations:
- Column 2: Annual coupon payment = 8% × $100 = $8
- Column 3 contains the present value of each cash flow.
  - The PV of the Year 10 cash flow ($108) is calculated as $108 / (1.104)^{10} = 40.154389$
- Column 4 shows the weight (i.e., the share of total market (present) value corresponding to each cash flow).
  - The weight of the Year 10 payment is calculated as 40.154389 / 85.503075 = 0.46963
- Column 5 multiplies the number of periods to receipt of the cash flow (Column 1) by the weight (Column 4). The sum of Column 5 (7.0029) is the Macaulay duration of this 10-year, 8% annual-pay bond.

Example 2-2: Calculating Macaulay Duration (for Semiannual-Pay Bond between Coupon Dates)

Consider a 7-year, 5% semiannual-pay bond that matures on September 15, 2020, which is purchased on January 3, 2014. The coupon payments are made on March 15 and September 15 each year. The yield-to-maturity is 5.00% quoted on a street-convention semiannual bond basis. Compute the bond's Macaulay duration at time of purchase.

Solution:

Period (1)	Time to Receipt (2)	Cash Flow (3) ($)	Present Value (4)	Weight (5)	Time × Weight (6)
1	0.4000	2.5	2.475429	0.02439	0.0097561
2	1.4000	2.5	2.415053	0.02380	0.0333135
3	2.4000	2.5	2.356149	0.02321	0.0557160
4	3.4000	2.5	2.298682	0.02265	0.0770058
5	4.4000	2.5	2.242616	0.02210	0.0972240
6	5.4000	2.5	2.187918	0.02156	0.1164101
7	6.4000	2.5	2.134555	0.02103	0.1346024
8	7.4000	2.5	2.082492	0.02052	0.1518381
9	8.4000	2.5	2.031700	0.02002	0.1681530
10	9.4000	2.5	1.982146	0.01953	0.1835816
11	10.4000	2.5	1.933801	0.01905	0.1981576
12	11.4000	2.5	1.886635	0.01859	0.2119134
13	12.4000	2.5	1.840620	0.01814	0.2248803
14	13.4000	102.5	73.624790	0.72542	9.7206330
			101.492586	**1.00000**	**11.383185**

Calculations:

- Column 1: There are 14 semiannual periods remaining until maturity (including the current period).
- Column 2 contains the number of semiannual periods to receipt of cash flow.
  - Payment 1 will be received in $1 - 108/180 = 0.4$ semiannual periods, Payment 2 will be received in $2 - 108/180 = 1.4$ semiannual periods, and so on.
- Column 3: The coupon payment per semiannual period is $2.50.
- Column 4: The annual yield-to-maturity is 5.00% so the yield per semiannual period is 2.50%. When this yield per semiannual period is used to compute the present value of each cash flow, the full price of the bond equals 101.492586 (sum of Column 4).
- Column 5 contains the weights (the shares of the full price corresponding to each cash flow).
- Column 6: The values in this column are obtained by multiplying the values in Column 2 by those in Column 5.

Macaulay duration equals the sum of the values in Column 6. However, note that the value obtained here (11.383185) is in terms of number of semiannual periods. Similar to coupon rates and yields-to-maturity, duration statistics are also annualized in practice. This is done by dividing the duration per period by the number of periods in the year. Therefore, in this example annualized Macaulay duration equals $11.383185 / 2 = 5.691592$ years.

Macaulay duration can also be computed using the following closed-form formula:

$$\text{MacDur} = \left\{ \frac{1+r}{r} - \frac{1+r+[N \times (c-r)]}{c \times \left[(1+r)^N - 1\right] + r} \right\} - (t/T) \quad \text{... (Equation 1)}$$

where:
c = Coupon rate per period (PMT/FV)

Note that Equation 1 uses the YTM *per period*, coupon rate *per period*, the number of *periods* until maturity, and the fraction of the current *period* that has elapsed. The number attained from applying the formula gives us the Macaulay duration **in terms of periods**, which can be annualized by dividing it by the number of periods in a year. See Example 2-3.

Example 2-3: Calculating Macaulay Duration Using the Closed-Form Formula

Determine the Macaulay duration of the fixed-rate bond in Example 2-2 using the general closed-form formula.

Solution:

$$\text{MacDur} = \left\{ \frac{1+r}{r} - \frac{1+r+[N \times (c-r)]}{c \times [(1+r)^N - 1] + r} \right\} - (t/T)$$

r = 0.025, c = 0.025, N = 14, and t/T = 108/180

Therefore,

$$\text{MacDur} = \left\{ \frac{1+0.025}{0.025} - \frac{1+0.025+[14 \times (0.025-0.025)]}{0.025 \times [(1+0.025)^{14} - 1] + 0.025} \right\} - (108/180)$$

MacDur = 11.383185 semiannual periods or 5.691592 years

Macaulay duration is typically not used as a measure of the interest rate sensitivity of a bond's price (since better measures such as modified duration exist). However, it does have has some useful applications, including measurement of the duration gap, which is discussed towards the end of the reading.

Modified Duration

Modified duration is calculated by dividing Macaulay duration by one plus the yield per period. See Example 2-4.

$$\text{ModDur} = \frac{\text{MacDur}}{1+r}$$

Example 2-4: Calculating Modified Duration

Determine the annual modified duration of the fixed-rate bond in Example 2-2 given that its Macaulay duration is 11.383185 semiannual periods.

Solution:

$$ModDur = \frac{MacDur}{1+r}$$

$$ModDur = \frac{11.38315}{1+(0.05/2)} = 11.1055146 \text{ semiannual periods}$$

The annualized modified duration of the bond is **5.552773** (= 11.1055146/2).

Note that we can also calculate the annualized modified duration of the bond as the annualized Macaulay duration divided by 1 plus the yield per semiannual period:

$$ModDur_{ANN} = \frac{MacDur_{ANN}}{1+r}$$

$$ModDur_{ANN} = \frac{5.691592}{1+(0.05/2)} = 5.552773$$

Modified duration has a very important application in risk management. It can be used to estimate the percentage price change for a bond in response to a change in its yield-to-maturity.

$$\%\Delta PV^{Full} \approx -AnnModDur \times \Delta Yield$$

Note that the formula above estimates the percentage price change in the **full price** of a bond, and uses the **annual** modified duration and the **annual** yield-to-maturity. Also, bond prices are *inversely* related to changes in yields, which explains the minus sign in the formula. See Example 2-5.

Example 2-5: Using Modified Duration to Estimate the Change in a Bond's Price

Given an annualized modified duration of 5.552773 for the bond in Example 2-2, estimate the change in value of the bond in response to (1) a 100 bp increase in yields and (2) a 100 bp decrease in yields.

Solution:

If the yield-to-maturity increases by 100 bps (to 6.00%), the estimated loss in the value will be:

$$\%\Delta PV^{Full} = -5.552773 \times 0.0100 = -0.05552773 \text{ or } -5.55\%$$

If the yield-to-maturity decreases by 100 bp (to 4.00%), the estimated loss in the value will be:

$$\%\Delta PV^{Full} = -5.552773 \times -0.0100 = 0.05552773 \text{ or } 5.55\%$$

Notice that the absolute value of the percentage change in the price of the bond is the same for either an increase or a decrease in yields (5.55%). Modified duration only provides a linear estimate of the change in the price of a bond in response to a change in yields. It provides good estimates for bond prices in response to relatively small changes in yields, but its estimating accuracy fades with larger changes in yields as the curvature (convexity) of the price-yield profile becomes more pronounced. Recall that given the coupon rate and term to maturity, the percentage increase in the price of a bond in response to a decrease in yields is *greater* than the percentage decrease in its price in response to an equivalent increase in yields. Later in this reading, we will study the convexity adjustment to account for the asymmetric response of bond prices to changes in yields.

If Macaulay duration is not already known, annual modified duration can be estimated using the following formula:

$$\text{ApproxModDur} = \frac{(PV_-) - (PV_+)}{2 \times (\Delta \text{Yield}) \times (PV_0)} \quad \text{... (Equation 2)}$$

This approximation basically estimates the slope of the line tangent to the price-yield profile for a bond at a particular yield level, as illustrated in Figure 2-1 (that follows Example 2-6). The value for approximate modified duration obtained by applying this formula gives us the percentage change in the price of a bond in response to a 100-bp (1%) change in yields. The percentage price change if yields were to change by 50 basis points would be half the figure obtained from applying the formula. Also note that the change in YTM (Δ Yield) must be entered as a decimal (not as a percentage) in Equation 2.

Example 2-6: Estimating Modified Duration

Using the bond that we worked with in Example 2-2, estimate its modified duration using the approximation formula. Compute PV_- and PV_+ by decreasing and increasing yields by 5 bps.

Solution:

Given that the yield-to-maturity is 5.00%, the full price ($PV0$) of a 7-year, 5% semiannual-pay corporate bond (maturing on September 15, 2020 and settling on January 3, 2014) is calculated as:

N = 14; PMT = –$2.50; FV = –$100; I/Y = 2.5%; CPT PV → PV = $100

$PV_0 = \$100 \times (1.025)^{108/180} = \textbf{\$101.492586}$

In order to compute PV_+, we raise the annual yield-to-maturity by 5 bps (from 5.00% to 5.05%). The yield per semiannual period therefore rises from 2.50% to 2.525%. PV_+ is calculated as:

N = 14; PMT = –$2.50; FV = –$100; I/Y = 2.525%; CPT PV → PV = $99.7082

$PV_+ = \$99.7082 \times (1.02525)^{108/180} = \textbf{\$101.211273}$

In order to compute PV_, we lower the annual yield-to-maturity by 5 bps (from 5.00% to 4.95%). The yield per semiannual period therefore falls from 2.50% to 2.475%. PV_ is calculated as:

N = 14; PMT = –$2.50; FV = –$100; I/Y = 2.475%; CPT PV → PV = $100.2928

$$PV_- = \$100.2928 \times (1.02475)^{108/180} = \mathbf{\$101.774839}$$

Now that we have computed PV_0, PV_+ and PV_- we can estimate the duration of the bond given $\Delta Yield = 0.0005$ as:

$$ApproxModDur = \frac{\$101,774839 - \$101.211273}{2 \times 0.0005 \times \$101.492586} = \mathbf{5.55278}$$

Figure 2-1: Approximate Modified Duration

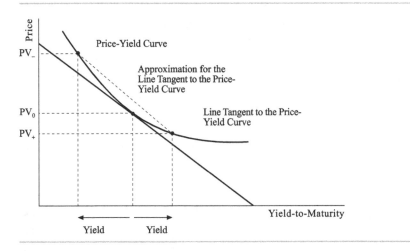

Important: Even though we computed the values of PV_+ and PV_- by moving yields up and down by 5 bps, the way that the modified duration formula is structured dictates that the value obtained for duration approximates the change in the value of a bond **for a 1% or 100-bp change in yields**. Therefore, we would interpret our value of modified duration as follows: If the market discount rate were to shift (up or down) by 1%, the estimated change in the value of the bond would be 5.55% (in the other direction).

Notice that our approximate value for modified duration, 5.55278% (using Equation 2 in Example 2-6) is very close to the actual value of 5.552773% (computed earlier in Example 2-4).

We can also use the approximate modified duration (ApproxModDur) to estimate Macaulay duration (ApproxMacDur) by applying the following formula:

$$\boxed{ApproxMacDur = ApproxModDur \times (1+r)} \quad ... \text{(Equation 3)}$$

Note that both Equation 2 and Equation 3 produce results for *annualized* modified and Macaulay durations. The frequency of payments and the periodicity of the yield-to-maturity are included in bond price calculations.

Effective Duration

Another approach for measuring a bond's interest rate risk is to compute effective duration (also known as OAS duration), which measures the sensitivity of a bond's price to a change in **the benchmark yield curve**.

$$EffDur = \frac{(PV_-)-(PV_+)}{2\times(\Delta Curve)\times(PV_0)} \quad \text{... (Equation 4)}$$

Note that:

- Effective duration is a **curve duration** statistic that measures interest rate risk in terms of a change in the benchmark yield curve (ΔCurve).
- Modified duration is a **yield duration** statistic that measures interest rate risk in terms of a change in the bond's own yield-to-maturity (ΔYield).

Effective duration is the appropriate measure of risk **for bonds with embedded call options**, including callable bonds (and mortgage-backed bonds). For such bonds, future cash flows are uncertain as they depend on the path taken by interest rates in the future. Generally speaking, if interest rates fall (rise) there is a greater (lower) likelihood that the issuer will call the bonds. Since future cash flows are contingent on future interest rates, there is no well-defined internal rate of return or yield-to-maturity on these bonds. Therefore, yield duration statistics (i.e., modified and Macaulay duration) do not apply. Effective duration, being a curve duration statistic, is the appropriate duration measure here.

> In case you were wondering, the sensitivity of a callable bond's price to a change in the yield-to-worst is also not an appropriate measure of duration either.

Option-pricing models are used to determine PV_- and PV_+, the inputs for computing effective duration for a callable bond. Note that these pricing models make use of several inputs, including (1) the length of the call protection period, (2) the schedule of call prices and call dates, (3) an assumption regarding credit spreads on top of benchmark yields, (4) an assumption about future interest rate volatility, and (5) the level of market interest rates (e.g., the government par curve). In order to compute PV_- and PV_+, the first four are held constant and then we change the fifth (by a specific number of bps). See Example 2-7.

Example 2-7: Computing Effective Duration

A callable bond is currently trading at 101.05 per 100 of par. When the government par curve is raised by 25 bps, the value of the bond falls to 99.04, and when it is lowered by 25 bps the value of the bond rises to 102.87. Compute the effective duration of this bond.

Solution:

- $PV_0 = 101.05$
- $PV_- = 102.87$
- $PV_+ = 99.04$
- $\Delta Curve = 0.0025$

$$EffDur = \frac{102.87-99.04}{2\times 0.0025\times 101.05} = 7.5804$$

Note that curve duration measures (including effective duration) indicate the sensitivity of a bond's price to the benchmark yield curve, **assuming no change in the credit (or liquidity) spread**. Practically speaking, an issuer can call a callable bond if its cost of financing falls due to (1) a fall in benchmark yields or (2) a decrease in the credit spread. It is important for you to understand that:

- Modified or Macaulay duration (essentially, just one statistic) can be computed to estimate the percentage price change for a **traditional fixed-rate bond** in response to a change in the benchmark yield and/or credit spread.
- On the other hand, **for bonds with embedded options** (where there is no well-defined internal rate of return), a curve duration statistic must be computed to measure the effects of a change in benchmark yields, and a separate measure (e.g., credit duration) must be computed to measure the effects of a change in the credit spread.

Further, note that unlike modified duration, effective duration does not necessarily provide more accurate estimates for changes in a bond's price if we use a smaller change in benchmark rates. This is because rates typically need to change by a relatively large amount for an issuer to call a bond or for a homeowner to refinance a mortgage loan (the interest savings must outweigh the transaction costs).

Finally, although effective duration is the appropriate interest rate risk measure for bonds with embedded options, it is also used for traditional bonds to supplement the information provided by modified and Macaulay duration. When it comes to a traditional fixed-rate bonds, modified duration and effective duration are generally not the same (unless the yield curve is completely flat, which is very rare). The difference between the two becomes smaller as:

- The yield curve is flatter.
- The time to maturity is shorter.
- The bond is priced closed to par (which means that the difference between the coupon rate and YTM is smaller).

LOS 54d: Define key rate duration and describe the use of key rate durations in measuring the sensitivity of bonds to changes in the shape of the benchmark yield curve. Vol 5, pg 549

Key Rate Duration

Key rate duration (or partial duration) is a measure of a bond's (or bond portfolio's) sensitivity to a change in the benchmark yield for a given maturity. Key rate durations are used to assess shaping or yield curve risk for a bond that is, the bond's sensitivity to changes in the shape of the benchmark yield curve, or nonparallel shifts in the yield curve (e.g., the yield curve becoming steeper or flatter). Recall that effective duration measures a bond's sensitivity to a parallel shift in the yield curve.

As an example, assume that the yield curve is currently upward sloping. An analyst expects benchmark rates at short maturities to rise by 25 bps, but rates at longer maturities to remain unchanged (i.e., she expects the yield curve to flatten). In order to compute the expected price change, the key rate duration for the short maturity will be multiplied by 0.0025 (note that price will fall since the yield has increased).

Finally, note that for parallel shifts in the benchmark yield curve, key rate durations will suggest the same interest rate sensitivity as effective duration.

LOS 54e: Explain how a bond's maturity, coupon, and yield level affect its interest rate risk. Vol 5, pp 549–554

Properties of Bond Durations

Earlier, we mentioned that for traditional fixed-rate bonds, Macaulay duration and modified duration are functions of (1) the coupon rate or payment per period, (2) the yield-to-maturity per period, (3) the number of periods to maturity (as of the beginning of the period), and (4) the fraction of the coupon period that has elapsed. We now study the relationship between Macaulay (and modified) duration and each one of these variables.

The Fraction of the Coupon Period That Has Elapsed (t/T)

All other things remaining the same, as time passes (or as the bond nears maturity) through the coupon period, Macaulay duration decreases smoothly as t goes from t = 0 (the last coupon payment date) to t = T (the next coupon payment date), creating a "saw-tooth" like pattern (illustrated in Figure 2-2). Notice how Macaulay duration falls as time passes through a coupon period (moving from right to left in Figure 2-2), and then jumps after each coupon payment.

Figure 2-2: Macaulay Duration between Coupon Payment Dates with Constant YTM

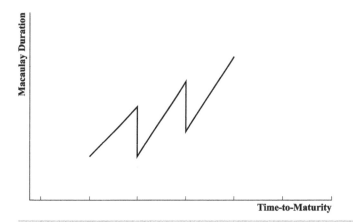

Time-to-Maturity
- For fixed-rate coupon bonds trading at par or premium to par, longer times-to-maturity correspond to a higher Macaulay duration.
    - However, Macaulay duration for these bonds never rises above a threshold level defined by MacDur = (1 + r)/r
- For fixed-rate coupon bonds trading at a discount, longer times-to-maturity **generally** correspond to a higher Macaulay duration.
    - Given a long enough time-to-maturity, Macaulay duration for discount bonds actually rises to a maximum level that lies above MacDur = (1 + r)/r.
    - However, after reaching its maximum level, as time-to-maturity further increases, Macaulay duration for discount bonds starts falling back towards (1 + r)/r, if the coupon rate is low relative to the yield-to-maturity.
- The Macaulay duration for a zero-coupon bond equals its time-to-maturity.
- For a noncallable perpetuity (or consol), that is, a bond that pays a fixed coupon forever,
- Macaulay duration equals the threshold level MacDur = (1 + r)/r. See Figure 2-3.

Figure 2-3: Properties of Macaulay Yield Duration

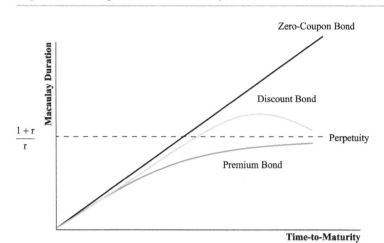

Coupon Rate

All other things remaining the same, a lower-coupon bond has higher duration and more interest rate risk than a higher-coupon bond.

Yield-to-Maturity

All other things remaining the same, a lower yield-to-maturity bond has higher duration and more interest rate risk than a higher yield-to-maturity bond. Think of it this way: A higher yield-to-maturity effectively reduces the weighted average of the time to receipt of promised cash flows.

Callable Bonds

Recall that modified and Macaulay duration cannot be used for callable bonds and mortgage-backed bonds (these securities have no well-defined yields-to-maturity because their cash flows are subject to change depending on future interest rates). As a result, we work with effective duration, which evaluates the impact of a change in the benchmark yield curve (ΔCurve) on the bond's price.

Figure 2-4 illustrates the impact of a change in the benchmark yield curve on the price of a callable bond and a noncallable bond, where the two have the same credit risk, coupon rate, payment frequency, and term-to-maturity.

Figure 2-4: Interest Rate Risk Characteristics of a Callable Bond

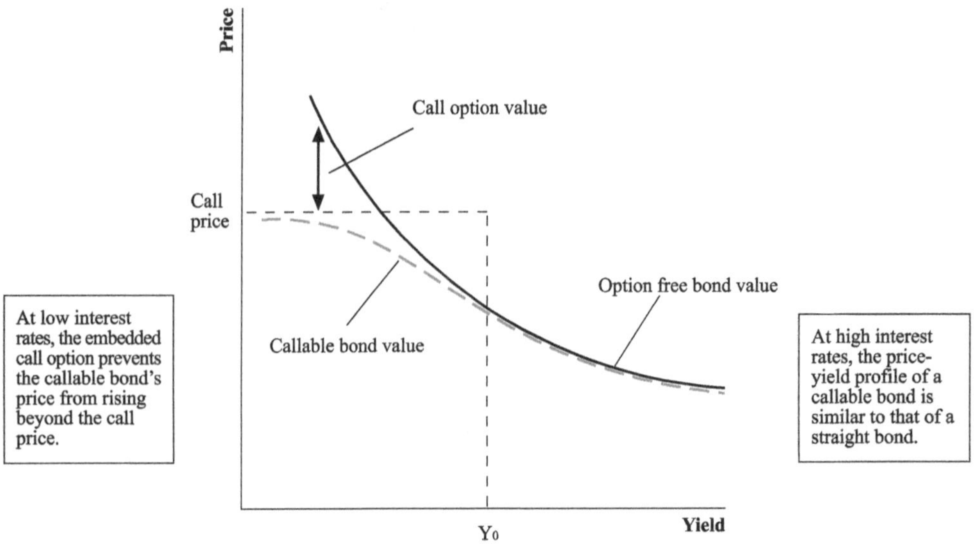

Notice the following:

- The price of a callable bond is always *lower* than the price of an otherwise identical noncallable bond. The difference represents the value of the embedded call option. Recall that the embedded call option favors the issuer, so an investor would pay less for a callable bond than for an otherwise identical noncallable bond.

When interest rates are **high** relative to the coupon rate:

- It is highly unlikely that the issuer will call the bond, so the value of the embedded call option is relatively low.
- Therefore, the effective durations (slopes of the price-yield profiles) of the callable and noncallable bonds are very similar.

When interest rates are **low** relative to the coupon rate:

- It becomes more likely that the issuer will call the bond (and exercise the option to refinance at a lower cost of funds), so the embedded call option gains value for the issuer.
- As interest rates fall, the callable bond suffers "price compression" as it becomes increasingly likely that the bond will be called, with the call price serving as a cap on the callable bond's value.
- The effective duration (slope of the price-yield profile) of the callable bond is *lower* than that of an otherwise identical noncallable bond—its expected life shortens as the weighted average time to receipt of cash is reduced.

When we talk about greater or lower slopes in the analysis here, we are referring to the absolute value of the slope of the price-yield profile.

Putable Bonds

Figure 2-5 illustrates the impact of a change in the benchmark yield curve on the price of a putable bond and a nonputable bond, where the two have the same credit risk, coupon rate, payment frequency, and term-to-maturity.

Figure 2-5: Interest Rate Risk Characteristics of a Putable Bond

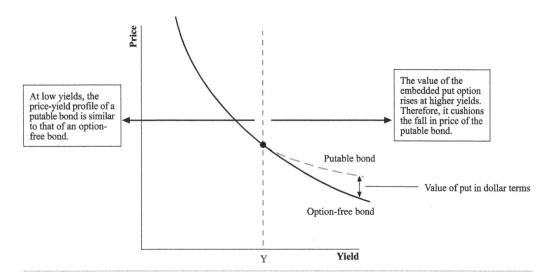

Notice the following:

- The price of a putable bond is always greater than the price of an otherwise identical nonputable bond. The difference represents the value of the embedded put option. Recall that the embedded put option favors the investor, so she would pay more for a putable bond than for an otherwise identical nonputable bond.

When interest rates are **low** relative to the coupon rate:

- It is highly unlikely that the investor will put the bond back to the issuer, so the value of the embedded put option is relatively low.
- Therefore, the effective durations (slopes of the price-yield profiles) of the putable and nonputable bonds are very similar.

When interest rates are **high** relative to the coupon rate:

- It becomes more likely that the investor will put the bond back to the issuer, so the embedded put option gains value for the investor.
- As interest rates rise, the putable bond does not lose as much value as an otherwise identical nonputable bond. The put price effectively serves as a floor on its value.
- The effective duration (slope of the price-yield profile) of the putable bond is lower than that of an otherwise identical nonputable bond—its expected life shortens as the weighted average time to receipt of cash is reduced.

To summarize, the presence of an embedded option (be it a call or a put) reduces the duration of the bond and makes it less sensitive to changes in the benchmark yield curve, assuming there is no change in credit risk.

LOS 54f: Calculate the duration of a portfolio and explain the limitations of portfolio duration. Vol 5, pp 555–556

Duration of a Bond Portfolio

There are two ways to compute the duration of a bond portfolio:

1. **Compute the weighted average of time to receipt of the portfolio's aggregate cash flows.**

   Under this method, projected cash flows on all (1) traditional bonds and (2) bonds with embedded options held in the portfolio are aggregated to determine the portfolio's cash flow yield (i.e., internal rate of return based on those *projected* cash flows), which is then used to compute Macaulay and modified duration for the portfolio. While theoretically accurate, this method is difficult to implement in practice because:

   - The cash flow yield is not usually calculated for bond portfolios.
   - The amount and timing of payments on bonds with embedded options and floating-rate bonds is uncertain.
   - Interest rate risk should be measured based on a change in benchmark interest rates, not on a change in the cash flow yield.
   - For an individual bond, the amount of change in its cash flow yield is not necessarily the same as the change in its yield-to-maturity.

2. **Compute the weighted average of the durations of the individual bonds held in the portfolio.**

   Under this method, Macaulay and modified duration statistics for a bond portfolio are computed as the weighted average of the statistics for the individual bonds that comprise the portfolio, where each bond's weight equals the proportion of the total portfolio's market value that it comprises (based on **full prices**).

   > Portfolio duration $= w_1 D_1 + w_2 D_2 + \ldots + w_N D_N$
   >
   > where:
   > N = Number of bonds in portfolio.
   > D_i = Duration of Bond i.
   > w_i = Market value of Bond i divided by the market value of portfolio.

   - This method is more popular among fixed-income portfolio managers.
   - It provides a very good approximation for the "theoretically correct" portfolio duration (computed using the first approach).
   - The approximation becomes more accurate if the differences between yields-to-maturity for bonds held in the portfolio are smaller.
   - When the yield curve is flat, the two approaches produce the same value for portfolio duration.
   - The advantage of this approach is that bonds with embedded options and floating-rate securities can be included in the calculation of portfolio duration by using effective durations for these securities.
   - Another (major) advantage of this approach is that the computed value for duration can be used as a measure of interest rate risk. From the computation in Example 2-8, we can assert that if the yields-to-maturity for bonds in the portfolio change by 100 bps (or 1%) the estimate change in portfolio value will be 4.38% (in the other direction).

- However, a related disadvantage is that this measure of duration assumes a parallel change in the yield curve (i.e., yields across all maturities change by the same amount and in the same direction). Portfolios of bonds are composed of a variety of bonds that may have different maturities, credit risks, and embedded options, and realistically speaking, there is no reason to expect the change in yields on all these bonds to be identical.

Example 2-8: Calculating Portfolio Duration

An investment fund contains the following three fixed-rate government bonds:

	Bond A	Bond B	Bond C
Par value	20,000,000	20,000,000	40,000,000
Coupon rate	7.0%	9.0%	6.0%
Time-to-maturity	3 years	5 years	7 years
Yield-to-maturity	7.21%	7.45%	7.71%
Market value (USD)	19,888,485	21,274,578	36,352,583
Macaulay duration	2.757	4.165	5.748

- The total market value of the portfolio is USD 77,515,646.
- Each bond is on a coupon date so that there is no accrued interest.
- The market values are the full prices given the par value.
- Coupons on all three bonds are paid semiannually.
- The yields-to-maturity are stated on a semiannual bond basis.
- The Macaulay durations are annualized.

1. Calculate the portfolio's (annual) modified duration using shares of market values as weights.
2. Estimate the percentage loss in the portfolio's market value if the (annual) yield-to-maturity on each bond goes up by 30 bps.

Solution:

1. First we must compute the annual modified durations for the three bonds. We are provided with annual Macaulay durations. To convert an annual Macaulay duration into an annual modified duration we:
   - Convert the Macaulay duration into the number of semiannual periods (by multiplying it by 2).
   - Divide this number of semiannual periods by 1 + yield per semiannual period.
   - Divide the resulting number by 2 to obtain annual modified duration.

   Notice how the first and third bullets cancel out, leaving us with:

   $$\text{Annual ModDur} = \frac{\text{Annual MacDur}}{1+r}$$

   r = yield per semiannual period

   $\text{ModDur}_A = 2.757/(1 + 0.0721/2) = 2.6611$
   $\text{ModDur}_B = 4.165/(1 + 0.0745/2) = 4.0154$
   $\text{ModDur}_C = 5.748/(1 + 0.0771/2) = 5.5346$

We now compute the weighted average of these ModDurs based on the share of each bond in the market value of the portfolio:

$$\text{ModDur}_{\text{Portfolio}} = 2.6611 \times \frac{19,888,485}{77,515,646} + 4.0154 \times \frac{21,274,578}{77,515,646}$$

$$+ 5.5346 \times \frac{36,352,583}{77,515,646} = 4.3804$$

2. The estimated decline in the market value of the portfolio if yields rise by 30 bps across the board is calculated as:

$$-4.3804 \times 0.0030 = -0.0131 \text{ or } 1.31\%$$

LOS 54g: Calculate and interpret the money duration of a bond and price value of a basis point (PVBP). Vol 5, pp 557–558

Money Duration

Money duration (or dollar duration) is a statistic closely related to modified duration. While modified duration is a measure of the *percentage change* in the price of a bond in response to a change in its yield-to-maturity, money duration is a measure of the *dollar* (or whichever currency the bond is denominated in) *price change* in response to a change in yields. Money duration can be stated per 100 of par or in terms of the actual size of the position. See Example 2-9. It is calculated as:

$$\boxed{\text{MoneyDur} = \text{AnnModDur} \times \text{PV}^{\text{Full}}}$$

The estimated (dollar) change in the price of the bond is calculated as:

$$\boxed{\Delta \text{PV}^{\text{Full}} = -\text{MoneyDur} \times \Delta \text{Yield}}$$

Example 2-9: Money Duration

Consider an 8-year, annual-pay bond with a par value of $3.5 million. The bond has a modified duration of 6.75 and a full price of 102.31 per 100 of par.

1. Calculate the money duration of the bond in terms of the actual size of the position and per 100 of par value.
2. Compute the impact of a 50-bp increase in yield-to-maturity on the dollar value of the position.

Solution:

1. Money duration in terms of the actual size of the position is calculated as:

$$\text{MoneyDur (in terms of actual size)} = \text{AnnModDur} \times \text{PV}^{\text{Full}}$$
$$= 6.75 \times \$3,500,000 \times 1.0231 = \$24,170,737.50$$

Money duration per 100 of par value is calculated as:

$$\text{MoneyDur(per 100 of par)} = \text{AnnModDur} \times \text{PV}^{\text{Full}} \text{(per 100 of par)}$$
$$= 6.75 \times 102.31 = \$690.59$$

2. If there were a 50-bp increase in yield-to-maturity, the change in the value of the overall position (in terms of dollars) would be calculated as:

$$\$24,170,737.50 \times 0.005 = \$120,853.69$$

The value of the position would fall by \$120,853.69 if yields were to rise by 50 basis points.

Price Value of a Basis Point

The price value of a basis point (PVBP) is another version of money duration. It estimates the change in the full price of a bond in response to a 1-bp change in its yield-to-maturity. The PVBP can be calculated as:

$$\text{PVBP} = \frac{(\text{PV}_-) - (\text{PV}_+)}{2}$$

PV_- and PV_+ are full prices calculated by decreasing and increasing yields by 1 bp (0.01%). See Example 2-10.

Example 2-10: Price Value of a Basis Point

Consider a newly-issued 10-year, 5% annual-pay bond that is priced at 92.64 per 100 of par to yield 6%. Calculate the price value of a basis point for this bond.

Solution:

PV_+ can be calculated as:

N = 10; FV = 100; PMT = 5; I/Y = 6.01; CPT PV; PV = \$92.57

PV_- can be calculated as:

N = 10; FV = 100; PMT = 5; I/Y = 5.99; CPT PV; PV = \$92.71

The price value of a basis point can be computed as:

$$\text{PVBP} = (92.71 - 92.57) / 2 = \$0.07 \text{ per 100 of par value}$$

Note that the PVBP is also referred to as PV01, present value of 01, and DV01, or dollar value of 01, where 01 means 1 bp. A related statistic is basis point value (BPV), which is calculated as:

$$\text{BPV} = \text{MoneyDur} \times 0.0001 (1 \text{ bp expressed as a decimal})$$

LOS 54h: Calculate and interpret approximate convexity and distinguish between approximate and effective convexity. Vol 5, pp 559–567

LOS 54i: Estimate the percentage price change of a bond for a specified change in yield, given the bond's approximate duration and convexity. Vol 5, pp 559–567

Bond Convexity

We know that the relationship between the price of a bond and its yield-to-maturity (the price-yield profile) is convex. We have also learned that duration is a linear measure of interest rate risk (i.e., it estimates the change in a bond's price along a straight line that is tangent to the [curved] price-yield profile). Duration provides a good approximation for changes in bond prices only for small changes in yields. For large changes in yields, duration *underestimates* the price increase caused by a reduction in yields, and *overestimates* the decrease in prices when yields rise. Therefore, price estimates of option-free bonds based on duration must be revised upward to bring them closer to their actual values. This revision is performed via the convexity adjustment. The more the curvature or convexity of the price-yield relationship, the more significant the convexity adjustment becomes. See Figure 2-6.

Figure 2-6: Convexity of a Traditional Fixed-Rate Bond

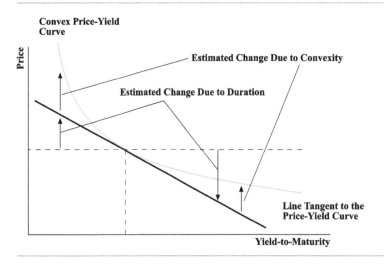

In order to compute the convexity adjustment, we must first calculate annual convexity (AnnConvexity). Annual convexity can be approximated using the following equation:

$$\text{ApproxCon} = \frac{(PV_-) - (PV_+) - [2 \times (PV_0)]}{(\Delta \text{Yield})^2 \times (PV_0)}$$

... (Equation 5)

Once we have an estimate for convexity, we can estimate the percentage change in a bond's full price as:

$$\%\Delta PV^{\text{Full}} \approx (-\text{AnnModDur} \times \Delta \text{Yield}) + \left[\frac{1}{2} \times \text{AnnConvexity} \times (\Delta \text{Yield})^2 \right]$$

... (Equation 6)

- The first part of Equation 6 captures the first-order (duration) effect. If there in an increase (decrease) in yields, the duration effect on a bond's price will be negative (positive).
- The second part of Equation 6 captures the second-order effect or convexity adjustment. Notice that the convexity adjustment has a positive impact on the bond price estimate for either an increase or a decrease in yields.

It will help you to remember that duration measures the slope of the price-yield profile (rate of change of bond value) at a given level of yields. Stated differently, duration is the first derivative of the price-yield function. Convexity is the second derivative of the price-yield function (i.e., it measures the rate of change of duration). See Example 2-11.

Example 2-11: The Convexity Adjustment

We continue with the bond we worked with in Examples 2-2 and 2-6. Relevant information from those examples is provided below:

- Initial YTM = 5%
- PV_0 = $101.492586
- PV_+ = $101.2110
- PV_- = $101.7750
- ΔYield = 0.0005
- ApproxModDur = 5.55278

1. Calculate approximate convexity.
2. Calculate the estimated convexity-adjusted percentage price change resulting from a 100 bp increase in the yield-to-maturity.
3. Compare the estimated percentage price change with the actual change, assuming the yield-to-maturity jumps to 6.00% on the settlement date.

Solution:

1. Approximate convexity can be calculated as:

$$ApproxCon = \frac{101.775 + 101.211 - (2 \times 101.492586)}{(0.0005)^2 \times 101.492586}$$

$$ApproxCon = 32.6329$$

2. The convexity-adjusted percentage price drop resulting from a 100-bp increase in the yield-to-maturity is calculated as:

$$\%\Delta PV^{Full} \approx (-5.55278 \times 0.01) + \left[\frac{1}{2} \times 32.6329 \times (0.01)^2 \right]$$

$$\%\Delta PV^{Full} = -0.0555278 + 0.00163165$$

$$\%\Delta PV^{Full} = -0.057159 \text{ or } 5.7159\%$$

Notice that modified duration alone estimates that the price of the bond will fall by 5.55278% (from Example 2-6). The convexity adjustment adds 16.32 bps to price estimate based on duration alone.

---

3. The new full price if the yield-to-maturity goes from 5% to 6% on the settlement date can be calculated as:

$N = 14$; $PMT = -\$2.50$; $FV = -\$100$; $I/Y = 3\%$; $CPT\ PV \rightarrow PV = \$94.35196$

$PV^{Full} = \$94.35196 \times (1.03)^{108/180} = \$96.040249$

$\%\Delta PV^{Full} = \dfrac{96.040249 - 101.492586}{101.492586} = -0.0537215$

- The actual percentage change in the bond price is −5.37215%.
- The convexity-adjusted estimate (the combines the duration effect and convexity adjustment) for the change in the bond's price is −5.36773%.
- The estimated change based on modified duration alone is −5.55278%.

Notice how performing the convexity adjustment brings the change in price estimate that is based on duration alone closer to the actual change in the price of the bond.

Another convexity-related statistic is money convexity. While money duration indicates the first-order effect on the full price of a bond (in dollar terms) given a change in the yield-to-maturity, money convexity (MoneyCon) is the second-order effect. The money convexity of a bond is its annual convexity multiplied by the full price of the bond such that:

$$\Delta PV^{Full} \approx (-MoneyDur \times \Delta Yield) + \left[\frac{1}{2} \times MoneyCon \times (\Delta Yield)^2 \right]$$

Factors that Affect Convexity

The factors that lead to greater duration also lead to greater convexity. All other things remaining the same, for a fixed-rate bond:

- The longer the term-to-maturity, the greater the convexity.
- The lower the coupon rate, the greater the convexity.
- The lower the yield-to-maturity, the greater the convexity.

Another factor is the degree to which payments are spread out over the bond's term. If two bonds have the same duration, the one with a greater dispersion of cash flows will have greater convexity.

The greater the convexity of a bond, the greater the price appreciation when yields decrease, and the lower the price depreciation when yields increase. Given the same price, yield-to-maturity, and modified duration, a more convex bond will outperform a less convex bond in both bull and bear markets.

Convexity for Bonds with Embedded Options

For callable bonds (and other bonds with embedded options) the first-order effect of a change in the benchmark yield curve is measured by **effective** duration, and the second-order effect of a change in the benchmark yield curve is measured by effective convexity. Effective convexity is a **curve convexity** statistic.

$$\text{EffCon} = \frac{[(PV-) + (PV_+)] - [2 \times (PV_0)]}{(\Delta \text{Curve})^2 \times (PV_0)} \qquad \text{... (Equation 7)}$$

A pricing model is used to determine PV_- and PV_+ when the benchmark yield curve is moved upward and downward by the same amount (ΔCurve). Note that the credit spread is assumed constant when computing PV_- and PV_+.

Also note that the difference between Equation 5 and Equation 7 is that Equation 5 (to approximate yield convexity) has the change in yield-to-maturity squared (ΔYield)^2 in the denominator, while Equation 7 (to estimate effective convexity) has the change in benchmark yield curve squared (ΔCurve)^2 in the denominator. See Example 2-12.

Example 2-12: Effective Convexity

Compute effective convexity for the callable bond we worked with in Example 2-7 (to illustrate the computation of effective duration). Relevant information is reproduced below:

- $PV_0 = 101.05$
- $PV_- = 102.87$
- $PV_+ = 99.04$
- ΔCurve $= 0.0025$

Solution:

$$\text{EffCon} = \frac{102.87 + 99.04 - (2 \times 101.05)}{(0.0025)^2 \times 101.05} = -300.84$$

Notice that the value of convexity for this callable bond is negative. Negative convexity (also known as concavity) is an important feature of callable bonds. We mentioned earlier that convexity (the second-order effect) indicates the change in the first-order effect (duration) as the benchmark yield curve is changed. Notice in Figure 2-4, that as the benchmark yield decreases (as we move to the left) the slope to the line tangent to the price-yield profile of the noncallable bond becomes steeper (i.e., the rate of change of duration is positive, which implies positive convexity). On the other hand, for the callable bond, the slope of the line tangent to the price-yield profile flattens (i.e., the rate of change of duration is negative, which implies negative convexity). The point of inflection here indicates the yield at which convexity for the callable bond goes from positive to negative.

To summarize, when the benchmark yield is high, callable and noncallable bonds experience similar price changes to changes in benchmark yields. However, as benchmark yields decline, there comes a point where the callable bond moves into negative convexity territory, where the embedded call option holds significant value to the issuer and is highly likely to be exercised. This is why the price of a callable bond experiences price compression at low yields—the call price effectively serves as a cap on its value.

Finally, note that putable bonds always have positive convexity.

LOS 54j: Describe how the term structure of yield volatility affects the interest rate risk of a bond. Vol 5, pp 567–569

Interest Rate Risk and the Investment Horizon

Yield Volatility

In this section, let's focus on a short-term investor who is concerned with the risk of a change in the value of a bond in response to a change in the yield-to-maturity. You might be correct in thinking that duration and convexity are useful measures of risk arising from changes in the yield-to-maturity, but that is only one part of the puzzle. Another important consideration for this investor would be the term structure of yield volatility.

Recall that in our discussion of duration and convexity, we often said "for a given change in the yield-to-maturity." In comparing two bonds based on duration/convexity it was assumed that (1) the given change in yields was the same for both securities and (2) that there were only parallel yield curve shifts. In practice however, the shape of the yield curve changes based on factors that affect supply and demand for short-term versus long-term securities. Further, the term structure of yield volatility (relationship between volatility of bond yields and time-to-maturity) is not flat (i.e., yield volatility for different maturities tends to be different).

Changes in bond prices result from two factors:

1. The impact per basis point change in the yield-to-maturity. This factor is captured by duration and convexity.
2. The number of basis points in the change in yield-to-maturity. This factor is captured by yield volatility.

To drive the point home, consider Equation 6, which is restated below:

$$\%\Delta PV^{Full} \approx (-AnnModDur \times \Delta Yield) + \left[\frac{1}{2} \times AnnConvexity \times (\Delta Yield)^2\right]$$

... (Equation 6)

Notice that the estimated percentage change in the price of the bond depends on modified duration and convexity, **as well as on the magnitude of the change in yield-to-maturity**. See Example 3-1.

Example 3-1: Ranking Bonds in Terms of Interest Rate Risk

A fixed-income analyst has been assigned the task of ranking three bonds in terms of interest rate risk (measured in terms of the potential percentage price depreciation given forecasted worst-case scenario changes in the yields).

Bond	Modified Duration	Convexity	ΔYield (bps)
A	9.2	147.0	15
B	7.8	38.5	20
C	5.9	12.1	25

- The modified duration and convexity statistics are annualized.
- ΔYield is the projected increase in the annual yield-to-maturity.

Rank the bonds in terms of interest rate risk.

Solution:

First, we calculate the approximate percentage price change for each bond given the projected increase in its yield:

Bond A: $(-9.2 \times 0.0015) + [1/2 \times 147.0 \times (0.0015)^2] = 0.013635$ or **–1.36%**

Bond B: $(-7.8 \times 0.002) + [1/2 \times 38.5 \times (0.002)^2] = 0.015523$ or **–1.55%**

Bond C: $(-5.9 \times 0.0025) + [1/2 \times 12.1 \times (0.0025)^2] = 0.014712$ or **–1.47%**

Based on these anticipated changes in yields, and the bonds' current modified duration and convexity measures, Bond B has the highest degree of interest rate risk (potential loss = 1.55%), followed by Bond C (potential loss = 1.47%) and Bond A (potential loss = 1.36%).

LOS 54k: Describe the relationships among a bond's holding period return, its duration, and the investment horizon. Vol 5, pp 569–573

Investment Horizon, Macaulay Duration, and Interest Rate Risk

In this section, our focus moves to a long-term investor who is concerned with the total return from her bond investment. Interest rate risk is important to this investor as she faces market price risk as well as coupon reinvestment risk.

Let's go back to Examples 1-1 through 1-6 earlier in the reading where we worked with a 10-year, 8% annual-pay bond that was priced at 85.503075 per 100 of par to yield 10.40%. Recall the following:

- Investor A (the buy-and-hold investor) only faced coupon reinvestment risk (no market price risk). She experienced a higher total return if interest rates increased (Example 1-3) and a lower total return if interest rates decreased (Example 1-5).
- Investor B (the short-term investor with a 4-year investment horizon) faced both market price risk and coupon reinvestment risk. She had a higher total return if interest rates decreased (Example 1-6) than if interest rates increased (Example 1-4), which suggests that given her investment horizon and the change in yields, market price risk dominated coupon reinvestment risk.

Now let's consider a third investor, Investor C, who has a 7-year investment horizon. We spare you the calculations here, but provide the following total return information for this investor in the three different yield scenarios to illustrate our point. Given her 7-year investment horizon:

- If interest rates remain at 10.40% (the bond's stated yield-to-maturity at purchase), her horizon yield would be 10.40%.
- If the yield-to-maturity were to rise to 11.40% (as was the case in Examples 1-3 and 4), her horizon yield would be 10.407%.
- If the yield-to-maturity were to fall to 9.40% (as was the case in Examples 1-5 and 1-6), her horizon yield would be 10.408%.

Notice that for Investor C (the 7-year investor), the horizon yields are almost the same in each of the three interest rate scenarios. Unlike Investors A and B (the 4- and 10-year investors), she achieves the same rate of return (around 10.40%) regardless of whether interest rates rise, fall, or stay the same.

This brings us to a very important property regarding Macaulay duration. Given a particular assumption about yield volatility, Macaulay duration indicates the investment horizon for which coupon reinvestment risk and market price risk offset each other. Recall that in Example 2-1, we computed the Macaulay duration of this bond to be 7.0029 years. This is one of the applications of duration where "years-based" interpretation is meaningful and where Macaulay duration is used rather than modified duration. See Figure 3-1.

> Note that the particular assumption about yield volatility that we make here is that there is a one-time parallel shift in the yield curve that occurs before the first coupon payment date.

Figure 3-1: Interest Rate Risk, Macaulay Duration, and the Investment Horizon

A. Interest Rates Rise

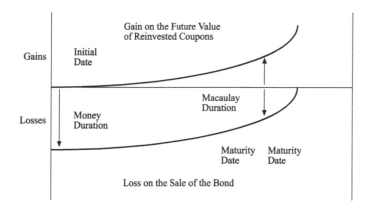

B. Interest Rates Falls

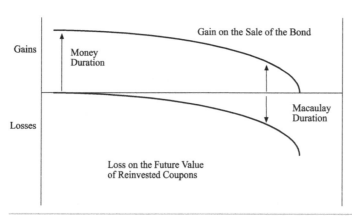

In Panel A, notice the following. When interest rates rise:

- Money duration measures the immediate decline in the value of the bond.
- Over time, the value of the bond is pulled up to par.
- The gain in future value of reinvested coupon starts out small, but increases at an increasing rate over time.
- At a certain point during the life of the bond, the gain on reinvested coupon and the loss on the sale of the bond offset each other. That point is the Macaulay duration of the bond.

> Note that the gain/loss on future value of reinvested coupon is measured relative to the future value of coupon reinvestment had interest rates not risen/fallen.

In Panel B, notice the following. When interest rates fall:

- Money duration measures the immediate increase in the value of the bond.
- Over time, the value of the bond is pulled down to par.
- The loss in future value of reinvested coupon starts out small, but increases at an increasing rate over time.
- At a certain point during the life of the bond, the gain on sale of the bond and the loss on the future value of reinvested coupon offset each other. That point is the Macaulay duration of the bond.

Based on the example and analyses above, we can make the following three general statements:

1. When the investment horizon is *greater* than the Macaulay duration of the bond, coupon reinvestment risk dominates market price risk. In this case, the investor is concerned about interest rates *falling*.
2. When the investment horizon is less than the Macaulay duration of the bond, market price risk dominates coupon reinvestment risk. In this case, the investor is concerned about interest rates *rising*.
3. When the investment horizon equals the Macaulay duration of the bond, coupon reinvestment risk and market price risk offset each other.

The difference between the Macaulay duration of a bond and the investment horizon is known as the duration gap.

> Duration gap = Macaulay duration − Investment horizon

- Investor A (with the 10-year horizon) has a *negative* duration gap and is currently at risk of *lower* interest rates.
- Investor B (with the 4-year horizon) has a *positive* duration gap and is currently at risk of *higher* interest rates.
- Investor C (with the 7-year horizon) has a duration gap of zero and is currently hedged against interest rate risk.

The word "currently" in the above statements is very important because interest rate risk is related to an immediate change in the bond's yield-to-maturity and coupon reinvestment rates. As time passes, (1) the investment horizon falls and (2) the Macaulay duration of the bond also changes, so the duration gap changes as well.

LOS 54l: Explain how changes in credit spread and liquidity affect yield-to-maturity of a bond and how duration and convexity can be used to estimate the price effect of the changes. Vol 5, pp 574–575

CREDIT AND LIQUIDITY RISK

Recall that the yield on a corporate bond is composed of (1) the government benchmark yield and (2) a spread on top of that benchmark. A change in a bond's yield-to-maturity can be caused by either of, or a combination of, the two. Also recall that the benchmark yield is composed of the expected real interest rate and expected inflation, while the credit spread is driven by credit risk and liquidity risk.

For a traditional fixed-rate bond, the same duration or convexity statistics apply regardless of whether a change in the yield-to-maturity is caused by a change in the benchmark yield or a change in the spread or both. For fixed-income securities, changes in the components of the overall yield-to-maturity do not occur in isolation (i.e., there is interaction between changes in benchmark yields and spreads, between changes in the expected inflation rate and the expected real interest rate, and between changes in credit and liquidity risk). The point here is that for a fixed-rate bond, "inflation duration" or a "credit duration" refer to the same number. Therefore, we can use modified duration and convexity to estimate the change in the value of a bond in response to any change in the yield-to-maturity regardless of the source of the yield-to-maturity change. See Example 3-2.

Example 3-2: Price Impact of a Change in the Credit Spread

Consider an annual-pay bond that is trading at 93.75 per 100 of par. The duration of the bond is 7.25 and its convexity is 34. Compute the percentage change in the price of the bond if a credit rating downgrade results in its spread relative to the benchmark increasing by 25 basis points.

Solution:

The change in spread equals 25 bps, so we compute the estimated change in the price of the bond given its duration and convexity and ΔYield = 0.0025.

$$l = (-7.25 \times 0.0025) + (0.5 \times 34 \times 0.0025^2) = -0.018125 + 0.00010625$$
$$= -0.018 \text{ or } -1.8\%$$

The bond's value will fall by approximately 1.8% in response to the 25-bp increase in its credit spread.

READING 55: FUNDAMENTALS OF CREDIT ANALYSIS

LESSON 1: CREDIT RISK, CAPITAL STRUCTURE, SENIORITY RANKING, AND RECOVERY RATES

LOS 55a: Describe credit risk and credit-related risks affecting corporate bonds. Vol 5, pp 592–594

LOS 55b: Describe default probability and loss severity as components of credit risk. Vol 5, pp 592–594

Credit risk refers to the risk of loss resulting from a borrower's failure to make full and timely payments of interest and/or principal. It has two components:

- Default risk or default probability: This refers to the probability of a borrower failing to meet its obligations to make full and timely payments of principal and interest under the terms of the bond indenture.
- Loss severity or loss given default: This refers to the portion of the bond's value that an investor would lose if a default actually occurred. A default does not necessarily mean that the investor will lose the entire amount invested. Typically, the investor can expect to recover a certain percentage of her investment from the issuer. The percentage of the principal amount plus unpaid interest that the investor is able to recover in the event of a default is called the recovery rate. Loss severity equals 1 minus the recovery rate.

The expected loss is calculated as the probability of default multiplied by loss severity. It can be stated in terms of a dollar amount or as a percentage of the bond's value.

$$\text{Expected loss} = \text{Default probability} \times \text{Loss severity given default}$$

Spread risk: Bonds with credit risk typically trade at a yield premium or spread relative to "risk-free" bonds that are issued by the U.S. Treasury and the German government. If a bond becomes more risky, the spread (or compensation) that the market will demand on top of the return required from a risk-free borrower will increase. This increase in the spread will translate into an increase in the required yield on the bond, resulting in a decrease in its market value. Spread risk refers to the risk of a widening of the yield spread on the bond. It encompasses:

- Downgrade risk or credit migration risk: This is the risk that the issuer's creditworthiness may deteriorate during the term of the bond, causing rating agencies to downgrade the credit rating of the issue. This would result in investors demanding a higher spread to compensate them for the higher risk inherent in the instrument, which in turn will reduce the market price of the bond.
- Market liquidity risk: This is the risk that an investor may have to sell her investment at a price lower than its market value due to insufficient volumes (liquidity) in the market. To compensate investors for this risk, the spread or yield premium on corporate bonds includes a market liquidity component. The primary measure of liquidity risk is the bid–ask spread. A higher bid–ask spread indicates low market liquidity and a higher level of liquidity risk. Two issuer-specific factors that affect liquidity risk are:
  - The size of the issuer (i.e., the amount of publicly traded debt an issuer has outstanding). Generally speaking, the lower the amount of publicly traded debt an issuer has outstanding, the less frequently its debt securities trade, and the higher the liquidity risk.
  - The credit quality of the issuer. Generally speaking, the lower the credit quality of the issuer, the higher the liquidity risk.

LOS 55c: Describe seniority rankings of corporate debt and explain the potential violation of the priority of claims in a bankruptcy proceeding. Vol 5, pp 595–600

A company's capital structure refers to the composition and distribution of debt and equity across its operating units.

Seniority Ranking

Companies may issue debt with different rankings in terms of seniority, where the most senior or highest-ranking debt has the first claim on the issuer's cash flows and assets in case of an issuer default or restructuring. Debt may be classified as:

- Secured debt: Holders of secured debt have a direct claim on certain assets and their associated cash flows.
- Unsecured debt or debentures: Holders of unsecured debt have only a general claim on the issuer's assets and cash flow. In the event of default, secured debt ranks higher than unsecured debt in the priority of claims.

Further, within each category of debt, there are sub-rankings.

For example, secured debt may be further classified as:

- First lien or first mortgage (where a specific asset is pledged).
- Senior secured.
- Junior secured, which is the lowest rank of secured debt.

Unsecured debt may be further divided into:

- Senior unsecured debt, which is the highest rank of unsecured debt.
- Senior subordinated debt.
- Subordinated debt.
- Junior subordinated debt.

Companies may issue secured debt because (1) it is required by investors given the company's perceived riskiness or (2) it is cheaper than unsecured debt due to its higher ranking in the priority of claims. On the other hand, companies may issue subordinated debt because (1) it is less expensive than issuing equity (and does not dilute existing shareholders' holdings), (2) it is usually less restrictive than issuing senior debt, and (3) investors may be willing to buy it if they believe that the offered yield adequately compensates them for the associated risk.

Recovery Rates

All creditors at the same level in the capital structure are treated as one class irrespective of (1) the coupon rate offered on their bonds, and (2) when their bonds are maturing. For example, in the event of bankruptcy, a senior unsecured bondholder whose bond matures in 10 years will have the same pro rata claim on the issuer's assets as another senior unsecured bondholder whose bond matures in just another 3 months. This is referred to as bonds ranking pari passu (i.e., on an equal footing) in right of payment.

Recovery rates are highest for the senior-most class of debt in the priority of claims and fall with each lower rank of seniority. Therefore, the lower the seniority of the bond, the greater the credit risk, and this is why investors demand a higher yield to invest in lower-ranked debt instruments.

Apart from the relative seniority of a particular bond, recovery rates also vary (1) by industry and (2) depending on when the default occurs in a credit cycle.

- Recovery rates are usually lower in industries that are in secular decline compared to industries that are experiencing a cyclical economic downturn.
- Recovery rates are usually lower at or near the bottom of a credit cycle (which is usually very closely linked with the economic cycle) than at other times in the cycle. This is because the volume of bankruptcies tends to be very high near the bottom of the cycle, which crowds the market for distressed securities, resulting in lower valuations.

Note that recovery rates can also vary greatly across companies within the same industry depending on the composition and proportion of debt in the issuer's capital structure. For example, all other things remaining the same, if a company has a relatively higher proportion of secured debt in its capital structure, recovery rates for lower-ranked debt will tend to be lower.

Priority of Claims: Not Always "Absolute"

Let's now return to the rule of absolute priority.

In principle, in the event of bankruptcy:

- Holders of secured debt have a direct claim on certain assets and their associated cash flows. If the value of the pledged property is less than the amount due to secured debt holders, the difference is treated as a senior unsecured claim.
- Holders of unsecured debt have a right to be paid in full before any payments are made to equity holders (both common and preferred shareholders).
- Senior creditors have a priority over junior (i.e., subordinated) creditors. Note that a creditor is senior unless it is explicitly stated that her claim is subordinated.

In practice, however, holders of junior and subordinated debt and even shareholders may recover some value on their interests without more senior creditors being paid in full. This is because during bankruptcy proceedings, all impaired classes of claimants (those that receive less than their full claim) get to vote to approve the reorganization plan. In trying to formulate a reorganization plan that is acceptable to all classes of claimants, several items may be debated upon, such as:

- The value of certain assets in the bankruptcy estate.
- The present value and timing of payouts.
- The value of debt issued to a certain class in the reorganized entity (that emerges from bankruptcy).

> Note that no single class of claimants can be too aggressive when negotiating because if all classes do not come to a compromise, the case would go to court where a bankruptcy judge would rule on the matter.

Resolution of these matters takes time, and can entail substantial legal and accounting fees. Further, the value of the entity may also suffer as key employees and customers leave the company. Therefore, in order to expedite matters, claimants usually negotiate and compromise. This often leads to relatively junior creditors receiving more consideration than they would be legally entitled to were the absolute priority rule strictly enforced.

Note that in the United States, there is a tendency toward reorganization and recovery of companies in bankruptcy, where claimants with relatively junior claims can fare relatively well in terms of recovery rates. In other jurisdictions such as the U.K., there is a bias toward liquidation of companies in bankruptcy, where banks and senior claimants tend to do very well in terms of recovering the amount of their respective interests.

LESSON 2: RATING AGENCIES, CREDIT RATINGS, AND THEIR ROLE IN DEBT MARKETS

LOS 55d: Distinguish between corporate issuer credit ratings and issue credit ratings and describe the rating agency practice of "notching."
Vol 5, pp 601–605

Credit Ratings

Rating agencies issue credit ratings, which reflect an opinion on the potential risk of default of a particular (1) bond issue or (2) bond issuer. Table 2-1 shows the long-term rating matrix used by Moody's, S&P, and Fitch.

Table 2-1 Long-Term Ratings Matrix: Investment Grade vs. Noninvestment Grade[1]

		Moody's	S&P	Fitch
Investment Grade	High-Quality Grade	Aaa	AAA	AAA
		Aa1	AA+	AA+
		Aa2	AA	AA
		Aa3	AA–	AA–
	Upper-Medium Grade	A1	A+	A+
		A2	A	A
		A3	A–	A–
	Low-Medium Grade	Baa1	BBB+	BBB+
		Baa2	BBB	BBB
		Baa3	BBB–	BBB–
Noninvestment Grade "Junk" or "High Yield"	Low Grade or Speculative Grade	Ba1	BB+	BB+
		Ba2	BB	BB
		Ba3	BB–	BB–
		B1	B+	B+
		B2	B	B
		B3	B–	B–
		Caa1	CCC+	CCC+
		Caa2	CCC	CCC
		Caa3	CCC–	CCC–
		Ca	CC	CC
		C	C	C
	Default	C	D	D

- Bonds rated triple-A (Aaa or AAA) are said to be "of the highest quality with minimal credit risk" and have the lowest probability of default.
- Bonds rated Baa3/BBB—or higher are known as investment grade bonds.
- Bonds rated lower than Baa3/BBB—are known as noninvestment grade or high-yield bonds.

Generally speaking, issuers of bonds rated investment grade are able to more easily access debt markets and borrow at lower rates than those rated below investment grade.

1 - Exhibit 4, Volume 5, CFA Program Curriculum 2018.

Rating agencies also usually provide outlooks on their respective ratings (i.e., positive, stable, or negative), and may sometimes provide indications on the potential future direction of ratings (e.g., "on review for a downgrade" or "on credit watch for an upgrade").

Issuer versus Issue Ratings

Rating agencies usually provide credit ratings for the **issuer** (referred to as a corporate family rating) and for different **issues** (referred to as corporate credit rating) as well.

- The corporate family rating (CFR) is based on the overall creditworthiness of the issuer (i.e., the ability and willingness of the issuer to make full and timely payments of interest and principal). These ratings are typically based on the issuer's senior unsecured debt.
- The corporate credit rating (CCR) applies to a specific financial obligation of the issuer and is based on factors such as the issue's relative seniority ranking in the priority of claims and covenants.

Most bonds contain cross-default provisions in the bond indenture. Under the terms of a cross-default provision, if there is a default event (such as nonpayment of interest) on any one bond issued by a company, default on all other debt that the company has outstanding is triggered automatically. The existence of cross-default provisions implies that the **probability of default** for all the different issues of a particular company is the same. However, different issues can be assigned different (higher or lower) credit ratings due to a ratings adjustment known as notching.

Notching

Rating agencies consider several factors when assigning ratings to specific issues of the same company. While the probability of default is one of the primary factors considered, other factors such as (1) the priority of payment in the event of default and (2) the potential loss severity in the event of default also play an important role.

Further, rating agencies also consider structural subordination, which arises when there is a holding company structure and both the parent and its subsidiary have outstanding debt. The parent company could be relying on cash flows from the subsidiary to service its debt, but covenants in the debt instruments issued by the subsidiary may preclude the subsidiary from passing on cash to the parent until its own debt has been serviced. In such a case, even though the parent's bonds are not junior to the subsidiary's bonds, the subsidiary's debt holders have a priority claim to the subsidiary's cash flows. As a result, the parent's bonds are effectively subordinate to the subsidiary's bonds.

In order to account for these different payment priorities, rating agencies have adopted the practice of notching, whereby they move credit ratings for specific issues up or down relative to the issuer rating (which applies to senior unsecured debt). Generally speaking:

- For more risky issuers (with lower credit ratings), a larger notching adjustment is applied across seniority rankings. For these issuers, the probability of default is higher, so the potential difference in loss from a lower or higher seniority ranking is a bigger consideration in assessing the issue's credit risk.
- For less risky issuers (with higher credit ratings), the probability of default is lower, so there is less of a need to notch ratings to capture any potential difference in loss severity.

LOS 55e: Explain risks in relying on ratings from credit rating agencies. Vol 5, pp 605–611

Risks in Relying on Agency Ratings

- **Credit ratings can be very dynamic:** Credit ratings can (and generally tend to) change significantly during a bond's term. Therefore, investors should not assume that a bond's credit rating will remain the same from the time of purchase through the entire holding period.
- **Rating agencies are not infallible:** Rating agencies also make mistakes. For example, they assigned inappropriately high credit ratings to subprime-backed mortgage securities (in the lead-up to the 2008 financial crisis), and failed to detect accounting fraud at large companies like Enron and WorldCom.
- **Other types of so-called idiosyncratic or event risk are difficult to capture in ratings:** Certain risks (e.g., litigation risk faced by tobacco companies, environmental and business risks faced by chemical companies) cannot be anticipated in advance. Rating agencies therefore fail to capture these risks in assigned credit ratings.
- **Ratings tend to lag market pricing of credit:** Bond prices and credit spreads tend to change more quickly (to reflect changes in perceived creditworthiness) than credit ratings assigned to bonds. Most of the time, credit rating changes are already "priced in" by the market.

Further, credit ratings primarily focus on the risk of default, whereas (especially for low-quality credits) market price depends more on expected loss (i.e., default probability times loss severity). Therefore, two bonds with similar default risk but different recovery rates will have similar ratings, but different market values.

LESSON 3: TRADITIONAL CREDIT ANALYSIS

LOS 55f: Explain the four Cs (Capacity, Collateral, Covenants, and Character) of traditional credit analysis. Vol 5, pp 611–628

The Four Cs of Credit Analysis: A Useful Framework

The aim of credit analysis is to assess an issuer's ability to satisfy its debt obligations. Analysts usually consider the four Cs of credit when performing credit analysis.

Capacity

Capacity refers to a borrower's ability to make its debt payments on time. An evaluation of capacity to pay usually starts with industry analysis and then moves down to company analysis.

Industry Structure

Michael Porter's "five forces framework" is typically used to conduct industry analysis.

- *Power of suppliers:* Generally speaking, an industry that relies on just a few suppliers has greater credit risk than an industry that has multiple suppliers. This is because powerful suppliers have the negotiating power to potentially capture a higher proportion of industry profits. Industries that have plenty of suppliers can play them off against each other to keep input prices in check.
- *Power of buyers/customers:* Generally speaking, industries that rely heavily on just a few customers have greater credit risk than those that sell to a large number of customers. Powerful buyers may force down prices, demand better quality products or services (driving up costs), or play industry participants off against each other.
- *Barriers to entry:* Generally speaking, the higher the barriers to entry, the lower the level of competition in an industry, and the lower the credit risk of industry participants. The entry of new firms brings additional capacity into the industry, and the desire of new firms to gain market share puts pressure on existing firms' profits.
- *Substitution risk:* Generally speaking, industries that offer products and services for which there are no good or cost-effective substitutes have greater pricing power and hence lower credit risk. Substitutes limit an industry's profitability by effectively placing a cap on prices unless industry participants can differentiate their products in terms of quality, performance, or marketing.
- *Level of competition:* Generally speaking, the greater the intensity of competition among companies in an industry, the lower the industry's profit potential. Therefore, highly competitive industries tend to entail higher credit risk.

Apart from these five forces, analysts should also consider the level of operating leverage in an industry when evaluating credit quality. Operating leverage refers to the proportion of fixed costs incurred by companies. If an industry is characterized by high fixed costs (e.g., airlines and hotels), companies would find it difficult to cut down costs if they are unable to generate sufficient revenue.

Industry Fundamentals

An analysis of industry fundamentals involves an assessment of the industry's sensitivity to macroeconomic factors, its growth prospects, its profitability, and reliance on debt financing. Evaluation of industry fundamentals is based on:

- *Industry cyclicality:* Cyclical industries are more sensitive to the performance of the broader economy and tend to have more volatile revenues, margins, and cash flows. Therefore, they are generally considered to be riskier than noncyclical industries.
- *Growth prospects:* Weaker companies in industries with little or no growth prospects may begin to struggle financially, resulting in greater credit risk for bondholders.
- *Published industry statistics:* Industry fundamentals and performance can be analyzed by studying statistics published by rating agencies, investment banks, industry publications, and so on.

Company Fundamentals

Analysis of company fundamentals involves an examination of the following:

- *Competitive position:* This involves an analysis of a company's current market share, potential for market share growth, cost structure relative to its peers, competitive strategy, and potential financing requirements going forward.
- *Track record/operating history:* This involves an analysis of trends in the company's revenues, profit margins, and cash flows during various phases of the business cycle. Analysts should also look at the company's balance sheet to assess changes in its use of debt versus equity over time.
- *Management's strategy and execution:* Analysts must evaluate management's business strategy and determine whether it makes sense given the current environment, how risky it is, how it is different from competitors' strategies, and whether management can execute the chosen strategy successfully.
- *Ratios and ratio analysis:* To evaluate a company's financial health, credit analysts calculate a number of ratios, examine trends in ratios over time, and compare them with those of competing firms to determine relative creditworthiness. Ratio analysis is discussed in more detail later in the reading.

Collateral

Collateral refers to the quality and value of assets that are pledged against the issuer's debt obligations. Analysts focus more on assessing collateral when the probability of default is significantly high (as is the case with companies with low creditworthiness). The value of collateral is used in estimating loss severity in the event of default. It is sometimes difficult to observe the value and quality of a company's assets directly, and analysts should consider the following factors:

- *The nature and amount of intangible assets on the balance sheet:* Some intangible assets, such as patents, can be sold easily and are more valuable than others such as goodwill, which cannot be separately sold. Further, a company's goodwill deteriorates if it performs poorly so it may have little or no value in the event of default.
- *The amount of depreciation an issuer takes relative to its capital expenditures:* If capital expenditures are low relative to depreciation expense, it could suggest that management is not investing in the business sufficiently. This would lead to lower-quality assets, potentially lower operating cash flow in the future, and higher loss severity in case of default.

Analysts evaluate the quality of a publicly traded company's assets and their ability to generate cash for debt service based on the company's equity market capitalization. For example, if a company's stock trades below its book value, it suggests that the actual value of company assets is lower than the value reported on its balance sheet.

It is even more difficult to evaluate collateral quality for service- or knowledge-based companies as they rely more on human and intellectual capital than on "hard assets." Such companies may generate a lot of cash flow, but the value of any collateral depends on whether there are valuable patents and other forms of intellectual property that can be sold separately in the event of default.

Covenants

Covenants refer to the terms and conditions in a bond's indenture that place restrictions (negative or restrictive covenants) or certain requirements (affirmative covenants) on the issuer.

- Examples of affirmative covenants include:
    - Making timely interest and principal payments.
    - Maintaining all properties used in the business in good condition.
    - Redeeming debt if the company gets acquired.
    - Keeping the ratio of debt to EBITDA below a specified level.
- Examples of negative covenants include:
    - Limiting the amount of cash that can be paid out to shareholders.
    - Limiting the amount of additional secured debt that can be issued.

While covenants protect bondholders by creating a binding framework for the repayment of debt obligations, they must offer management sufficient flexibility to run the business. It is also important to note that since the bond-buying investor base (1) is very large and diverse and (2) is legally not allowed to act as a syndicate, it is relatively difficult for bond investors to negotiate strong covenants on most new bond issues. Therefore, covenants provide only limited protection to investment-grade bondholders and slightly stronger protection to high-yield investors. Further, covenants tend to be stronger for bonds that are issued in weak economic times (to induce investors to purchase them).

Character

Character refers to the quality and integrity of management. When evaluating management's character, analysts should:

- Evaluate the suitability and reliability of management's strategy.
- Assess management's track record in executing strategies successfully, while keeping the companies they run clear of bankruptcy, restructuring, and other distressed situations. A company run by management whose previous ventures have resulted in distress may still be able to obtain debt financing, but it will likely have to borrow on a secured basis and/or pay a higher interest rate.
- Identify the use of aggressive accounting policies and/or tax strategies. Use of significant off-balance-sheet financing, revenue and expense recognition issues, and frequent changes in auditors are potential red flags.
- Look for any history of fraud or malfeasance.
- Look for instances of poor treatment of bondholders in the past. Examples of management actions that can benefit shareholders at the expense of bondholders include debt-financed acquisitions, payments of special dividends to shareholders, and debt-financed stock repurchases.

LOS 55g: Calculate and interpret financial ratios used in credit analysis. Vol 5, pp 615–618

LOS 55h: Evaluate the credit quality of a corporate bond issuer and a bond of that issuer, given key financial ratios for the issuer and the industry. Vol 5, pp 618–625

Ratios and Ratio Analysis

Analysis of financial statements using ratios has been covered in detail at Level I in the readings on Financial Reporting and Analysis. The focus of our discussion here is on credit analysis from the perspective of a bondholder.

Credit analysts calculate a number of ratios to assess a company's financial strength, identify trends over time, and make comparisons with peer companies. These ratios can be categorized as:

- Profitability and cash flow measures.
- Leverage ratios.
- Coverage ratios.

> The values of these ratios vary widely across industries due to differences in industry characteristics such as competitive structure, economic cyclicality, regulation, and so on.

Profitability and Cash Flow Measures

These measures are important because at the end of the day, it is profits and cash flows generated by the company that are used to service debt obligations. Four profit and cash flow measures that are commonly used by credit analysts are the following:

- *Earnings before interest, taxes, depreciation, and amortization (EBITDA):* EBITDA is calculated as operating income (EBIT) plus depreciation and amortization. A drawback of using EBITDA as a measure of cash flow is that it ignores certain cash expenses such as capital expenditures and investment in working capital.
- *Funds from operations (FFO):* FFO is calculated as net income from continuing operations plus depreciation, amortization, deferred income taxes, and other noncash items. It is similar to cash flow from operations (CFO) except that it does not consider changes in working capital.
- *Free cash flow before dividends:* This is the amount of cash flow that the company can use to pay out dividends or pay down debt. It is calculated as net income plus depreciation and amortization minus capital expenditures minus investment in noncash working capital. Note that it excludes non-recurring items. Companies that have negative FCF before dividends will need additional financing, so they entail higher credit risk.
- *Free cash flow after dividends:* This is the amount of cash flow that the company can use to pay down debt. It is calculated as FCF before dividends minus dividends. A positive FCF after dividends can be used to pay down debt or build up cash.

Leverage Ratios

To compute leverage ratios, credit analysts usually adjust the company's reported debt levels for other debt-like liabilities such as underfunded pension plans and operating leases. Commonly used leverage ratios include:

- *Debt/Capital:* Total capital equals total debt plus shareholders' equity. The debt-capital ratio reflects the proportion of a company's capital base that is financed with debt. The higher the ratio, the higher the credit risk. If the company reports significant intangible assets that are subject to devaluation, analysts should compute an adjusted debt-capital ratio based on the written-down, after-tax value of these assets.
- *Debt/EBITDA:* The higher the debt-EBITDA ratio, the higher the credit risk. Note that this ratio can be quite volatile over time for companies with high volatility of cash flows (e.g., companies in cyclical industries and those with high operating leverage).
- *FFO/Debt:* The higher the FFO-debt ratio, the lower the credit risk.

Coverage Ratios

Coverage ratios are used to evaluate an issuer's ability to make interest payments. Higher coverage ratios indicate better credit quality. Commonly used coverage ratios include:

- EBITDA/Interest expense
- EBIT/Interest expense

EBIT/interest expense is the more conservative ratio of the two, as it subtracts depreciation and amortization expense from earnings. However, EBITDA/interest expense is used more frequently.

Issuer Liquidity

When evaluating credit quality, analysts also look at an issuer's access to liquidity in times of cash flow stress. All other things remaining the same, companies with ready access to liquidity represent lower credit risk. When assessing an issuer's liquidity, analysts look at the following:

- Cash on the balance sheet.
- Net working capital.
- Operating cash flow.
- Committed bank lines of credit.
- Debt coming due in the near term.
- Committed capital expenditures in the near term.

Generally speaking, issuer liquidity is a bigger factor when evaluating credit risk for high-yield companies than for investment-grade companies. See Example 3-1.

Example 3-1: Credit Analysis

An analyst wants to compare the creditworthiness of two companies, Alpha and Beta. He gathers the following information:

Alpha

	2013	2011	2010
Operating profit margin	20.55%	18.75%	19.28%
Debt/EBITDA	1.04	1.15	1.24
EBITDA/Interest expense	29.24	27.87	26.91
FCF/Debt	27.65%	28.94%	26.82%
Debt/Capital	24.70%	25.25%	26.60%

Beta

	2013	2011	2010
Operating profit margin	15.25%	14.98%	12.66%
Debt/EBITDA	1.79	1.84	1.90
EBITDA/Interest expense	18.68	18.91	19.08
FCF/Debt	18.34%	19.99%	19.28%
Debt/Capital	30.73%	29.31%	29.58%

Which company has lower credit risk? Explain your answer.

Solution:

It appears that Alpha has lower credit risk. Over the three-year period:

- Alpha has a higher (better) and less volatile (better) operating profit margin.
- It has a lower (better) debt/EBITDA ratio.
- It has a higher (better) EBITDA/interest expense ratio.
- It has a higher (better) FCF/debt ratio.
- It has a lower (better) debt/capital ratio.

LOS 55i: Describe factors that influence the level and volatility of yield spreads. Vol 5, pp 628–637

The yield on risk-free bonds that are extremely liquid can be decomposed into (1) the real interest rate, (2) the expected inflation rate, and (3) a maturity premium. The yield for option-free corporate bonds includes these three factors *plus* a liquidity premium and a credit spread. Therefore, the yield on a corporate bond can be expressed as:

> Yield on a corporate bond = Real risk-free interest rate + Expected inflation rate
> + Maturity premium + Liquidity premium + Credit spread

Investors in corporate bonds are primarily interested in the yield spread relative to comparable risk-free bonds. This yield spread is composed of the liquidity premium and credit spread.

> Yield spread = Liquidity premium + Credit spread

Yield spreads on corporate bonds are affected by the following:

- *Credit cycle:* Credit spreads widen as the credit cycle deteriorates, and they narrow as the credit cycle improves. They are widest at or near the bottom of the credit cycle when financial markets believe that risk is high, and tightest at or near the top when risk is low.
- *Broader economic conditions:* Investors demand a higher risk premium in relatively weak economic conditions, which drives overall credit spreads wider. On the other hand, credit spreads tend to narrow as the economy recovers.
- *Financial market performance overall, including equities:* Credit spreads widen in weak financial markets, and narrow in strong markets. Credit spreads also narrow in relatively stable, low-volatility market conditions as investors search for yield.
- *Broker-dealers' willingness to provide sufficient capital for market making:* Bonds are primarily traded in over-the-counter markets, where broker-dealers play a very important role in bringing liquidity. Credit spreads are narrow when broker-dealers bring sufficient capital to the market, but tend to widen when there is a reduction in broker-provided capital available for market-making purposes.
- *General market supply and demand:* Credit spreads tend to widen when there is an excess supply of new issues, and tend to narrow when there is excess demand for bonds.

Finally, note that yield spreads on low credit quality bonds tend to be wider that those on high credit quality bonds.

Investors in high-grade corporate bonds are not too concerned by default risk (as defaults on high-quality bonds have historically been very low), but are more concerned by spread risk (i.e., how the price of a bond changes in response to changes in spreads). The return impact of a change in the credit spread depends on:

1. The magnitude of the change in the spread (ΔSpread).
2. The sensitivity of the price of the bond to changes in interest rates.

For small, instantaneous changes in the yield spread, the return impact (i.e., the percentage change in price, including accrued interest) can be estimated using the following formula:

$$\text{Return impact} \approx -\text{Modified duration} \times \Delta\text{Spread}$$

Note that if the spread change is expressed in basis points, then the return impact will also be in basis points. On the other hand, if the spread change is expressed as a decimal, then the return impact will also be a decimal.

- Modified duration is an estimate of the percentage change in the price of a bond in response to a 100bp change in yields assuming that the bond's cash flows do not change when yields change.
- The negative sign in the above equation reflects the inverse relationship between bond prices and yields. Narrowing spreads lead to an increase in bond prices, while widening spreads lead to a decrease in bond prices.

For larger changes in the yield spread, we must also incorporate the (positive) impact of convexity into our estimate of the return impact:

$$\text{Return impact} \approx -(\text{MDur} \times \Delta\text{Spread}) + (1/2 \times \text{Convexity} \times \Delta\text{Spread}^2)$$

- When applying this formula, ensure that convexity is appropriately scaled. For option-free bonds, convexity should have the same order of magnitude as modified duration squared. For example, if we are given modified duration of 5 and convexity of 0.345, then, since modified duration squared equals 25, the appropriately scaled convexity would be 34.5.
- Also notice that convexity is divided in half here, while in another fixed income reading the convexity adjustment was not divided in half. For the exam, use one-half times convexity whenever the question asks you for the return impact. See Example 4-1.

Example 4-1: Estimating Return Impact

A 15-year corporate bond with a coupon rate of 6% is currently trading at $105.25. Due to improved economic conditions, the yield spread on the bond narrows by 150 basis points. Given a modified duration of 5.8 and a convexity of 0.645, estimate the return impact on the bond.

Solution:

First, the given convexity must be scaled appropriately. Since modified duration squared equals 33.64, the appropriately scaled convexity would be 64.5.

$$\text{Return impact} \approx -(\text{MDur} \times \Delta\text{Spread}) + (1/2 \times \text{Convexity} \times \Delta\text{Spread}^2)$$

$$\approx -[(5.8 \times (-0.0150)] + [1/2 \times 64.5 \times (-0.0150)^2]$$

$$\approx 0.0943$$

Since we expressed the change in the yield spread as a decimal (not in terms of bp), our answer is also in the form of a decimal. We can convert the decimal into a percentage by multiplying it by 100. Therefore, we can say that if spreads tighten by 150 basis points, the bond's price will increase by 9.43%.

Note that for a given change in the yield spread, the change in price is generally more substantial for a longer-duration bond than for a shorter-duration bond. This indicates that longer-duration bonds are generally more sensitive to changes in the yield spread.

Longer-maturity bonds entail more uncertainly than shorter-maturity bonds as it is relatively more difficult to forecast future creditworthiness for these bonds. Investors therefore require a higher return on longer-maturity bonds. As a result, compared to shorter-maturity bonds, longer-maturity bonds of a given issuer typically trade at wider yield spreads to comparable-maturity government bonds. This is why spread curves (also referred to as credit curves) are generally upward sloping.

LESSON 5: SPECIAL CONSIDERATIONS OF HIGH-YIELD, SOVEREIGN, AND MUNICIPAL CREDIT ANALYSIS

LOS 55j: Explain special considerations when evaluating the credit of high-yield, sovereign, and non-sovereign debt issuers and issues. Vol 5, pp 638–652

High-Yield Corporate Debt

High-yield corporate bonds (also referred to as noninvestment-grade corporate bonds or junk bonds) are those that are rated below Baa3/BBB—by the credit rating agencies. Companies may be rated below investment grade for the following reasons:

- Highly leveraged capital structure.
- Weak or limited operating history.
- Limited or negative free cash flow.
- High sensitivity to business cycles.
- Poor management.
- Risky financial policies.
- Lack of scale and/or competitive advantage.
- Large off-balance-sheet liabilities.
- Bleak industry outlook.

High-yield bonds entail a greater risk of default than investment-grade bonds. As a result, credit analysts pay more attention to recovery analysis (or loss severity in the event of default) when evaluating these bonds. The following factors are given special consideration when analyzing high-yield corporate bonds:

- Liquidity: While having cash or the ability to generate cash is important for all debt issuers, it is absolutely critical for high-yield debt issuers. Investment-grade companies typically have several sources of liquidity that allow them to roll over (refinance) maturing debt quite easily. However, high-yield companies only have access to limited sources of liquidity. The sources of liquidity for high-yield companies, from strongest to weakest, are the following:
  - *Cash on the balance sheet:* This is the strongest source of cash for repaying debt for high-yield companies.
  - *Working capital:* This can be either a large source or a use of liquidity, depending on the company's cash conversion cycle and efficiency of overall operations.
  - *Operating cash flow:* Cash flow generated from operations is a ready source of liquidity.
  - *Bank credit facilities:* These can be an important source of liquidity for high-yield issuers, but may come with some covenants.
  - *Equity issuance:* This may not be a reliable option for high-yield companies if they are privately held, or if market conditions are not favorable.
  - *Asset sales:* This is the most unreliable source of liquidity because both the potential value of assets and the actual time of closing can be highly uncertain.

Analysts should evaluate the availability and significance of these avenues as sources of liquidity for the company in light of the amount and timing of upcoming debt payments. If there is a mismatch (i.e., a large amount of debt is coming due when liquidity is expected to be insufficient), there will be concerns that the issuer will default if investors do not subscribe to new bonds (whose proceeds would be used to pay off maturing debt) issued by the company.

- Financial projections: Analysts should forecast earnings and cash flows several years into the future to assess whether the issuer's credit profile will remain stable, improve, or deteriorate. Analysts should also incorporate required capital expenditures, changes in working capital, and realistic "stress" scenarios in their analysis to identify any vulnerabilities in the business.
- Debt structure: High-yield companies usually have many layers of debt in their capital structures, with each layer having a different seniority ranking and hence entailing a different potential recovery rate in the event of default. Examples of these different layers of debt include secured bank debt, second lien debt, senior unsecured debt, subordinated debt (which may be convertible into equity), and preferred stock.

To evaluate the credit risk of a high-yield issuer with many layers of debt in its capital structure, analysts must calculate leverage for each level of the debt structure.

High-yield companies with a relatively high proportion of secured debt (typically bank debt) in their capital structure are said to be "top-heavy." It is generally difficult for such companies to take on more debt in the event of financial stress because of (1) the stringent covenants associated with bank debt and (2) the relatively short maturity of bank debt relative to other forms of debt. Both these factors contribute to a higher risk of default for these companies and lower recovery rates for less secured creditors. See Example 5-1.

Example 5-1: Debt Structure and Leverage

An analyst wants to compare the creditworthiness of two companies and gathers the following information:

In $'000	Alpha	Beta
Cash	1,610	2,248
Interest expense	750	1,015
EBITDA	1,300	1,820
Secured debt (bank loan and bonds)	4,285	2,390
Senior unsecured bonds	2,030	2,945
Subordinated bonds	570	4,305
Total debt	6,885	9,640

1. Calculate the total financial leverage through each level of debt for both companies.
2. Calculate the net leverage through the total debt structure for both companies.
3. Comment on the creditworthiness of both companies from the point of view of an unsecured debt investor.

Solution:

1. Secured debt leverage = Total secured debt/EBITDA

   Alpha: 4,285/1,300 = 3.30 times
   Beta: 2,390/1,820 = 1.31 times

   Senior unsecured leverage = (Secured debt + Senior unsecured debt)/EBITDA

   Alpha: (4,285 + 2,030)/1,300 = 4.86 times
   Beta: (2,390 + 2,945)/1,820 = 2.93 times

   Total leverage = Total debt/EBITDA

   Alpha: 6,885/1,300 = 5.30 times
   Beta: 9,640/1,820 = 5.30 times

2. Net leverage = (Total debt – Cash)/EBITDA

   Alpha: (6,885 – 1,610)/1,300 = 4.06 times
   Beta: (9,640 – 2,248)/1,820 = 4.06 times

3. Both companies have the same total leverage and net leverage. However, Alpha has more secured debt than Beta. Beta's capital structure is less "top-heavy" than Alpha's so it could potentially take on more bank debt in times of financial difficulty.

- Corporate structure: Credit analysis becomes a little more complicated for companies that have a holding company structure.

  In the holding company structure, the parent owns stock in the subsidiaries and relies on dividends from these operating subsidiaries to service its own debt. However, if the subsidiary is not performing very well, or if it is limited by covenants on its own debt from passing on cash to the parent in the form of dividends or a loan, the parent's ability to meet its debt obligations may become impaired. The reliance on cash flows from its subsidiaries means that the parent's debt becomes structurally subordinated to the subsidiaries' debt, and will therefore usually have a lower recovery rate in the event of default.

  The scenario can be further complicated by one or more intermediate holding companies, each carrying its own debt. This structure must be examined very carefully and is often seen in high-yield companies that arise from mergers and acquisitions or leveraged buyouts.

  High-yield investors need to assess whether debt has been issued by the parent or its subsidiary, and how cash can move between the two. They should compute leverage ratios for each of the debt-issuing entities individually and on a consolidated basis.

  Finally, note that even though the debt of the operating subsidiary would be more directly and hence better secured than the debt of the parent, the credit quality of the parent may still be higher because the parent has access to the diversified cash flow from all its operating subsidiaries. Therefore, credit quality is not determined solely by debt provisions and liens.

- Covenant analysis: Analysis of covenants takes on even more significance for high-yield bonds than for investment-grade bonds. Some of the important covenants for high-yield issuers are described next:
  - *Change of control put:* Under this covenant, if the issuer is acquired by another company, investors obtain the right to sell their bonds back to the issuer at par or at some premium to par value. This provision is meant to protect creditors from being exposed to a weaker or more indebted borrower as a result of an acquisition.
  - *Restricted payments:* This covenant protects creditors by limiting the amount of cash the company can pay out to its shareholders over time.
  - *Limitations on liens and additional indebtedness:* This covenant protects unsecured creditors by placing a limit on the amount of secured debt the company can issue.
  - *Restricted versus unrestricted subsidiaries:* Holding companies may classify their subsidiaries as restricted or unrestricted. Restricted subsidiaries are those that guarantee holding company debt. This guarantee effectively puts the parent's debt holders on an equal footing (pari passu) with the subsidiaries' own debt holders, instead of being structurally subordinated. Generally speaking, restricted subsidiaries tend to be the issuer's larger subsidiaries in terms of assets and cash flow. It is very important for analysts to examine the definitions of restricted and unrestricted subsidiaries in the bond indenture because sometimes the language can allow the parent to reclassify subsidiaries from one type to another through a simple vote by the board of directors.

It is also important to analyze covenants in a high-yield issuer's bank credit agreements. Bank covenants can be more restrictive than bond covenants and may include maintenance covenants (e.g., leverage tests). If a maintenance covenant is breached (e.g., if a leverage ratio such as debt/EBITA exceeds a specified level), the bank attains the right to block further loans under the agreement until the company remedies the situation. The bank may also trigger default by demanding early repayment of the loan.

Equity-like Approach to High-Yield Analysis

High-yield bonds can be viewed as a hybrid between investment-grade bonds and equity securities.

- Movements in prices and spreads for high-yield bonds are less influenced by interest rate changes compared to investment-grade bonds.
- Returns on high-yield bonds are highly correlated with movements in equity markets.

Therefore, an equity-like approach can be useful for analyzing high-yield bonds. One such approach is to calculate multiples (e.g., EV/EBITDA and debt/EBITDA) and compare them across several issuers. Enterprise value (EV) is calculated as equity market capitalization plus total debt minus excess cash. It is used as a measure of the worth of a business. For a given issuer, if there is only a small difference between the EV/EBITDA and debt/EBITDA ratios, it indicates that the issuer has a relatively small "equity cushion," which means higher risk for bond investors.

Sovereign Debt

Sovereign debt refers to debt issued by national governments. Credit analysis of sovereign bonds entails an evaluation of the government's ability and willingness to service its debt. An assessment of willingness to service debt is particularly important for sovereign debt, as bondholders typically have no legal recourse if a national government is unwilling to meet its debt obligations.

A basic framework for evaluating sovereign credit risk is built around the following:

- Political and economic profile.
  - Effectiveness, stability, and predictability of policy making and institutions.
  - Perceived commitment to honor debts.
  - Economic structure and growth prospects.
- Flexibility and performance profile.
  - External liquidity and international investment position.
  - Fiscal performance, flexibility, and debt burden.
- Monetary flexibility.
  - Ability to use monetary policy to address domestic economic objectives.
  - Credibility of monetary policy.
  - Effectiveness of monetary policy transmission via domestic capital markets.

Credit rating agencies typically assign a local currency debt rating and a foreign currency debt rating to sovereign issuers. This is because defaults on foreign currency-denominated sovereign bonds have tended to exceed defaults on local currency-denominated sovereign bonds. Local currency bonds can be serviced by raising taxes, by controlling domestic spending, or by printing local currency. For foreign currency bonds, however, the government would have to sell domestic currency to purchase foreign currency to service the bonds, which exposes the country's currency to significant risk of depreciation. Therefore, ratings on foreign currency bonds can be up to two notches lower than on local currency bonds for the same country.

> Sovereigns are best able to service both external and local debt by running "twin surpluses" (i.e., a government budget surplus and a current account surplus).

Municipal Debt

Non-sovereign (or subsovereign) government entities include local and state governments as well as various agencies and authorities created by them. The majority of municipal bonds are either general obligation bonds or revenue bonds.

General Obligation (GO) Bonds

GO bonds are unsecured bonds issued with the full faith and credit of the issuing entity, and are supported by the taxing authority of the issuer. Credit analysis of GO bonds is quite similar to that of sovereign bonds. However, municipalities must balance their operating budgets annually, as they do not have the ability to use monetary policy (print money) the way many sovereigns can. The economic analysis of GO bonds focuses on:

- Employment.
- Per capita debt.
- Tax base.
- Demographics.
- Infrastructure and location for attracting and supporting new jobs.
- Volatility and variability of tax revenues during times of both economic strength and weakness. Overreliance on a particularly volatile source of revenue (e.g., capital gains taxes or sales taxes) can indicate higher credit risk.
- Unfunded pension and post-retirement obligations. These do not typically show up on the issuer's balance sheet, but analysts should add them to reported debt levels to obtain a more complete understanding of the issuer's long-term commitments.
- The issuer's ability to operate within its budget.

Revenue Bonds

> Revenue bonds are considered to be riskier than GO bonds as they are dependent on a single source of revenue.

These are issued for financing a specific project (e.g., a toll road, bridge, hospital, etc.) and are serviced with revenues generated from the project. Therefore, analysis of revenue bonds is similar to analysis of corporate bonds. It focuses on the cash-generating ability of the particular project and on the economic base supporting the project (sources of finance).

A key ratio used to analyze revenue-backed municipal bonds is the debt service coverage ratio (DSCR), which measures how much revenue is available to cover debt payments (interest and principal) after meeting operating expenses. Many revenue bonds come with a minimum DSCR ratio covenant. The higher the ratio, the lower the credit risk of the bond.

READING 56: DERIVATIVE MARKETS AND INSTRUMENTS

LESSON 1: DERIVATIVE MARKETS, FORWARD COMMITMENTS, AND CONTINGENT CLAIMS

LOS 56a: Define a derivative and distinguish between exchange-traded and over-the-counter derivatives. Vol 6, pp 6–14

INTRODUCTION

A derivative is a financial contract or instrument that derives its value from the value of something else (known as the underlying). The underlying on which a derivative is based can be an asset (e.g., stocks and bonds), an index (e.g., S&P 500), or something else (e.g., interest rates).

> The most widely used derivative contracts are written on underlying assets that are financial (e.g., Treasuries and stock indices).

Note that certain investment instruments like mutual funds and exchange-traded funds may meet this definition of a derivative (even though they are not actually derivatives). Therefore, you should keep in mind that, strictly speaking, derivatives *transform* the performance of the underlying asset before paying out in the derivatives transaction. Mutual funds and exchange-traded funds simply *pass on* the returns on their underlying securities. While the formal definition of derivatives does not highlight this characteristic, you should note that this is an important factor that distinguishes derivatives from mutual funds, exchange-traded funds, and other straight pass-through instruments.

Derivatives are created and traded in two different types of markets: exchanges and over-the-counter markets.

Exchange-Traded Derivatives Markets

Exchange-traded derivatives (e.g., futures contracts) are traded on specialized derivatives exchanges or other exchanges. The contracts are standardized and backed by a clearinghouse.

- Standardization facilitates the creation of a more liquid market for derivatives. However, it comes at the cost of flexibility.
    - Note that liquidity is a function of (1) trading interest and (2) level of uncertainty. Little trading interest and a high level of uncertainty lead to low liquidity.
- Market makers and speculators play an important role in these markets.
    - Market makers stand ready to buy at one (low) price and sell at another (high) price in order to lock in small short-term profits (known as scalping).
    - Speculators are willing to take educated risks to earn profits.
- The exchange is responsible for clearing and settlement through its clearinghouse. The clearinghouse is able to provide a credit guarantee to market participants. (More on this in the reading on derivative pricing.)
- Exchange markets also have transparency (i.e., information regarding all transactions is disclosed to regulatory bodies). This regulation does bring certain benefits, but also means a loss of privacy.

Over-the-Counter (OTC) Derivatives Markets

OTC derivatives (e.g., forward contracts) do not trade in a centralized market; instead, they trade in an *informal* market. OTC derivatives are customized instruments. Dealers (typically banks) play an important role in OTC markets as they buy and sell these customized derivatives to market participants, and then look to hedge (or lay off) their risks. Due to the customized nature of OTC derivatives, dealers are typically unable to find identical offsetting transactions. Therefore, they turn to similar transactions to lay off some of the risk, and use their specialized knowledge and complex models to manage any remaining exposure.

- Note that there is a tendency to think that the OTC market is less liquid than the exchange market. This is not necessarily true. It is worth repeating that liquidity is primarily driven by trading interest, which can be weak in both types of markets.
- OTC derivative markets are less regulated than exchange-traded derivative markets (even though regulation of OTC derivative markets has increased since the financial crisis of 2007).
- OTC markets offer more privacy and flexibility than exchange markets.

LOS 56b: Contrast forward commitments and contingent claims. Vol 6, pg 7

LOS 56c: Define forward contracts, futures contracts, options (calls and puts), swaps, and credit derivatives and compare their basic characteristics. Vol 6, pp 14–35

Forward Commitments

> Please note that defining characteristics of forwards, futures, options, and swaps are discussed in detail in the reading on derivative pricing, so we will only be providing brief definitions here. We recommend you attempt the practice questions within the curriculum chapter, and at the end of the curriculum chapter, only after you have studied all the derivatives readings.

A forward commitment is a legally binding **obligation** to engage in a certain transaction in the spot market at a future date at terms agreed upon today. Forward commitments can be made on exchange-traded derivatives and over-the-counter derivatives. They include forward contracts, futures contracts, and swap contracts.

Forwards: These are customized and private contracts between two parties, where one party has an obligation to buy an asset, and the counterparty has an obligation to sell the asset, at a price and future date that are agreed upon signing of the contract. If the price of the asset increases after inception of the contract, the buyer benefits while the seller loses out. Forward contracts can be written on equities, bonds, assets, or interest rates.

Futures: These are standardized derivative contracts where one party, the buyer, will purchase an underlying asset from the other party, the seller, at a later date at a price agreed upon contract initiation. For futures contracts, there is daily settlement of gains and losses, and the futures exchange (through its clearinghouse) provides a credit guarantee.

As their definitions suggest, forwards and futures are quite similar in that they both establish terms for a spot transaction that will be completed later. However, forwards are customized, less transparent, less regulated, and subject to higher counterparty default risk, while futures are standardized, more transparent, more regulated, and generally immune to counterparty credit risk.

A swap is an over-the-counter derivative contract in which two parties agree to exchange a series of cash flows whereby one party pays a variable series that will be determined by an underlying asset or rate, and the counterparty pays either 1) a variable series determined by a different underlying asset or rate or 2) a fixed series. For example, in a plain-vanilla interest rate swap, one party is obligated to make floating-rate interest payments on a notional principal amount, while the other party makes fixed-rate interest payments on the same amount. Essentially, a swap contract is equivalent to a series of forward contracts.

CONTINGENT CLAIMS

A contingent claim is a derivative in which the outcome or payoff is determined by the outcome or payoff of an underlying asset, conditional on some event occurring. Contingent claims include options, credit derivatives, and asset-backed securities.

Options are contingent claims because their payoffs depend on the underlying's value in the future. Options are derivative instruments that give their holders the **choice** (not the obligation) to buy or sell the underlying from or to the seller (writer) of the option. The option to buy the underlying asset is known as a call option, while the option to sell the underlying asset is known as a put option. The exercise of a call or put option is contingent upon the future price of the underlying asset. Options can be customized, over-the-counter contracts or standardized, exchange-traded contracts.

A credit derivative is a contract that transfers credit risk from one party (the credit protection buyer) to another party (the credit protection seller), where the latter protects the former against a specific credit loss.

Most credit derivatives take the form of credit default swaps. A credit default swap (CDS) is a bilateral contract between two parties that transfers the credit risk embedded in a reference obligation from one party to another. It is essentially an insurance contract.

- The reference obligation is the fixed-income security on which the protection is written (or whose credit risk is transferred). This is usually a bond, but can also be a loan in some cases.
- The protection buyer makes a series of periodic payments (think of them as periodic insurance premium payments) to the protection seller during the term of the CDS. In return for this series of periodic premium payments (known as the CDS fee or CDS spread), the protection buyer obtains protection against default risk embedded in the reference obligation.
- The protection seller earns the CDS spread over the term of the CDS in return for assuming the credit risk in the reference obligation. If a credit event occurs, the protection seller is obligated to compensate the protection buyer for credit losses by means of a specified settlement procedure.

Illustration of a CDS

To illustrate how CDSs work, assume that we purchase $10 million worth of five-year bonds issued by ABC Company at par. In order to insulate our portfolio from ABC's credit risk, we enter a CDS on ABC Company as the protection buyer. This CDS has a notional amount of $10 million, a five-year term, and a CDS premium of 60 bps (payable quarterly).

- If a credit event does not occur during the tenor of the swap, we will pay the swap counterparty a quarterly premium worth $0.006/4 \times \$10,000,000 = \$15,000$.
- In the case of a credit event, we would stop making premium payments and the CDS would be settled immediately.
  - In a physical settlement, we (as the protection buyer) would:
    - Receive the notional amount ($10,000,000) from the swap counterparty (protection seller).
    - Deliver the ABC Company bonds that we hold (reference obligation) to the protection seller.
  - In a cash settlement we would:
    - Receive a cash payment from the protection seller equal to the difference between the par value of the bonds and the post-default market value of the reference obligation.
    - For example, if ABC Company declared bankruptcy and the post-default value of the bonds were determined to be $4,500,000 in an auction (approximately 45% recovery rate of the par amount), we would receive a payment of $10,000,000 – 4,500,000 = \$5,500,000$.

Other types of credit derivatives include:

- Total return swaps, in which the underlying is a bond or a loan. The protection buyer pays the protection seller the total return on the underlying bond (interest, principal, and changes in market value), while the protection seller pays the protection buyer either a fixed or floating interest rate. If there is a default, the protection seller will continue to make payments, while receiving a very low or negative return (which would entail making another payment to the protection buyer).
- Credit spread options, which typically are call options based on a bond's yield spread relative to a benchmark. If there is an increase in the yield spread (e.g., due to a decline in the bond's credit quality), the call holder receives a positive payoff from her position. The instrument is essentially a call option in which the underlying is an entity's credit spread.
- Credit-linked notes, which have been described in the fixed-income section.

An asset-backed security (ABS) is a derivative in which a portfolio of debt instruments is pooled and claims are issued on the portfolio in the form of tranches, which have different priorities of claims on the payments that come in from the pool of debt securities. Asset-backed securities are discussed in detail in the fixed-income section.

LESSON 2: BENEFITS AND CRITICISMS OF DERIVATIVES, AND ARBITRAGE

LOS 56d: Describe purposes of, and controversies related to, derivative markets. Vol 6, pp 39–45

Purposes and Benefits of Derivatives

Risk Allocation, Transfer, and Management

- Derivatives allow investors to hedge away risks without trading the underlying itself.
- They improve risk allocation within markets as parties who do not want exposure to a particular risk can transfer it to those who do.

Information Discovery
- Certain forms of derivative contracts (e.g., futures) provide an indication of the direction of the underlying. For example, the S&P futures price is a good indicator of where the stock market will actually open when trading commences.
- Since derivative transactions involve less capital, information can sometimes be reflected in derivatives prices more quickly than in spot prices.
- Certain derivatives (e.g., options) can be used to implement strategies that cannot be implemented with the underlying alone. Further, option market prices can be used to infer implied volatility, which can be used to measure the risk of the underlying.

Operational Advantages
- Derivatives entail lower transaction costs (relative to the value of the underlying) than comparable spot market transactions.
- Derivative markets are typically more liquid than the underlying spot markets.
- Derivatives offer an easy way to take a short position on the underlying. With derivatives, it is as easy to take a short position on the underlying as it is to go long. With some underlying assets (e.g., commodities) it is typically much more difficult to go short.
- Derivatives allow users to engage in highly leveraged transactions, as a relatively small amount of money must be invested to take a position on a derivative compared to taking a position directly in the underlying.

Market Efficiency
- When asset prices deviate from the fundamental values, derivative markets offer a less costly of taking advantage of the mispricing as less capital is required, transaction costs are lower, and short selling is easier.
- The ability to hedge various risks through derivatives increases the willingness of market participants to trade and improves liquidity in the market.

Criticisms and Misuses of Derivatives

Destabilization and systematic risk: The argument here is that the very benefits of derivatives (low cost, low capital requirements, and ease of going short) result in an excessive amount of speculative trading that brings instability to the market. If they end up on the wrong side of a trade, speculators can incur huge losses. These losses can trigger defaults on their creditors, creditors' creditors, and so on, spreading instability throughout financial markets and the economy. In the past, governments have had to step in and bail out large banks and insurance companies to restore the smooth functioning of the financial system, so there is definitely an argument to be made for controlling derivatives trading. At the same time, however, it must be kept in mind that market crashes (e.g., the stock market crash of 1929) have existed long before the advent of derivatives, so while derivatives may seem dangerous, there are other relatively innocuous ways to take on leverage that can be just as risky.

Speculation and gambling: For hedging to work, there must be someone willing to take on the risk. This role is performed by speculators (e.g., professional traders and hedge funds), whose willingness to accept risk has resulted in a decline in the costs of hedging over time. Unfortunately, however, speculators are typically seen in an unfavorable light, and often compared to gamblers. This harsh stance fails to recognize that gambling benefits only a limited number of participants, with no benefit to society as a whole. Derivatives trading brings many benefits as discussed earlier.

Complexity: The mechanics behind derivative contracts can be complex and difficult to understand. Lack of understanding on part of users can result in significant losses.

LOS 56e: Explain arbitrage and the role it plays in determining prices and promoting market efficiency. Vol 6, pp 47–52

Arbitrage

Arbitrage opportunities exist whenever similar assets or combinations of assets are selling for different prices. In other words, these opportunities abound when assets are mispriced. Arbitrageurs exploit these opportunities and trade on mispricings until they are eliminated and asset prices converge to their "correct" levels (where no arbitrage opportunities exist).

Arbitrage plays an important role in the study of derivatives. It is an important feature of efficient markets because it helps:

- Determine prices.
- Improve market efficiency.

The first role is based on the "law of one price," which states that two securities that will generate identical cash flows in the future, regardless of future events, should have the same price today. For example, if Asset X and Asset Y offer identical cash flows regardless of future events, they should have the same price. If they are trading at different prices, arbitrageurs would profit. For example, if X is priced lower than Y, then one could make an immediate profit by purchasing X and selling Y. The cash flows from owning X would offset the liabilities associated with being short on Y.

The second role of arbitrage is that it promotes market efficiency. Let's continue with the previous example to explain this point. The difference in prices between Asset X and Asset Y will increase demand for X and reduce demand for Y. This will cause the price of X to rise and the price of Y to fall. Arbitrage will continue to bring the two assets' prices closer until parity is established. Accurate pricing is a feature of efficient markets.

Detailed examples of arbitrage are provided in the reading on derivatives pricing and valuation.

READING 57: BASICS OF DERIVATIVE PRICING AND VALUATION

LESSON 1: FUNDAMENTAL CONCEPTS AND PRICE VERSUS VALUE

Before getting into this reading, please note that I have included a lot of introductory content here so that the material is easier to understand. I have also included a lot more figures and examples, and in certain sections I have also gone into a lot more detail than the curriculum. A solid foundation in derivatives is crucial to success at all three levels of the CFA Program, and I feel that the current Level I curriculum reading fails to deliver on this front.

LOS 57a: Explain how the concepts of arbitrage, replication, and risk neutrality are used in pricing derivatives. Vol 6, pp 60–73

Fundamental Concepts of Derivative Pricing

Make sure that you are familiar with all the basic concepts regarding derivatives that were covered in the previous reading ("Derivative Markets and Instruments") before moving into this reading.

As mentioned in the previous reading, a derivative is a financial instrument that derives its value from the performance of an underlying asset. The four main types of underlying on which derivatives are based are equities, fixed-income securities/interest rates, currencies, and commodities.

> Equities, fixed-income securities, currencies, and commodities are all assets. An interest rate is not an asset, but it can still be structured as the underlying of a derivative.

Pricing the Underlying

The price or value of a financial asset is determined as the present value of expected future price plus (minus) any benefits (costs) of holding the asset, discounted at a rate appropriate for the risk assumed. When making a trading/investing decision, an investor compares this fundamental value of the asset to its current market price, and then gauges the profit potential (net of trading costs) in light of the level of confidence she has in her valuation model.

The price (or fundamental value) of an asset (S_0) that incurs costs (θ) and generates benefits (γ) is calculated as:

$$S_0 = \left[\frac{E(S_T)}{(1+r+\lambda)^T} \right] - \theta + \gamma$$

- The investor's best prediction of the spot price in the future (expected future price of the asset) is denoted by $E(S_T)$.
- The required rate of return (also referred to as the expected rate of return) is the rate that is used to discount the expected future price of the asset. It is denoted by k.
  - At the minimum, this rate will include the risk-free rate, which is denoted by r.
  - For risky assets, it also includes a risk premium, which is denoted by λ. Investors are generally risk-averse (i.e., they require a premium for bearing risk). All things being equal, an investment with a higher risk premium will have a lower price. Please note that risk premia are not automatically earned; they are only expectations, and actual outcomes can differ. For

example, stocks that declined in value over a particular period did not earn risk premia (even though someone obviously bought them with the expectation that they would). The point is that risk premia must exist in the long run to entice risk-averse investors to accept risk.

- Many assets may generate/incur monetary and nonmonetary benefits/costs to their owners. For example, equities offer dividend payments, bonds make coupon payments, investments in foreign currency generate the foreign risk-free rate of return, investments in commodities may offer convenience yield, but they also entail costs of storage. We use the symbol θ (theta) to denote the present value of costs and γ (gamma) to denote the present value of any benefits associated with holding the asset. The net of these costs and benefits is often referred to by the term carry (or cost of carry).
  - Note that we shall assume that the costs and benefits from the underlying asset are known with certainty, so they are discounted at the risk-free rate to obtain their present values.

To summarize, the price of the underlying asset depends on expectations, risk, and the costs and benefits associated with holding it. In the next section, we move into derivative pricing, which requires us to establish a link between the derivative market and the spot market. This linkage occurs through arbitrage.

The Principle of Arbitrage

Please note that we introduced arbitrage, the law of one price, and market efficiency in the previous reading. Make sure you are comfortable with those concepts before moving ahead. Figure 1-1 provides a recap of executing an arbitrage transaction.

Figure 1-1: Illustration of Arbitrage

Given: Assets X and Y produce the same values at time T.
However, Asset X is selling for less than Asset Y at time t = 0.

$S_0^X < S_0^Y$:
Buy X at S_0^X
Sell Y at S_0^Y
Cash inflow = $S_0^Y - S_0^X$

$S_T^X = S_T^Y$:
Sell X at S_T^X
Buy Y at S_T^Y
Cash flow = $S_T^X - S_T^Y = 0$

t = 0   t = T

Whenever arbitrage opportunities arise, traders look to exploit them as quickly as they can. The increased demand for the underpriced asset results in an increase in its price, while the increased supply of the overpriced asset results in a decline in its price, until the prices converge. Note that practically speaking, prices may not converge precisely, or as quickly as you might think, because the cost of trading (transaction costs) on the mispricing may exceed the benefit.

Arbitrage and Derivatives

Since the value of a derivative is directly related to the price of its underlying, the derivative can be used to hedge a position on the underlying. When the underlying is combined with the derivative to create a perfectly hedged portfolio, all of the price risk is eliminated and the position should earn the risk-free rate. See Figure 1-2.

- If the hedged portfolio generates a return in excess of the risk-free rate, arbitrageurs will borrow at the risk-free rate and go long on the hedged portfolio.

- If the hedged portfolio generates a return less than the risk-free rate, arbitrageurs will short the hedged portfolio and invest the proceeds at the risk-free rate.
- Any mispricings will be exploited until prices are pushed back in line such that both risk-free transactions earn the risk-free rate; not less, not more.

Figure 1-2: Hedging the Underlying with a Derivative

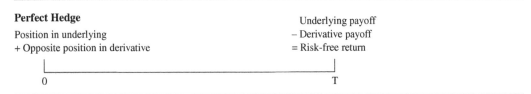

Most derivative pricing models are established on the assumption that no arbitrage opportunities can exist. The price of the derivative price is the unique price that precludes arbitrage opportunities. You will see this concept much more clearly when we illustrate the pricing of forward contracts later in this reading.

Arbitrage and Replication

Replication refers to the exercise of creating an asset or a portfolio from another asset, portfolio, and/or derivative. Starting with what we have just explained regarding the assumption employed in pricing a derivative (asset + derivative = hedged portfolio = risk-free asset), we can come up with the following replication strategies:

Asset + Derivative = Risk-free asset

Asset – Risk-free asset = – Derivative

Derivative – Risk-free asset = – Asset

We will illustrate the application of these replication strategies in the section on forward contracts. We will also show you how positions on swaps can be replicated using (1) forward contracts and (2) assets later in the section on swaps.

Risk Aversion, Risk Neutrality, and Arbitrage-Free Pricing

When it comes to pricing derivatives, we do not discount the expected payoff of the security at a rate that includes a risk premium commensurate with the uncertainty of the payoff (as we do in pricing underlying assets). The fact that a derivative can be combined with an asset to produce a risk-free position can be used to infer its price (as we will soon see). This means that the investor's risk aversion is not a factor in determining the derivative price, so in pricing derivatives, we can assume that investors are risk-neutral.

Therefore, derivative pricing models discount the expected payoff of the derivative at the risk-free rate rather than the risk-free rate plus a risk premium. Further (as you will learn later in the section on binomial option pricing), the expected payoff is calculated based on what are known as risk-neutral probabilities (not actual or true probabilities of possible outcomes). For now, just remember that while the risk aversion of investors is relevant to pricing assets, it is not relevant to pricing derivatives. As such, derivatives pricing is sometimes called risk-neutral pricing.

Limits to Arbitrage

Earlier in the reading, we mentioned significant transaction costs as one reason for an arbitrage opportunity remaining unexploited. Other reasons include the following:

- The transaction may require a very large amount of capital, which the arbitrageur may not have access to.
- The transaction may require additional capital down the line to maintain the position.
- The transaction may require shorting assets that are difficult to short.
- The transaction may entail significant risk, especially if the relevant derivative pricing models are based on complex models whose parameters are subject to modeling risk.

LOS 57b: Distinguish between value and price of forward and futures contracts. Vol 6, pp 73–74

The Concept of Pricing versus Valuation

Let's start with the equity market. The price of a stock refers to its current market price, while the value of a stock refers to its intrinsic or fundamental value, which is generally estimated through some valuation model (discounted cash flow, price multiples, etc.). When it comes to the derivate market, the notion that value represents fundamental value remains valid, but the interpretation of price is different.

> Please bear with me. If you are not familiar with derivatives (and we assume that you aren't), all of these points will become very clear once we get into subsequent sections of this reading.

- Price, as it relates to forwards, futures, and swaps (note that options are not a problem in this regard), refers to the fixed price (that is agreed upon at contract initiation) at which the underlying transaction will take place in the future. These securities do not require an outlay of cash at contract initiation, so there is no concept of a price being paid at the beginning.
- On the other hand, the value of these contract fluctuates in response to changes in the price of the underlying.

The takeaway is that value and price are not comparable when it comes to derivatives.

LESSON 2: FORWARD CONTRACTS

LOS 57c: Explain how the value and price of a forward contract are determined at expiration, during the life of the contract, and at initiation. Vol 6, pp 74–80

LOS 57d: Describe monetary and nonmonetary benefits and costs associated with holding the underlying asset, and explain how they affect the value and price of a forward contract. Vol 6, pp 75–77

Introduction

A forward is a contract between two parties, where one (the long position) has the **obligation** to buy and the other (the short position) has an **obligation** to sell an underlying asset at a fixed forward price (that established at the inception of the contract) at a future date. Typically, no cash changes hands at inception. The long position benefits when the price of the underlying asset increases, while the short benefits when the price of the underlying asset falls.

Let's work with an example. Suppose that Jane enters a forward contract with Michael to buy a share of GGLE stock after 30 days for $600 (this is the forward price). Jane has a long position while Michael has a short position. Neither of them pays any money to enter this forward contract. There are two ways to settle the forward contract at expiration. We will illustrate the two settlement methods assuming that GGLE stock is valued at $800 at the settlement date (after 30 days).

1. Jane pays Michael $600 and gets the GGLE share (underlying asset) in return. This mode of settlement is called physical delivery. The price increase is beneficial for Jane (long position) because she is able to acquire the share from Michael for $600, when its market value is higher ($800).
2. Michael pays $200 to Jane, which equals the difference between the price of GGLE stock at contract expiration ($800), and the agreed-upon forward price ($600). This method of settlement is known as cash settlement.

> Cash-settled forwards are also known as non-deliverable forwards (NDFs) or contracts for differences. Both cash-settled and delivery-based forwards have the same economic effects.

It is important to understand the element of counterparty risk in forward contracts. If the party that is adversely affected by price movements defaults on its commitment, the counterparty with the favorable position faces default risk. This is true for both deliverable and cash settled forward contracts. In our example, if Michael fails to perform on his obligations under the forward contract, Jane effectively loses the $200 gain. See Figure 2-1.

Figure 2-1: Illustration of Forward Contract

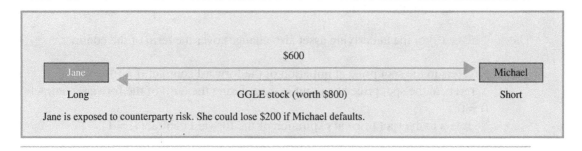

Jane is exposed to counterparty risk. She could lose $200 if Michael defaults.

Finally, notice how forwards are a zero-sum game: One party's gain is the other party's loss. In the example above, Jane has a gain of $200, while Michael incurs a loss of $200.

Pricing and Valuation of Forward Contracts

The price of a forward contract is the fixed price or rate at which the underlying transaction will occur at contract expiration. The forward price is agreed upon at initiation of the forward contract. Pricing a forward contract means determining this forward price.

The value of a forward contract is the amount that a counterparty would need to pay, or would expect to receive, to get out of its (already-assumed) forward position.

We will first work with a generic example to introduce you to the concepts and mechanics behind pricing and valuing forward contracts.

- The contract initiation date is denoted by t = 0.
- The contract expiration date is denoted by t = T.
- Any point in time between the contract initiation and expiration dates is denoted by t = t.

Contract Initiation:
Forward price F(0,T) is
agreed upon at this point
in time.

Contract Expiration:
Underlying transaction is
executed at F(0,T) is this
point in time.

The forward price (F) is determined at contract initiation. It does not change over the term of the contract.

- The term $F(0,T)$ is used to refer to the forward price for a contract that was initiated at t = 0 and expires at t = T.

The value (V) of the forward contract changes over the term of the contract as the price of the underlying asset changes.

- $V_0(0,T)$ refers to the value of a forward contract (initiated at t = 0 and expiring at t = T) at initiation (t = 0).
- $V_t(0,T)$ refers to the value of a forward contract (initiated at t = 0 and expiring at t = T) at a point in time during the term of the contract (t = t).
- $V_T(0,T)$ refers to the value of a forward contract (initiated at t = 0 and expiring at t = T) at expiration (t = T).

The spot price (S) of the underlying asset also changes over the term of the contract.

- S_0 refers to the spot price at initiation of the forward contract (t = 0).
- S_t refers to the spot price at a point in time during the term of the forward contract (t = t).
- S_T refers to the spot price at expiration of the forward contract (t = T).

In the following sections, we illustrate how forward contracts are valued at various points in time. Note that we will be taking the perspective of the long position on the contract when valuing a forward. Once the value of the long position has been determined, the value of the short can be determined by simply changing the sign.

Valuing a Forward Contract at Expiration (t = T)

The long position on the forward has an obligation to buy the underlying asset for the agreed-upon (at contract initiation) price of $F(0,T)$ at contract expiration. The price of the underlying asset at expiration of the forward equals S_T. Therefore, the value of the long position on the forward contract at expiration equals the difference between:

- The current worth of the asset, S_T, which represents the price at which the underlying asset can be sold; and
- The price that the long position in the forward must pay to acquire the asset, $F(0,T)$.

$$V_T(0,T) = S_T - F(0,T)$$

If the value at expiration does not equal this amount, arbitrage profits can be made. For example, if the forward price established at contract initiation equals \$30 and the spot price at contract expiration equals \$35, then the value of the forward contract must equal \$35 − \$30 = \$5 at expiration.

- If the contract value at expiration were greater than \$5, it would mean that someone is willing to pay more than \$5 to obtain an obligation to buy something worth \$35 for \$30, which wouldn't make sense.
- If the contract value were less than \$5, it would mean that someone is willing to accept less than \$5 to give up an obligation to buy something worth \$35 for \$30, which wouldn't make sense, either.

Table 2-1 summarizes the payoffs at expiration to the counterparties in a forward contract, while Figure 2-2 illustrates these payoffs.

Table 2-1: Forward Contract Payoffs

	$S_T > F(0,T)$	$S_T < F(0,T)$
Long position	$S_T - F(0,T)$ (Positive payoff)	$S_T - F(0,T)$ (Negative payoff)
Short position	$-[S_T - F(0,T)]$ (Negative payoff)	$-[S_T - F(0,T)]$ (Positive payoff)

Figure 2-2: Payoffs from a Forward Contract

A. Payoff from buying = $S_T - F(0,T)$

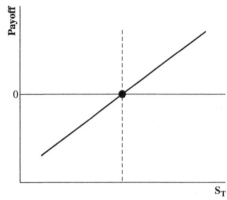

B. Payoff from selling = $-[S_T - F(0,T)]$

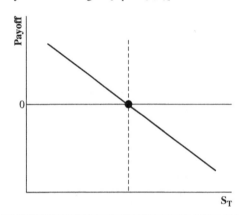

Finally, note that a forward contract initiated right at the instant of expiration would have forward price that equals the spot price. Essentially, such a contract would be a spot transaction.

Valuing a Forward Contract at Initiation

Now let's work with a forward contract that has a term of one year. The price (S_0) of the asset underlying the contract is currently $100 and the risk-free rate (r) is 8%. Let's determine the value of the contract at initiation, $V_0(0,1)$, given that:

1. The forward price, $F(0,1)$, equals $110.
2. The forward price, $F(0,1)$, equals $106.

Note that no money changes hands at origination of the forward contract.

Scenario 1: F(0,1) = $110

In this scenario, arbitrage profits can be made through cash and carry arbitrage by undertaking the following steps:

- Borrow $100 at 8%.
- Purchase the underlying asset at the current spot price of $100.
- Sell the underlying asset forward by taking the short position on the forward contract at a forward price of $110.

The following table illustrates the computation of arbitrage profits from this strategy:

t = 0 (Contract Origination)		t = T (Contract Expiration)	
Transaction	**Cash Flow**	**Transaction**	**Cash Flow**
Borrow $100 @ 8%	$100	Deliver the asset under the terms of the forward contract in return for	$110
Buy asset at current price S_0	($100)	F(0,1)	
Take the short position in a forward contract on the asset with a forward price, F(0,1), of $110	$0	Repay loan plus interest	($108)
Net Cash Flow	**0**	**Net Cash Flow**	**$2**

Scenario 2: F(0,1) = $106

In this scenario arbitrage profits can be made through reverse cash and carry arbitrage by undertaking the following steps:

- Short the underlying asset at the current spot price of $100.
- Invest the proceeds at 8%.
- Buy the underlying asset forward by taking the long position on the forward contract at the forward price of $106.

The following table illustrates the computation of arbitrage profits from this strategy:

t = 0 (Contract Origination)		t = T (Contract Expiration)	
Transaction	**Cash Flow**	**Transaction**	**Cash Flow**
Short the underlying asset at S0	$100	Take delivery of the asset under the terms of the forward contract by paying F(0,1)	($106)
Invest $100 @ 8%	($100)		
Take the long position in a forward contract on the asset with a forward price, F(0,1), of $106	$0	Receive investment amount plus interest	$108
Net Cash Flow	**0**	Net Cash Flow	**$2**

Now let's understand the value of a forward contract. Recall that we are taking the perspective of the long position.

- The long position has the obligation to pay the forward price, F(0,T), and take delivery of the underlying asset at contract expiration.
  - The value of this obligation at contract initiation equals $F(0,T) / (1 + r)^T$.

Get yourselves to think of the value to the long position as the current price of the underlying asset minus the present value of the obligation (forward price).

- At expiration, the long position will receive the underlying asset, which will be worth S_T.
  - The value of this underlying asset at contract initiation equals S_0.
- Therefore, the value of the forward contract to the long position at contract initiation equals the current worth of the asset minus the present value of the obligation.
  - $V_0(0,T) = S_0 - [F(0,T)/(1+r)^T]$

In Scenario 1, the value of the forward contract at initiation is calculated as:

$$V_0(0,T) = S_0 - [F(0,T)/(1+r)^T]$$
$$V_0(0,1) = 100 - [110/(1+0.08)^1] = -\$1.85$$

In Scenario 2, the value of the forward contract at initiation is calculated as:

$$V_0(0,T) = S_0 - [F(0,T)/(1+r)^T]$$
$$V_0(0,1) = 100 - [106/(1+0.08)^1] = \$1.85$$

> The negative value to the long position in Scenario 1 implies that a positive value of $1.85 accrues to the short position.

These nonzero values at contract initiation would entice traders to engage in arbitrage until the price of the forward contract equals the no-arbitrage forward price.

The forward price at contract initiation is the unique price that yields zero value to both the long and short positions at the inception of the contract. This is why we call it a no-arbitrage forward price. Since $V_0(0,T) = 0$, we can express the forward price in terms of the spot price of the asset as:

$$V_0(0,T) = S_0 - [F(0,T)/(1+r)^T] = 0$$
$$F(0,T) = S_0(1+r)^T \qquad \text{... Equation 1}$$

Notice how the risk premium on the asset does not directly appear in determining the price of a forward (it only appears implicitly as it influences the spot price of the asset). Since we know the spot price, there is no need to determine the risk premium. The derivative market can simply let the spot market derive the risk premium. Also note that although the forward price is fixed for a particular forward contract, a new contract calling for delivery of the same asset at the same point in time will have a different forward price (depending on the current spot price).

Now let's assume that the underlying generates benefits and incurs storage costs. The forward price can then be calculated as:

$$F(0,T) = (S_0 - \gamma + \theta)(1+r)^T$$

or

$$F(0,T) = S_0(1+r)^T - (\gamma - \theta)(1+r)^T$$

> Note that benefits (γ) and costs (θ) are expressed in terms of present value.

To understand this formula, let's work with a forward contract on an asset that only delivers benefits and entails no costs. To acquire a position in this asset at time T, the investor could either:

- Buy the asset today and hold it until time T, or
- Take a long position on a forward contract on the asset at a price of $F(0,T)$.

Either way, the investor would end up holding the asset at time T, but if she engages in a spot market transaction, she would get the benefits of the asset, while if she takes a long position on the forward, she does not reap the benefits associated with the spot asset through the term of the forward contract (as she does not really own the asset). Since the forward transaction would return less than the spot transaction, we adjust the forward price downward. Stated differently, acquiring the asset in the forward market should be cheaper as it forgoes the associated benefits. Note that this does not mean that the forward transaction would be better; it only costs less because it delivers less. Similarly, if the spot asset only incurred costs (or if costs incurred exceeded benefits) the forward price would be higher because, through a forward contract, the investor is able to avoid the costs associated with holding the spot asset.

Make sure you take away the following important points from this section:

1. Because neither the long nor the short pays anything to the other at initiation of a forward contract, the value of a forward contract when initiated is zero.
2. The forward price is the spot price compounded at the risk-free rate over the life of the contract.
3. The forward price of an asset with benefits (costs) is the spot price compounded at the risk-free rate over the life of the contract minus (plus) the future value of those benefits (costs).

Valuing a Forward Contract during Its Life

By now you should have digested that the value of the forward contract to the long position equals the asset's current price minus the present value of the forward price. We now use this logic to derive the expression for the value of the forward contract at any point in time (t) during its life.

- The long position has an obligation to pay the forward price, $F(0,T)$, and take delivery of the underlying asset at contract expiration.
  - The value of this obligation at any point in time during the term of the contract equals $F(0,T) / (1 + r)^{T-t}$.
- At expiration, the long position will receive the underlying asset, which will be worth S_T.
  - The value of this asset at any point in time during the term of the contract equals S_t.
- Therefore, the value of the forward contract to the long position at any point in time during the term of the contract equals the current value of the asset minus the present value of the obligation.
  - $V_t(0,T) = S_t - [F(0,T) / (1+r)^{T-t}]$
- If the underlying asset entails benefits/costs, we adjust the formula above for those benefits/costs:
  - $V_t(0,T) = S_t - (\gamma - \theta)(1+r)^t - [F(0,T) / (1+r)^{T-t}]$
  - Recall that benefits and costs from the underlying asset (γ and θ) are expressed in terms of present value as of time $t = 0$ (contract initiation). We need to adjust the current spot price of the asset for their value at time t, which is why they are compounded at the risk-free rate from 0 to t.

Just one more thing that we need to reemphasize before moving on to a few examples: $F(0,T)$ represents the forward price that is agreed upon at the inception of the contract. Both spot and forward prices continue to fluctuate after inception of the contract, but in order to determine the value of a particular forward contract at any point in time, we compare the "then-current" spot price of the underlying asset to the present value of the initially agreed-upon (or fixed) forward price. Table 2-2 summarizes what we have learned so far.

Table 2-2: Value of a Forward Contract

Time	Long Position Value	Short Position Value
At initiation	Zero, as the contract is priced to prevent arbitrage	Zero, as the contract is priced to prevent arbitrage
During life of the contract	$S_t - \left[\dfrac{F(0,T)}{(1+r)^{T-t}} \right]$	$\left[\dfrac{F(0,T)}{(1+r)^{T-t}} \right] - S_t$
At expiration	$S_T - F(0,T)$	$F(0,T) - S_T$

Example 2-1: Calculating the Forward Price

Amanda holds an asset worth $250, which she plans to sell in six months. To eliminate the price risk, she decides to take the short position in a forward contract on the asset. Given an annual risk-free rate of 5%, calculate the no-arbitrage forward price of the contract.

Solution:

Forwards are priced to have zero value to either party at origination. Therefore, the forward price is calculated as:

$$F(0,T) = S_0 (1+r)^T$$

$$F(0,6/12) = 250 \times (1+0.05)^{0.5} = \$256.17$$

Example 2-2: Calculating the Value of a Forward Contract during its Life

In Example 2-1 we calculated the forward price as $256.17. Suppose that two months into the term of the forward the spot price of the underlying asset is $262. Given an annual risk-free rate of 5%, calculate the value of the long and short positions in the forward contract.

Solution:

The value of the long position in the forward contract is calculated as:

$$V_t(0,T) = S_t - [F(0,T)/(1+r)^{T-t}]$$

$$V_{2/12}(0,6/12) = 262 - [256.17/(1+0.05)^{6/12-2/12}] = \$9.96$$

The value of the short position is just the opposite of the value of the long position. Therefore, the value of the short position equals –$9.96.

Example 2-3: Calculating the Value of a Forward Contract at Expiration

Continuing from Example 2-1, suppose that the spot price of the underlying asset at contract expiration is actually $247. Given an annual risk-free rate of 5%, calculate the value of the long position.

Solution:

At expiration, the value of the long position in a forward contract is calculated as:

$$V_T(0,T) = S_T - F(0,T)$$
$$V_T(0,6/12) = 247 - 256.17 = -\$9.17$$

Example 2-4: Calculating the Price of a Forward Contract on Dividend-Paying Stock

Sasha wants to purchase a stock of ABC Company in 150 days. The stock is currently priced at $40. It is expected to pay a dividend of $0.60 in 30 days, $0.80 in 120 days, and $0.70 in 210 days. To hedge the interim price risk, Sasha enters the long position on a forward contract on the stock today. Given an annual risk-free rate of 5%, calculate the no-arbitrage forward price.

Solution:

We would expect the expiration of the forward contract to coincide with the point in time that Sasha wants to take delivery of the stock (T = 150/365). Therefore, we ignore the dividend expected to be paid in 210 days, as it will be paid **after** the expiration of the forward contract.

In order to compute the forward price, we first compute the present value (as of the contract initiation date) of dividends/benefits (γ) expected to be paid on the stock during the term of the forward contract.

$$\gamma = 0.60 / 1.05^{30/365} + 0.80 / 1.05^{120/365}$$
$$= 0.5976 + 0.7873 = \$1.3849$$

And then apply the formula for computing the forward price:

$$F(0,T) = [S_0 - \gamma](1 + r)^T$$
$$F(0,150/365) = (40 - 1.3849) \times (1 + 0.05)^{150/365} = \$39.3972$$

LOS 57e: Define a forward rate agreement and describe its uses. Vol 6, pp 77–78

Forward Contracts on Interest Rates (Forward Rate Agreements)

A forward rate agreement (FRA) is a forward contract where the underlying is an interest rate (usually LIBOR). It might help you if you think about the long position in an FRA as the party that has committed to take a hypothetical loan, and the short as the party that has committed to give out a hypothetical loan, at the FRA rate. However, no actual loan is made at FRA expiration so there is no need to consider the creditworthiness of the parties in determining the FRA rate. The play here is simply on interest rate movements.

> Recall that LIBOR represents the rate of return on a Eurodollar time deposit, a loan in USD from one London bank to another.

The payoffs on FRAs are determined by market interest rates (LIBOR) at FRA expiration.

- If LIBOR at FRA expiration is *greater* than the FRA rate, the long benefits. Effectively, the long has access to a loan at lower-than-market rates, while the short is obligated to give out a loan at lower-than-market interest rates.
- If LIBOR at FRA expiration is *lower* than the FRA rate, the short benefits. Effectively, the short position is able to invest her funds at higher-than-market interest rates, while the long is obligated to take a loan at higher-than-market interest rates.

The whole point of getting into an FRA is to hedge against interest rate risk. A borrower (who would like to lock in a borrowing rate) would take a long position on an FRA, while a lender (who would like to lock in a rate of return) would take a short position on an FRA. The interesting thing about FRAs is that the underlying is not an asset (it is an interest rate). However, they can be duplicated (i.e., synthetic FRAs can be created) by taking opposing positions on two Eurodollar time deposits with different terms to maturity. This is illustrated in the example in the next section.

Pricing a Forward Rate Agreement

The price of an FRA (forward price) represents the interest rate at which the long (short) position has the obligation to borrow (lend) funds for a specified period (term of the underlying hypothetical loan) starting at FRA expiration. Therefore, pricing an FRA is a simple exercise of determining the forward rate consistent with two (given) spot rates, as illustrated in Example 2-5.

Example 2-5: Calculating the Price of an FRA

Thirty days from today Orix Inc. will need to borrow $1 million for 120 days. In order to hedge the interest rate risk associated with the anticipated borrowing, Orix takes the long position on an FRA. Current 30-day LIBOR is 5% and 150-day LIBOR is 6%. Determine the price (forward rate) of this FRA.

Solution:

We are looking to establish the no-arbitrage forward rate (120-day LIBOR) that would make an investor indifferent between (1) borrowing for 150 days today at current 150-day LIBOR and (2) borrowing for 150 days by first borrowing for 30 days at current 30-day LIBOR and then (after 30 days) rolling over into another loan for 120 days at prevailing 120-day LIBOR.

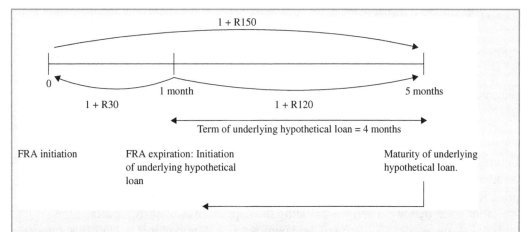

The first thing that we need to do is to unannualize the 30-day and 150-day LIBOR rates that are given.

Unannualized rate on the 30-day loan = R30 = 0.05 × (30/360) = 0.004167
Unannualized rate on the 150-day loan = R150 = 0.06 × (150/360) = 0.025

Based on the unannualized 30-day and 150-day rates, we can calculate the un-annualized interest rate applicable on a 120-day loan that will be taken 30 days from today (the annualized version of which represents the price of the FRA) as follows:

$$(1 + R30)(1 + R120) = (1 + R150)$$

$$
\begin{aligned}
\text{Unannualized price of FRA or R120} &= [(1 + R150) / (1 + R30)] - 1 \\
&= [(1 + 0.025) / (1 + 0.004167)] - 1 \\
&= 0.02075
\end{aligned}
$$

$$
\begin{aligned}
\text{Annualized price of FRA} &= 0.02075 \times 360/120 \\
&= 0.0622 \text{ or } 6.22\%
\end{aligned}
$$

Takeaway: The FRA rate is really just a forward rate derived from the term structure of interest rates (or spot rates), even though the underlying is not an asset. Essentially, taking the long position on an FRA is equivalent to holding a longer-term Eurodollar time deposit and at the same time shorting (or owing) a shorter-term Eurodollar time deposit. In our example, the investor would take a long position on the 150-day Eurodollar time deposit and short the 30-day Eurodollar time deposit. This leaves the investor with no interest rate exposure over the initial 30-day period, and then, after 30 days, she actually has exposure to interest rate changes over the next 120 days.

Note that the curriculum (perhaps confusingly for some of you) defines FRAs as "forward contracts that allow participants to make a known interest payment at a later date and receive in return an unknown interest payment." To relate this definition to our definition and example, understand that the known interest payment refers to the interest payment (based on 30-day LIBOR) on the shorter-term Eurodollar deposit that we owe, and the unknown interest payment that we receive will be based on 120-day LIBOR on the FRA expiration date (t = 30). We would strongly advise that you stick to our definition. Also note that Example 2-5 was provided for illustrative purposes only (the curriculum no longer includes an example on FRAs). Just make sure you understand the takeaways.

LESSON 3: FUTURES CONTRACTS

LOS 57f: Explain why forward and futures prices differ. Vol 6, pp 80–82

Characteristics of Futures Contracts

Standardization

Futures contracts are specialized versions of forward contracts that have been standardized and trade on a futures exchange. In the futures market, the futures price is the only term set by the two parties involved in the contract; all other terms are established by the exchange, including the expiration date of the contract, the underlying, the mode of settlement, and contract size. For example, a NYMEX futures contract on oil covers 1,000 barrels. A contract price of $45 essentially indicates a price of $45/barrel and makes each contract worth $45,000. The maximum allowable price movement during a trading day and trading times for the contract are also determined by the exchange.

The standardized nature of futures contracts make them acceptable to a wider variety of users as it tells traders exactly what is being traded and fixes the terms of the transaction.

Clearinghouse

Every futures exchange has a clearinghouse, which guarantees that participants on the exchange will meet their obligations. The clearinghouse accomplishes this by taking the opposite side of every trade on the exchange (i.e., it takes the short position for every long, and the long position for every short). This comforts traders in that they know that they will be able to exit their positions, as the clearinghouse is a willing counterparty to any contract. Further, they do not have to worry about counterparty defaults. We will see how the clearinghouse protects itself against trader defaults later in this reading.

Futures Margins

In the futures market, the initial margin is the amount that must be deposited by each party—the long and the short—into her account to be able to trade in the market. The initial margin requirement in the futures market is a relatively low proportion of the contract's total value, and is usually based on the historical daily price volatility of the underlying. Let's assume that we are dealing with a futures contract with one share of Reliance Industries Ltd. (RIL), which is trading at Rs.300/share, as the underlying. If the initial margin requirement on the futures contract is 10%, an investor wanting to take a long position in RIL futures would have to deposit Rs.30 into her futures account. It is important to note that no loan is taken to fund the remainder of the contract's value (Rs.270). Margin in the futures market is more like a performance bond or a down payment.

In the securities market, a margin transaction will allow the investor to partially fund the purchase of RIL stock with borrowed funds. An initial margin requirement of 50% would require the investor to put in Rs.150 of her own money, while the rest of the amount (Rs.150) would be borrowed through her broker. Therefore, the investor would also be charged interest on the loan for the number of days she holds on to the stock.

The maintenance margin is the minimum balance that must be maintained in an investor's account to avoid a margin call (a call for more funds to be deposited in the account). In the case of RIL futures, a maintenance margin of 5% would require a minimum balance of Rs.15 for every contract that the investor has a position on. If the balance falls below this level, she will receive a margin call to increase the balance in her account back to the initial margin level. For example, if the RIL futures contract closes at Rs.284, a loss of Rs.16 will be posted to the long's account and her margin balance will fall from Rs.30 to Rs.14. Now that the account balance is below the maintenance margin level (Rs.15), she will be required to deposit Rs.16 to restore the initial margin (Rs.30) if she wants to keep her position "open." Alternatively, the investor could simply close out her position, but she would still be responsible for any further losses incurred if prices move further before the closing transaction is executed. If the balance in the investor's account exceeds the initial margin requirement, funds can be withdrawn from the account or used to take additional futures positions.

In contrast to the futures market, if the margin balance in a securities market transaction falls below the maintenance margin, the investor must deposit enough funds to satisfy only the maintenance margin requirement.

To provide a fair mark-to-market process (described below), the clearinghouse designates an official settlement price on the basis of which gains and losses on futures positions are determined. The settlement price is usually calculated as the average of all trades during the closing period (which is defined by the exchange). The settlement price is determined in this manner because the closing price is subject to manipulation by unscrupulous traders.

Marking-to-Market

Marking-to-market is the process of adjusting the balance in an investor's futures account to reflect the change in value of her futures position since the last mark-to-market adjustment was conducted. Most exchanges require daily marking-to-market based on the settlement price. This periodic settlement through the mark-to-market process prevents the accumulation of losses in investors' accounts and ensures that the party that earns a profit from a futures transaction will not have to worry about collecting the money, thereby eliminating default risk.

Example 3-1: The Mark-to-Market Process in Futures Markets

Samantha takes a long position in 10 futures contracts, where each contract is worth $100. The initial margin requirement is $5/contract, and the maintenance margin is $4/contract. Based on settlement prices, the value of each contract for the next three days is $98, $99, and $98.50. Samantha meets all margin calls, and does not withdraw any excess margin. Determine the balance in her margin account at the end of each trading day.

Solution:

Samantha's initial margin requirement is $50 (10 contracts multiplied by a margin requirement of $5 per contract) and her maintenance margin requirement is $40.

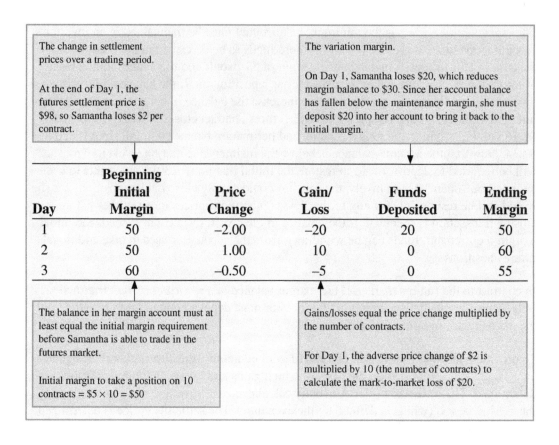

Day	Beginning Initial Margin	Price Change	Gain/ Loss	Funds Deposited	Ending Margin
1	50	−2.00	−20	20	50
2	50	1.00	10	0	60
3	60	−0.50	−5	0	55

The change in settlement prices over a trading period.

At the end of Day 1, the futures settlement price is $98, so Samantha loses $2 per contract.

The variation margin.

On Day 1, Samantha loses $20, which reduces margin balance to $30. Since her account balance has fallen below the maintenance margin, she must deposit $20 into her account to bring it back to the initial margin.

The balance in her margin account must at least equal the initial margin requirement before Samantha is able to trade in the futures market.

Initial margin to take a position on 10 contracts = $5 × 10 = $50

Gains/losses equal the price change multiplied by the number of contracts.

For Day 1, the adverse price change of $2 is multiplied by 10 (the number of contracts) to calculate the mark-to-market loss of $20.

The clearinghouse is the counterparty to every trade on the exchange. It acts as the short for every long position, and as the long for every short position. Taking the position as the counterparty to every trade combined with the ability to enforce periodic mark-to-market adjustments for all market participants makes for a very efficient mechanism for controlling default risk. This mechanism does not guarantee that defaults will not occur. Defaults do occur, but the clearinghouse is responsible for paying off the opposite party through a reserve fund or taxes on members. Figure 3-1 illustrates the role of a clearinghouse in futures trades.

Figure 3-1: Futures Trades

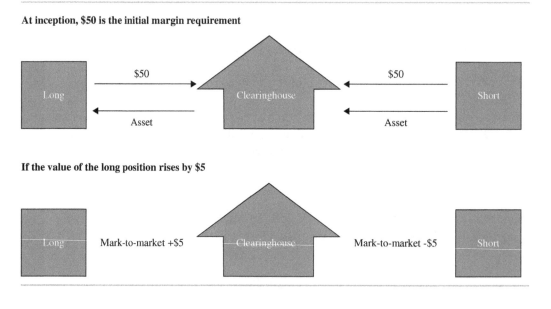

Price Limits

Some futures contracts have price limits. These limits are set by the exchange to restrict the change in the settlement price of a contract from one day to the next. No trading is allowed at prices beyond these limits. Continuing with our example of RIL futures, if the previous settlement price were Rs.284 and an Rs.30 price limit were in place, there would be no trading at prices below Rs.254 and prices above Rs.314. If the futures price hits its upper ceiling, the contract is said to be limit up, and if the price falls to its lower limit it is said to be limit down. If traders cannot transact because of a limit move, either up or down, the price is said to be locked limit.

Cash Flows on Forwards and Futures Contracts

Example 3-2 describes the cash flows from positions on forwards and futures contracts.

Example 3-2: Forwards versus Futures

Investor A and Investor B want to take long positions on ABC Stock through derivative contracts. They both want to purchase the stock for $50 in two days. Investor A decides to take a long position on a forward contract on ABC, while Investor B chooses to go long on a futures contract. Both the contracts expire in two days, and have forward/futures prices of $50.

1. Describe the cash flows on each investor's position given that the settlement price at the end of Day 1 is $49, and at the end of Day 2 (at contract expiration) is $52.

Solution:

Investor A's position on the forward contract:

There are no mark-to-market adjustments on forward contracts. The (only) settlement payment occurs at the expiration of the contract. The forward contract gives Investor A the ability to purchase the stock for $50 (forward price) even though it is priced at $52 in the market. She would receive a $2 profit in cash if the contract were cash-settled, or would receive the stock in return for a payment of $50 if it called for physical delivery. Either way, she would earn a profit of $2.

Investor B's position on the futures contract:

The future's price at contract expiration would converge to the asset's spot price ($52). However, the futures position would require a mark-to-market adjustment daily. At the end of Day 1, Investor B's account would be marked-to-market for a loss of $1 because the settlement price is $49. On Day 2, her position would be marked from $49 to $52, resulting in a gain of $3. Her net gain over the two days equals $2 (same as Investor A's).

Notice that that once the value of the futures contract (i.e., the mark-to-market adjustment) is paid out in the daily settlement, the futures price is effectively reset to the settlement price and the value of the contract goes to zero. In calculating the mark-to-market adjustment on the final day, we began with a futures price of $49, not the initial futures price of $50.

Note that interest can be earned/paid on that daily mark-to-market adjustments on any futures position. This can cause a difference between forward and futures prices on contracts that otherwise have identical parameters.

- If underlying asset prices are positively correlated with interest rates, any gains from the mark-to-market adjustment can be reinvested at higher interest rates, while any losses from the adjustment can be financed at lower borrowing rates. In such cases, traders prefer futures over forwards, which results in the futures price being higher than the forward price.
- If underlying asset prices are negatively correlated with interest rates, any gains from the mark-to-market adjustment must be reinvested at lower interest rates, while any losses from the adjustment must be financed at higher borrowing rates. In such cases, traders prefer forwards over futures, which results in the forward price being higher than the futures price.
- If interest rates are constant, forwards and futures would have the same prices. Further, if futures prices are uncorrelated with interest rates, forwards and futures would have the same prices. Note that forward and futures prices would be different if the volatility of the forward price is different from the volatility of the futures price.

Practically speaking, the derivatives industry makes no distinction between futures and forward price. Therefore, we will generally make no distinction between futures and forward pricing.

LESSON 4: SWAP CONTRACTS

LOS 57g: Explain how swap contracts are similar to but different from a series of forward contracts. Vol 6, pp 82–85

LOS 57h: Distinguish between the value and price of swaps. Vol 6, pp 82–85

SWAPS

Introduction

A swap is an agreement to exchange a series of cash flows at periodic settlement dates over a certain period of time (known as the tenor of the swap). The simplest kind of a swap is a plain-vanilla interest rate swap. Let's quickly illustrate a scenario in which such a swap is frequently used.

Suppose a company wants to borrow some money from a bank. The bank only offers floating-rate loans, but the company would much rather make fixed-interest payments. In such a situation, the company can add a swap to effectively convert its floating-rate loan to a fixed-rate loan (as illustrated in Figure 4-1).

Figure 4-1: Converting a Floating-Rate Loan to a Fixed-Rate Loan via a Swap

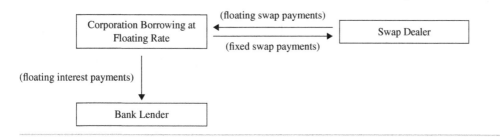

The company will take the pay-fixed/receive-floating side of a plain-vanilla interest rate swap.

- It will make fixed interest payments based on the notional principal of the swap.
- It will receive floating interest payments from the swap counterparty.
- It will pass on those floating-rate receipts to the bank to fulfill its obligations on the original loan.
- Overall, the company will just make fixed-rate payments (as it originally desired).

Plain-Vanilla Interest Rate Swaps

- A plain-vanilla interest rate swap involves the exchange of fixed interest payments for floating-rate payments.
- The party that wants to receive floating-rate payments agrees to make fixed-rate payments is known as the pay-fixed side of the swap or the fixed-rate payer/ floating-rate receiver.
- The party that wants to receive fixed payments and make floating-rate payments is the pay-floating side of the swap or the floating-rate payer/fixed-rate receiver.
- Note that there is no exchange of notional principal at initiation or expiration of the swap. The notional principal is simply used to determine the interest payment on each leg of the swap.
- Interest payments are not exchanged in full at each settlement date. Interest payments are netted, and the party that owes more in interest at a particular settlement date makes a payment equal to the difference to the other.
- As with forward contracts, there is an element of counterparty credit risk in swaps as the party that owes the lower amount can default.
- The floating rate is usually quoted in terms of LIBOR plus a spread. The floating rate for any period is known at the beginning of the period, while the settlement payment is actually made at the end of each period. (See Example 4-1.)

The formula for the net payment made (received) by the fixed-rate payer is given by:

$$\text{Net fixed rate payment}_t = [\text{Swap fixed rate} - (\text{LIBOR}_{t-1} + \text{spread})] \times (\text{No. of days}/360) \times \text{Notional principal}$$

Example 4-1: Settlement Payments on an Interest Rate Swap

AFC Bank enters into a $5,000,000 quarterly-pay, plain-vanilla interest rate swap as the fixed-rate payer at a swap rate of 5% based on a 360-day year. The floating-rate payer agrees to make payments at 90-day LIBOR plus a 0.50% spread (also known as margin). Ninety-day LIBOR currently stands at 3%.

LIBOR-90 rates are:
- 3.50%   90 days from today
- 4.50%   180 days from today
- 5.00%   270 days from today
- 5.50%   360 days from today

Calculate the amounts that AFC pays or receives:

1.   90 days from now.
2.   270 days from now.
3.   360 days from now.

Solution:

When working with LIBOR-based instruments, remember that the LIBOR rate at a particular reset date determines the interest payment due on the next reset date. Therefore, the floating interest rate payment on Day 90 of the swap will be based on LIBOR-90 at swap inception (Day 0). Similarly, the interest payment on Day 180 will be based on LIBOR-90 on Day 90 of the swap, and so on.

1.   The payment on Day 90 depends on LIBOR-90 at Day 0, which is 3.00%.

   Net fixed rate payment$_{90}$ = Swap fixed rate – (LIBOR$_0$ + Margin)
   $\times$ (No. of days/360) $\times$ (NP)

   Net fixed-rate payment$_{90}$ = [0.05 – (0.03 + 0.005)] (90/360)
   $\times$ \$5,000,000 = \$18,750.

2.   The payment on Day 270 depends on LIBOR-90 on Day 180, which is 4.50%.

   Net fixed-rate payment$_{270}$ = [0.05 – (0.045 + 0.005)] (90/360) $\times$ \$5,000,000 = \$0

   The floating-rate equals the fixed-rate so there is no settlement payment on Day 270.

3.   The payment on Day 360 depends on LIBOR-90 on Day 270, is 5.00%.

   Net fixed-rate payment$_{360}$ = [0.05 – (0.05 + 0.005)] (90/360) $\times$ \$5,000,000 = –\$6,250

   The floating-rate exceeds the fixed-rate. Therefore, AFC Bank will **receive** $6,250 on Day 360.

Pricing versus Valuation of Swaps

The distinction between the price and value of a swap is comparable to the distinction that we made between the price and value of a forward contract earlier in the reading. The price of a forward is the forward rate/price that results in zero value to either party at initiation of the contract. Subsequently, over the term of contract, the value of the forward to the long/short position fluctuates as the price/rate of the underlying changes.

We shall again work with a plain-vanilla interest rate swap to illustrate the difference between the price and value of a swap.

- At the initiation of the swap, the swap fixed rate is set at a level at which the present value of the floating-rate payments (based on the current term structure of interest rates) equals the present value of fixed rate payments so that there is zero value to either party. This swap fixed rate therefore represents the price of the swap.
- Over the term of the swap, as there are changes in the term structure of interest rates, the value of the swap will fluctuate.
  - If interest rates increase after swap initiation, the present value of floating-rate payments (based on the new term structure) will exceed the present value of fixed rate payments (based on the swap fixed rate).
    - The swap will have a positive value for the fixed-rate payer (floating-rate receiver).
    - The swap will be an asset to the fixed-rate payer and a liability for the floating-rate payer.
  - If interest rates decrease after swap initiation, the present value of floating-rate payments will be lower than the present value of fixed-rate payments.
    - The swap will have a positive value for the floating-rate payer (fixed-rate receiver).
    - In this case, the swap will be an asset to the floating-rate payer and a liability for the fixed-rate payer.

Swaps and Forward Contracts

A forward contract is a commitment by one party to make a fixed payment to the other in return for a variable payment at the expiration of the contract. A swap essentially combines a series of forward contracts into a single transaction. For example, a plain-vanilla interest rate swap is a combination of FRAs, where one FRA expires on each settlement date over the tenor of the swap and the FRA rate (forward price) for each FRA equals the swap fixed rate (swap price). The example below illustrates how the payoffs on the pay-fixed side of an interest rate swap can be replicated through long positions on FRAs.

Consider a quarterly reset, two-year plain-vanilla interest rate swap that carries a fixed rate of 5% and a floating rate based on LIBOR-90.

- On a given reset date, if LIBOR-90 is *greater* than the swap fixed rate, the fixed-rate payer would be entitled to *receive* the interest savings (difference between the floating rate and swap fixed rate multiplied by the notional principal).
- On a given reset date, if LIBOR-90 is *lower* than the swap fixed rate, the fixed-rate payer would be obligated to *make a payment* equal to the interest savings.

The payoff to the pay-fixed side of the swap can be replicated by taking the long position on a series of FRAs, where one FRA expires on each swap settlement date, and the FRA rate for each of the FRAs equals the swap fixed rate (5%).

- On the FRA expiration date, if LIBOR-90 is *greater* than the FRA rate, the long position on the FRA would be entitled to *receive* a payment equal to the interest savings.
- On the FRA expiration date, if LIBOR-90 is *lower* than the FRA rate, the long position on the FRA would be obligated to *make a payment* equal to the interest savings.

Recall that FRAs are priced based on implied forward rates given the term structure of expected future interest rates. Unless the term structure is flat, the implied forward rates (FRA rates) for FRAs that expire at different points in time (corresponding to swap settlement dates) will tend to be different. Since we require each of the FRAs to have an FRA rate equal to the swap fixed rate to replicate the payoffs of the interest rate swap, we would actually have to use off-market FRAs to replicate a swap. In an off market-FRA, the forward is set to have a nonzero value at inception. If the value is positive (negative), the long (short) pays the amount up front to the short (long). For the swap to have zero value at inception, some of the off-market FRAs that it comprises will have positive values at inception, while others will have negative values, such that the combined overall value is zero.

Pricing and valuation of swaps are simple exercises based on the concepts of replication and no-arbitrage. Let's continue working with plain-vanilla interest rate swaps to illustrate how positions on swaps can be replicated with bonds. The payoffs to the pay-fixed (receive floating) side of a plain-vanilla interest rate swap are as follows:

- A payment must be made if interest rates fall below the swap fixed rate.
- A payment is received if interest rates rise above the swap fixed rate.

Therefore, the payoffs of the pay-fixed side of an interest rate swap are similar to those of a strategy of issuing a fixed-rate bond (on which fixed-payments must be made) and using the proceeds to purchase a floating-rate bond (which will return floating-interest payments). On the other hand, the payoffs of the pay-floating side are similar to issuing a floating-rate bond and using the proceeds to purchase a fixed-rate bond.

- If interest rates increase, the fixed-rate payer benefits as there is a positive difference between her (floating-rate) receipts and (fixed-rate) payments.
  - In terms of the positions on bonds, the value of the fixed-rate bond decreases as interest rates increase, but the value of the floating rate bond remains at par. Since the fixed-rate payer is long on the floating-rate bond and short on the fixed-rate bond, she benefits from the increase in interest rates.
  - The swap will hold positive value to the fixed-rate payer. This value would equal the difference between the value of the floating-rate bond and the fixed-rate bond.
- If interest rates decrease, the fixed-rate payer loses out, as there is a negative difference between (floating-rate) receipts and (fixed-rate) payments.
  - In terms of the positions on bonds, the value of the fixed-rate bond increases as interest rates decrease, but the value of the floating rate bond remains at par. Since the fixed-rate payer is long on the floating-rate bond and short on the fixed-rate bond, she loses out as a result of the decrease in interest rates.
  - The swap will hold positive value for the floating-rate payer. This value would equal the difference between the value of the fixed-rate bond and the floating-rate bond.

> Recall from the fixed-income section that a floating-rate bond trades at par at every reset date.

Please note that we have gone well above and truly beyond the requirements of the Level I curriculum in illustrating how a position on a swap can be replicated through (1) FRAs and (2) bonds. The problem is that the curriculum reading mentions a lot of concepts without adequately explaining them. This may get you by at Level I, but Levels II and III will be very difficult if you do not have a decent understanding of each of these derivative securities. Our lecture video on this Reading will also explain everything in detail so that not only will you be very comfortable with Level I derivatives, but you will build a solid base for Levels II and III at the same time.

LESSON 5: OPTION CONTRACTS PART 1: EUROPEAN OPTION PRICING

LOS 57i: Explain how the value of a European option is determined at expiration. Vol 6, pp 86

LOS 57j: Explain the exercise value, time value, and moneyness of an option. Vol 6, pp 86–87, 90

LOS 57k: Identify the factors that determine the value of an option and explain how each factor affects the value of an option. Vol 6, pp 87–94

LOS 57l: Explain put-call parity for European options. Vol 6, pp 94–98

Options

Introduction

- A European option is one that can only be exercised at the option's expiration date.
- An American option can be exercised at any point in time up to and including the option's expiration date.

For most of this reading, we will be working with European options (i.e., options that can only be exercised at their expiration dates). We will also be using the following notations for European and American put and call options.

For calls:

c_0 = Value (price) of European call today
c_T = Value (price) of European call at expiration
C_0 = Value (price) of American call today
C_T = Value (price) of American call at expiration

For puts:

p_0 = Value (price) of European put today
p_T = Value (price) of European put at expiration
P_0 = Value (price) of American put today
P_T = Value (price) of American put at expiration

Call Options

A call option gives the **holder/buyer** the **right** to **buy** (or call) the underlying asset, for the given exercise price at the expiration date of the option.

A call option **writer/seller** has the **obligation** to **sell** the asset to the holder of the call option, for the given exercise price, should the option holder choose to exercise the option.

Let's work with an example to illustrate how call options work. Assume that Rahul has bought a call option on CSC stock from Betty for $2. The call option grants Rahul the right to purchase a share of CSC for $20 from Betty six months from today.

The $2 that Rahul pays Betty for the option is known as the option premium. The price at which the two parties can trade the underlying asset ($20) at the expiration of the option (six months from today) is known as the strike or exercise price.

We will work with two scenarios for CSC stock price at option expiration to illustrate the payoffs for Rahul (the call option holder) and Betty (the call option writer):

1. Scenario A: CSC stock price equals $35.
2. Scenario B: CSC stock price equals $15.

Scenario A: CSC's price at option expiration = $35

At option expiration, Rahul has to choose whether he should exercise his option to buy CSC stock from Betty at the exercise price, or let the option expire without exercising it. Is it profitable for him to purchase a share of CSC from Betty for $20 (the exercise price of the option) when the market price is $35? Of course it is! Rahul can exercise the option, purchase a share of CSC from Betty for $20, sell it in the market for $35, and realize a payoff equal to $15 ($35 – $20) on the option. His profit on the entire trade equals his payoff adjusted for the cost of the option.

S_T = Asset price at option expiration
X = Exercise price of the option
T = Time of option expiration
c_0 = Price of European call option (option premium)

- Payoff for call option holder = Asset price at option expiration – Exercise price
$$= S_T - X = \$35 - \$20 = \$15$$
- Profit (loss) for call option holder = Payoff – Call option premium
$$= (S_T - X) - c_0 = \$15 - \$2 = \$13$$

Betty, as the writer or seller of the option, is obligated to perform on the terms of the option. If Rahul (the option holder) chooses to exercise the option, Betty would have to deliver an asset worth $35 in the market to Rahul in exchange for a payment of only $20 (the exercise price). Betty's payoff in this scenario is negative (–$15). Her profit (loss) on the entire trade equals the payoff adjusted for the income from selling the option.

- Payoff for call option writer = – (Asset price at option expiration – Exercise price)
$$= - (S_T - X) = - (\$20 - \$35) = (\$15)$$
- Profit (loss) for call option writer = Payoff + Option premium
$$= - (S_T - X) + c_0 = (\$15) + \$2 = (\$13)$$

Remember that Rahul has not taken on any commitments by getting into the option contract. At the expiration date, he can choose to exercise his option, or to let it expire without exercising it. Betty however, is obligated to perform on the terms of the option if Rahul chooses to exercise the option. Also notice the following important points:

- Any positive payoff for the call option holder means that a negative payoff of equal magnitude is borne by the call writer.
- Any profit for the call holder means that a loss of equal magnitude is borne by the call writer.

Scenario B: CSC's price at option expiration = $15

In this scenario, the market price of CSC at option expiration is less than the exercise price of the option. Rahul can purchase CSC stock cheaper from the market ($15) than from Betty ($20). Therefore, Rahul will not exercise the call option, and receive no payoff from the option at expiration.

- Payoff for call option holder = 0
- Profit (loss) for call option holder = Payoff – Call option premium = $0 – $2 = ($2)

Because Rahul does not exercise the option, Betty also has zero payoffs from the option.

- Payoff for call option writer = 0
- Profit (loss) for call option writer = Payoff + Option premium = $0 + $2 = $2

Table 5-1 summarizes call option holder and writer payoffs.

Table 5-1: Call Option Payoffs

Option Position	Descriptions	Payoff	
		$S_T > X$	$S_T < X$
		Option holder exercises the option	Option holder does not exercise the option
Call option holder	Choice to buy the underlying asset for X	$S_T - X$	0
Call option writer	Obligation to sell the underlying asset for X if the option holder chooses to exercise the option	$-(S_T - X)$	0

Table 5-2 lists the payoffs to the call option holder and the call option writer under various scenarios.

Exercising the call option when the market price is less than the exercise price will result in a negative payoff for the call option holder. Therefore, he chooses not to exercise the option.

Table 5-2: Call Option Payoffs

CSC Market Price at Option Expiration (S_t) $	Exercise Price of Option (X) $	Call Option Holder's Payoff [(Max (0, $S_T - X$)] $	Put Option Writer's Payoff – [(Max (0, $S_T - X$)] $
5	20	0	0
10	20	0	0
15	20	0	0
20	20	0	0
25	20	5	–5
30	20	10	–10
35	20	15	–15
40	20	20	–20

Mapping the call option holder's and writer's payoffs on to a graph (Figure 5-1) results in the following payoff diagrams:

Figure 5-1: Call Option Payoff Diagrams

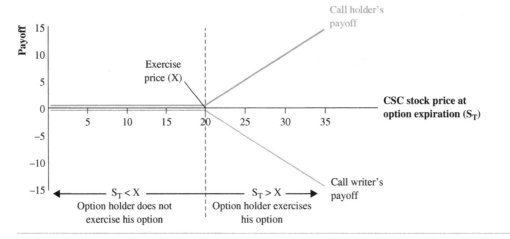

> If the market price is greater than the exercise price, the call option holder will exercise the option. The payoff to the option writer is the opposite of the payoff to the option holder.

Moneyness refers to whether an option is in-the-money or out-of-the-money.

- An option is in-the-money when immediate exercise of the option will generate a positive payoff for the holder.
- An option is out-of-the-money when immediate exercise will generate a negative payoff for the holder.
- An option is at-the-money when immediate exercise will result in neither a positive nor a negative payoff for the holder.

> Notice that for a stock, intrinsic value is a measure of fundamental or true value. For options, however, intrinsic value simply measures the amount by which the option is in-the-money. As you will see later, an option with time left until expiration will be worth more than this intrinsic value.

The intrinsic value or exercise value of an option is the amount an option is in-the-money by. It is the amount that would be received by the option holder if he were to exercise the option immediately. An option has zero intrinsic value if it is at, or out-of-the money. Therefore, the expression for the intrinsic value of a call option is given as:

$$\text{Intrinsic value of call} = \text{Max} [0, (S_t - X)]$$

Table 5-3 summarizes moneyness and intrinsic value of call options under different scenarios:

Table 5-3: Moneyness and Exercise Value of a Call Option

Moneyness	Current Market Price (S_t) versus Exercise Price (X)	Intrinsic Value Max $[0, (S_t - X)]$
In-the-money	S_t is greater than X	$S_t - X$
At-the-money	S_t equals X	0
Out-of-the-money	S_t is less than X	0

Put Options
- A put option gives the **holder/buyer** the **right** to **sell** (or put) the underlying asset, for the given exercise price, at the option's expiration date.
- A put option **writer/seller** has the **obligation** to **buy** the asset from the put option holder at the option's expiration date, for the given exercise price, should the holder choose to exercise the option.

Let's assume that Chang has purchased a put option from Sarah for $5. The put option grants Chang the right to sell a share of PSP stock for $50 (the exercise price) to Sarah, 12 months from today (option expiration). We shall go through two scenarios to illustrate the payoffs and profits from the put option position to the holder and the writer.

1. Scenario A: PSP stock price equals $30.
2. Scenario B: PSP stock price equals $85.

Scenario A: PSP's price at option expiration date = $30

The market price ($30) is less than the price that Chang can sell PSP stock to Sarah for by exercising the option ($50). Will Chang exercise the option?

Yes, he will. Chang will be able to sell a stock worth only $30 in the market to Sarah for $50. He will receive a positive payoff of $20 on the transaction, and his profit on the option position will be $15 (payoff adjusted for the cost of the put option).

- Payoff for put option holder = Exercise price – Asset price at option expiration
$$= X - S_T = \$50 - \$30 = \$20$$
- Profit (loss) for put option holder = Payoff – Option premium
$$= (X - S_T) - p_0 = \$20 - \$5 = \$15$$

The fact that Chang will exercise his option means that Sarah will be obligated to buy PSP stock from him for $50 (the option's exercise price) when the market price is only $30. Sarah will incur a negative payoff of $20, and a loss on the option position of $15.

- Payoff for put option writer = – (Exercise price – Asset price at option expiration)
$$= - (X - S_T) = - (\$50 - \$30) = (\$20)$$
- Profit (loss) for put option writer = Payoff + Option premium
$$= - (X - S_T) + p_0 = (\$20) + \$5 = (\$15)$$

Scenario B: PSP's price at option expiration date = $85

Chang must decide whether to sell a share of PSP to Sarah for $50 (by exercising the option) when the market price is $85. If Chang wants to sell the share, he would rather sell it in the market for $85 than to Sarah for only $50. Being the option holder, Chang will choose not to exercise the option. His payoff from the option will be zero, and his loss on the option position will equal $5.

- Payoff for put option holder = 0
- Profit (loss) for put option holder = Payoff – Option premium = $0 – $5 = ($5)

Because Chang chooses not to exercise the option, Sarah's payoff also equals zero, and she makes a profit equal to the premium she collected when she wrote (sold) the option.

- Payoff for put option writer = 0
- Profit (loss) for put option writer = Payoff + Option premium = $0 + $5 = $5

Remember that Chang has not taken on any commitment by purchasing the put option. At the expiration date, he can choose to exercise his option or to let it expire without exercising it. Sarah, however, is obligated to perform on the terms of the option if Chang chooses to exercise it. Also notice that:

- Any positive payoff for the put option holder means that a negative payoff of equal magnitude is borne by the put writer.
- Any profit for the put holder means that a loss of equal magnitude is borne by the put writer.

Table 5-4 provides a summary of put option holder and writer payoffs:

Table 5-4: Put Option Payoffs

Option Position	Descriptions	Payoff	
		$S_T < X$	$S_T > X$
		Option holder exercises the option	Option holder does not exercise the option
Put option holder	Choice to sell the underlying asset for X	$X - S_T$	0
Put option writer	Obligation to buy the underlying asset for X if the option holder chooses to exercise the option	$-(X - S_T)$	0

The intrinsic value of a put option equals Max $[0, (X - S_t)]$. Table 5-5 lists the payoffs to the put option holder and the put option writer under various scenarios:

Table 5-5: Put Option Payoffs

PSP Market Price at Option Expiration (S_t) $	Exercise Price of Option (X) $	Put Option Holder's Payoff [(Max $(0, X - S_T)$)] $	Put Option Writer's Payoff – [(Max $(0, X - S_T)$)] $
10	50	40	−40
20	50	30	−30
30	50	20	−20
40	50	10	−10
50	50	0	0
60	50	0	0
70	50	0	0
80	50	0	0

When the market price is less than the exercise price, the put option holder exercises the option.

When the market price is greater than the exercise price, the put option holder does not exercise the option.

Mapping the put option holder's and writer's payoffs onto a graph (Figure 5-2) results in the following payoff diagrams:

Figure 5-2: Put Option Payoff Diagrams

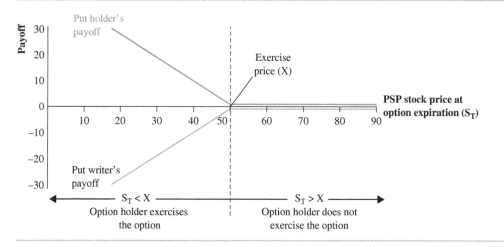

We have already defined intrinsic value and moneyness. Table 5-6 summarizes the intrinsic value and moneyness of a put option in different scenarios.

Table 5-6: Moneyness and Exercise Value of a Put Option

Moneyness	Current Market Price (S_t) versus Exercise Price (X)	Intrinsic Value Max $[0, (X - S_t)]$
In-the-money	S_t is less than X	$X - S_t$
At-the-money	S_t equals X	0
Out-of-the-money	S_t is greater than X	0

Put-Call Parity

Suppose we have two portfolios: Portfolio A and Portfolio B.

Portfolio A is composed of (1) a call option on a stock and (2) a zero-coupon riskless bond that pays X at maturity (face value equals X). This portfolio is also known as a fiduciary call.

Portfolio B is composed of (1) a European put option on a stock and (2) a share of the same stock. This portfolio is also known as a protective put.

Further:

- The call and put option, and the zero-coupon bond have the same time to maturity/expiration (T).
- The exercise price of the call and the put, and the face value of the zero-coupon bond are the same (X).
- The call and the put are options on the same underlying asset as the one held in Portfolio B (S). This asset makes no cash payments and has no carrying costs.
- The call and put can be exercised only at expiration (i.e., they are European options).

At option expiration, there are two possible scenarios: The stock price (S_T) can be greater than exercise price (X) or it can be less than the exercise price.

> Current price of call = c_0
>
> Current price of bond = $X/(1+R_F)^T$
>
> Current price of put = p_0
>
> Current price of stock = S_0

Let's determine the value of each of these four securities at option expiration under both scenarios.

If the stock price is greater than the exercise price:

- The call option is exercised for a payoff of $S_T - X$.
- The zero-coupon bond is worth X (i.e., its face value).
- The put option is not exercised because it is out-of-the money so it is worth zero.
- The share of stock is worth S_T (i.e. its value at option expiration date).

If the stock price is less than the exercise price:

- The call option is not exercised because it is out-of-the-money.
- The zero-coupon bond is worth X.
- The put option is exercised for a payoff equal to $X - S_T$.
- The share of stock is worth S_T.

Table 5-7 summarizes the value of the two portfolios in both scenarios.

Table 5-7: Fiduciary Call and Protective Put Payoffs

Security	Value if $S_T > X$	Value if $S_T < X$
Call option	$S_T - X$	Zero
Zero-coupon bond	X	X
Fiduciary call payoff	S_T	X
Put option	Zero	$X - S_T$
Stock	S_T	S_T
Protective put payoff	S_T	X

Notice that in both scenarios, the payoffs on the fiduciary call and the protective put are identical (also see Figure 5-3). Two portfolios that have exactly the same payoff at maturity should have the same value/cost today. If the values of the two portfolios are not identical, arbitrage profits can be made by purchasing the relatively cheaper portfolio and selling the overpriced one. Therefore, at any point in the time, the value of a portfolio composed of a call option and the zero-coupon bond (a fiduciary call) must be the same as the value of a portfolio consisting of a put option and the underlying asset (protective put).

Put-Call Parity

$$c_0 + \frac{X}{(1+R_F)^T} = p_0 + S_0 \quad \text{... (Equation 2)}$$

Figure 5-3: Protection Put (Asset Plus Long Put) and Fiduciary Call (Long Call Plus Risk-Free Bond)

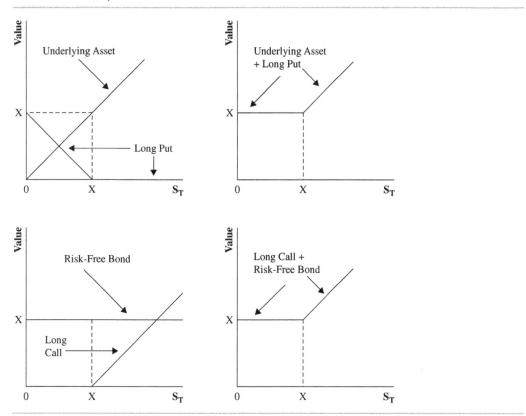

If we know the values for three of the securities in the put-call parity equation, we can determine the value of the fourth security using the equation above. Put-call parity can also be used to generate synthetic options and securities. For example, a synthetic call option can be created by purchasing a put and the underlying stock and selling the zero-coupon bond. Of course, each of the four conditions that we stated for put-call parity must hold. Table 5-8 lists the combinations of different securities that can be used to create synthetic securities.

Table 5-8: Combining Portfolios to Make Synthetic Securities

Strategy	Consisting of	Value	Equals	Strategy	Consisting of	Value
Fiduciary call	long call + long bond	$c_0 + \dfrac{X}{(1+R_F)^T}$	=	Protective put	long put + long underlying asset	$p_0 + S_0$
Long call	long call	c_0	=	Synthetic call	long put + long underlying asset + short bond	$p_0 + S_0 - \dfrac{X}{(1+R_F)^T}$
Long put	long put	p_0	=	Synthetic put	long call + short underlying asset + long bond	$c_0 - S_0 + \dfrac{X}{(1+R_F)^T}$
Long underlying asset	long underlying asset	S_0	=	Synthetic underlying asset	long call + long bond + short put	$c_0 + \dfrac{X}{(1+R_F)^T} - p_0$
Long bond	long bond	$\dfrac{X}{(1+R_F)^T}$	=	Synthetic bond	long put + long underlying asset + short call	$p_0 + S_0 - c_0$

Example 5-1: Using Put-Call Parity to Exploit Arbitrage Opportunities

The stock of Aldoro Inc. is currently trading at $60. A six-month call option on the stock is selling for $5.80, while a six-month put option on the stock is selling for $4.30. Given a risk-free rate of 6%:

1. Identify the mispricing by comparing the actual price of the call with the value of a synthetic call.
2. Demonstrate how this violation of put-call parity can be exploited to earn arbitrage profits.

Solution:

1. The price of the synthetic call can be calculated as:

$$c_0 = p_0 + S_0 - \frac{X}{(1+R_F)^T}$$
$$= 4.30 + 60 - 60/(1+0.06)6/12 = \$6.0228$$

The call option is underpriced as it is selling for less than the value of the synthetic call ($5.80 versus $6.02).

2. To exploit the mispricing, we go long on the relatively underpriced actual call and go short on the relatively overpriced synthetic call. Going short on the synthetic call requires taking (1) a short position on the put option, (2) a short position on the underlying stock, and (3) a long position on the zero-coupon bond.

The payoffs on the positions at option expiration will offset each other and we will be left with a risk-free profit of $6.0228 – $5.80 = $0.2228 today.

Today

Transaction	Cash Flow ($)
Long call option	–5.8000
Cost of long position	–5.8000
Short put option	4.3000
Short stock	60.0000
Invest in zero-coupon bond	–58.2772
Proceeds from short synthetic call	6.0228
Net cash flow (arbitrage profit)	0.2228

Payoffs at Expiration

	$S_T < 60$	$S_T > 60$
Long call	0	$S_T - 60$
Short put	$-(60 - S_T)$	0
Short stock	$-S_T$	$-S_T$
Long bond	60	60
Total	0	0

We now turn our attention to various factors that affect the value of an option.

Effect of the Value of the Underlying

A call option grants the holder the right to buy the underlying for predetermined exercise price. The greater (lower) the value of the underlying, the greater (lower) the exercise value of the call option, and the greater its price/value.

A put option grants the holder the right to sell the underlying for predetermined exercise price. The lower (greater) the value of the underlying, the greater (lower) the exercise value of the put option, and the greater its price/value.

Note that the value of the underlying serves as an upper boundary on the price of a call option. It would not make sense to pay more for the right to buy the underlying asset than the value of the underlying asset itself. Therefore, American and European call options have a maximum value equal to the price of the underlying.

Takeaways:

- The value of a call option is *directly* related to the value of the underlying.
- The value of a put option is *inversely* related to the value of the underlying.
- $C_t, c_t \leq S_t$

Effect of Exercise Price

For call options, the higher the exercise price, the *lower* the exercise value of the option. Given two call options on the same underlying asset and with the same expiration date, we would pay more for an option with an exercise price of $10 than for one with an exercise price of $20 because the former has a higher exercise value and a higher probability of expiring in-the-money. To put it simply, you would pay *more* for the option to **buy** for *less*.

For put options, the higher the exercise price, the *higher* the intrinsic value. Given two put options on the same underlying asset and with the same expiration date, we would pay more for a put option with an exercise price of $80 than for one with an exercise price of $60 because the former has a higher exercise value and a greater probability of expiring in-the-money. To put it simply, you would pay *more* for the option to **sell** for *more*.

Note that the exercise price helps form the upper bound for a European put option. The best outcome for the holder of a put option is for the underlying's value to fall to zero (e.g., if the underlying is stock, the best-case scenario for a put option holder is for the company to dissolve), because it would result in a payoff equal to the exercise price ($X - S_t = X$ since $S_t = 0$) at option expiration. In the case of the European put, the holder would have to wait until expiration to exercise the option, so the maximum value anyone would pay for a European put option today would be the present value of its exercise price, $X/(1 + RFR)^T$.

Takeaways:

- Call option values and exercise prices are *inversely* related.
- Put options values and exercise prices are *directly* related.
- $p_0 \leq X/(1 + RFR)^T$

Effect of the Risk-Free Rate of Interest

When interest rates decrease, call option prices *decrease*, while put option prices *increase*. Some simple math helps us arrive at this conclusion.

From put-call parity, we know that:

$$c_0 = S_0 + p_0 - X/(1 + RFR)^T \quad \text{and that} \quad p_0 = c_0 - S_0 + X/(1 + RFR)^T$$

A decrease in interest rates (RFR) will *increase* the value of $X/(1+RFR)^T$, resulting in a *decrease* in the value of the call and an *increase* in the value of the put. However, remember that this rule may not apply to interest rate options or to options on bonds or T-bills, where the change in interest rates directly affects the value of the underlying.

Takeaways:

- The value of a call option is *directly* related to the risk-free rate.
- The value of a put option is *inversely* related to the risk-free rate.

The Effect of Time to Expiration

Call options always benefit from a longer time to expiration. With a longer time to expiration, there is a higher probability that the price of the underlying will rise above the option's exercise price and generate a positive payoff for the option holder. Of course, there is also the possibility that the price of the underlying will fall and that the option will expire out-of-the-money, but a call option holder would not be overly concerned about this possibility. This is because call option holders do not participate in the downside of the stock; they participate only in the upside. This one-sided feature of option payoffs makes them worth more if there is a longer time to expiration.

Given the relation between a call option's price and time to expiration you would be tempted to think that the same direct relationship would hold between put options and time to expiration. However, this is not necessarily true. A put option holder suffers from a subtle penalty from additional time in that she is awaiting a cash inflow (equal to the exercise price) from sale of the underlying. The longer she has to wait, the lower the present value of this receipt. Further, the higher the risk-free rate and the higher the value of the payoff (excess of the exercise price over the price of the underlying), the greater the negative effect of a longer time to expiration. Note, however, that typically, the positive effect of time is more dominant.

Takeaways:

- The value of a European call option is *directly* related to the time to expiration.
- The value of a European put option can be either *directly* or *inversely* related to the time to expiration. Typically, the direct effect holds, but the inverse effect can prevail if a longer time to expiration comes with a higher risk-free rate, and if the option is deep in-the-money.

Effect of Volatility of the Underlying

Greater volatility in the price of the underlying asset *increases* the value of both calls and puts. Higher volatility increases possible upside values and possible downside values for the underlying asset.

- An increase in the upside helps calls (as their exercise value increases) and does not hurt puts (as the loss resulting from an increase in the value of the underlying is limited to the put premium paid).
- An increase in the downside does not hurt calls (as the loss resulting from a decrease in the value of the underlying is limited to the call premium paid) and helps puts (as the exercise value increases).

Option payoffs are one-sided and their value cannot fall lower than zero, so the increased volatility results in greater profit potential for both calls and puts.

Takeaway:

- Both call and put prices are *directly* related to volatility of the underlying.

The effects of volatility and time give rise to the time value of an option. At any point in time before expiration, an option is worth at least as much as its exercise value. However, on top of its exercise value, there is also an element of speculative value in the option to account for the possibility that the underlying asset's price could move favorably over the remaining time to expiration and result in a payoff greater than the current exercise value. This speculative value is known as the time value of an option, which increases with volatility, but decreases as the option nears expiration (known as time value decay). At expiration, no time value remains, and the option is worth its exercise value.

Effects of Payments from the Underlying and the Cost of Carry

As we learned earlier in the reading, assets that serve as the underlying for derivatives may offer benefits (e.g., dividend payments and convenience yield) and/or incur costs (e.g., maintenance and storage costs).

Let's first consider the impact of benefits from the underlying on option prices. To make things simple, we'll work with stocks. Dividend payments reduce the value of stocks, and dividend payments do not flow through to the owners of options (because they do not actually own the underlying). As a result, for call option holders, benefits from the underlying (such as dividend payments), which cause a decline in the value of the underlying, are a negative because they lead to a decline in the exercise value. For put option holders, on the other hand, benefits from the underlying are a positive (as the value of the underlying falls).

Carrying costs have the opposite effect: They increase the cost of holding the asset. Call options allow investors to participate in movements in the underlying without incurring these costs, so carrying costs are a positive for call options. On the other hand, holding put options is a relatively more expensive way to participate in movements in the underlying relative to short selling (because short sellers benefit from carrying costs, which are borne by owners of the asset). Therefore, costs of carry are a negative for puts.

Lowest Prices of Calls and Puts

At a fairly basic level, the minimum value of any option is zero. An option cannot sell for less than its exercise value, and no option can have a negative value (in that case the writer would have to pay the buyer). Therefore, as a starting point to this exercise, you must understand that all American and European put and call options cannot have a value less than zero.

$$C_0, c_0, P_0, p_0 \geq 0$$

Now let us try to refine these minimum values of put and call options. We will just work with European options for now, starting with call options. From put-call parity we know that:

$$p_0 = c_0 + \frac{X}{(1+R_F)^T} - S_0 \quad \text{... Equation 2}$$

We also now know that a European put option cannot be worth less than zero (i.e., $p_0 \geq 0$).

Therefore, the right-hand side of Equation 2 can also not be worth less than zero:

$$c_0 + \frac{X}{(1+R_F)^T} - S_0 \geq 0$$

Rearranging the above inequality, we are left with:

$$c_0 \geq S_0 - \frac{X}{(1+R_F)^T}$$

The above expression specifies the lowest possible value of a European call option (subject to some further refinement). Notice that if S_0 is less than $X/(1 + RFR)^T$ we would be saying that the lowest value can be a negative number. We already know that a call option can never be worth less than zero, so the (refined) minimum value of a European call option can be expressed as:

$$c_0 \geq \text{Max} \left[0, S_0 - \frac{X}{(1+R_F)^T} \right]$$

To find the minimum value of a European put option, we once again start with (a rearranged version of) put-call parity.

$$c_0 = p_0 - \frac{X}{(1+R_F)^T} + S_0 \quad \text{... Equation 3}$$

We also now know that a European call option cannot be worth less than zero (i.e., $c_0 \geq 0$).

Therefore, the right-hand side of Equation 3 can also not be worth less than zero:

$$p_0 - \frac{X}{(1+R_F)^T} + S_0 \geq 0$$

Rearranging the above inequality, we are left with:

$$p_0 \geq \frac{X}{(1+R_F)^T} - S_0$$

The above expression specifies the lowest possible value of a put option (subject to some refinement). Notice that if S_0 is greater than $X/(1 + RFR)^T$, we would be saying that the lowest value can be a negative number. We already know that a put option can never be worth less than zero, so the (refined) minimum value of a European put option can be expressed as:

$$p_0 \geq \text{Max} \left[0, \frac{X}{(1+R_F)^T} - S_0 \right]$$

Takeaways:

- The lowest value of a European call is the greater of (1) zero and (2) the value of the underlying minus the present value of the exercise price.
- The lowest value of a European put is the greater of (1) zero and (2) the present value of the exercise price minus the value of the underlying.

Put-Call Forward Parity

Deriving put-call forward parity is very straightforward (assuming you are very comfortable with the derivation of put-call parity). Recall that put-call parity was derived by matching the payoffs of two portfolios, a fiduciary call (call option plus zero-coupon bond) and a protective put (put option plus underlying stock). In order to derive put-call forward parity, we assume that instead of holding the underlying stock in our protective put, we (1) take a long position on a forward contract on the underlying stock and (2) hold a risk-free bond that has a face value equal to the forward price. We refer to this combination of the put option, long position on the forward, and zero-coupon bond as a protective put with a forward contract.

Before getting into the cost of this portfolio and payoffs, note that:

- The price of the forward contract on the underlying is given by $F(0,T)$.
- The put and the call options expire at the same time as the forward contract.
- X represents the exercise price of the call and put options.
- The options are European options.
- The options and the forward contract are based on the same underlying asset.

The cost of the protective put with a forward contract today equals $F(0,T)/(1 + RFR)^T + p_0$.

- Taking a long position on the forward contract does not cost anything.
- The price of a zero-coupon bond with a face value of $F(0,T)$ is $F(0,T)/(1 + RFR)^T$.
- The put option costs the put premium, p_0.

At expiration of the options/forward, if the stock price is *greater* than the exercise price, the payoff on the protective put with a forward contract will equal S_T.

- The long forward position will be worth $S_T - F(0,T)$.
- The zero-coupon bond will be worth $F(0,T)$.
- The put option will expire out-of-the-money.

At expiration of the options/forward, if the stock price is *lower* than the exercise price, the payoff on the protective put with a forward contract will equal X.

- The long forward position will be worth $S_T - F(0,T)$.
- The zero-coupon bond will be worth $F(0,T)$.
- The put option will be worth $X - S_T$.

Notice that the payoffs on this protective put with a forward contract are the same as those on (1) the fiduciary call and (2) the protective put with the asset (which were described in the section on put-call parity) in both scenarios ($S_T < X$ and $S_T > X$) as shown in Table 5-9.

Table 5-9: Payoffs

	Outcome at T	
	$S_T < X$ Put Expires In-the-Money Call Expires Out-of-the-Money	$S_T > X$ Call Expires In-the-Money Put Expires out-of-the-Money
Protective put with forward contract		
Risk-free bond	$F(0,T)$	$F(0,T)$
Forward contract	$S_T - F(0,T)$	$S_T - F(0,T)$
Long put	$X - S_T$	0
Total	X	S_T
Protective put with asset		
Asset	S_T	S_T
Long put	$X - S_T$	0
Total	X	S_T
Fiduciary call		
Call	0	$S_T - X$
Risk-free bond	X	X
Total	X	S_T

Therefore, we can attain the expression for put-call forward parity by equating the cost of the protective put with the forward contract to the fiduciary call:

$$\frac{F(0,T)}{(1+R_F)^T} + p_0 = c_0 + \frac{X}{(1+R_F)^T}$$, which can be rearranged and expressed as:

Put-call forward parity

$$\boxed{p_0 - c_0 = \frac{[X - F(0,T)]}{(1+R_F)^T}}$$

Shortcut: You can simply derive the expression for put-call forward parity by starting with the expression for put-call parity and replacing S_0 in the put-call parity equation with $F(0,T)/(1 + RFR)^T$.

- $F(0,T) = S_0 \times (1 + RFR)^T$ so $S_0 = F(0,T) / (1 + RFR)^T$ ... (See Equation 1)

LOS 57n: Explain how the value of an option is determined using a one-period binomial model. Vol 6, pp 100–104

Binomial Valuation of Options

Assumptions

- Time moves in discrete (not continuous) increments.
- Given the current price of the underlying asset, over the next period the price can move to one of two possible new prices.

The One-Period Binomial Model

In the one-period binomial model, the price of the underlying stock starts off at a given level, S, and can either:

- Move up by a factor of u to a new price, S^+, one period later with a probability of q; or
- Move down by a factor of d to a new price, S^-, one period later with a probability of $1 - q$.
- Note that q and $1 - q$ are actual or real probabilities of the up and down movements respectively.

Therefore:

- $u = S^+/S$ and $d = S^-/S$; and
- $S^+ = Su$ and $S^- = Sd$.

Now let's bring in a European call option on the stock that expires in the next period and has an exercise price denoted by X. (See Figure 6-1.)

- If the price of the stock in the next period equals S^+, the value of the call option (c^+) will equal $Max(0, S^+ - X)$, which represents its exercise value or the payoff at expiration.
- If the price of the stock in the next period equals S^-, the value of the call option (c^-) will equal $Max(0, S^- - X)$, which represents its exercise value or the payoff at expiration.

The aim of this exercise is to determine the price of the call option today (c).

Figure 6-1: One-Period Binomial Model

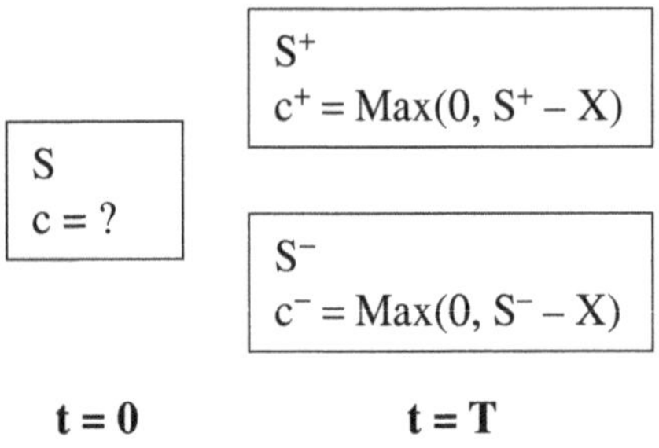

S c = ?	S^+ $c^+ = Max(0, S^+ - X)$
	S^- $c^- = Max(0, S^- - X)$

t = 0   **t = T**

Now suppose that we are given the following information:

- S = $100
- u = 1.75
- d = 0.75
- X = 100

We can calculate c^+ and c^- as follows:

- $S^+ = 100 (1.75) = \$175$
- $c^+ = \text{Max} (0, 175 - 100) = \$75$
- $S^- = 100 (0.75) = \$75$
- $c^- = \text{Max} (0, 75 - 100) = \$0$

The call can take a value of $75 (if the stock price goes up) or $0 (if the stock price goes down) at expiration. Therefore, the call is a risky investment. Now suppose that we want to (1) **short** this call option today and (2) go **long** on n number of stocks such that the overall portfolio is risk-free (i.e., it maintains the same value regardless of the stock price in the next time period). Our portfolio (we'll call it Portfolio H) can be represented by nS – c.

$$H = nS - c$$

- If the stock price goes up (to $175) in the next period, the value of our portfolio will be $H^+ = nS^+ - c^+ = n(175) - 75$
  - The value of the stock holding will be n times the new stock price, $175.
  - The call will be in-the-money so our short position on the call will result in a payoff of –$75.
- If the stock price goes down (to $75) in the next period, the value of our portfolio will be $H^- = nS^- - c^- = n(75) - 0$
  - The value of the stock holding will be n times the new stock price, $75.
  - The call will be out-of-the money so our short position on the call will result in a payoff of 0.

In order for this portfolio to be risk-free (i.e., for the overall portfolio value to be the same in either scenario—that is, regardless of the stock price), n(175) – 75 must equal n(75) – 0. We can therefore, solve for the value of n that results in a risk-free portfolio:

$$n(175) - 75 = n(75) - 0$$
$$n = 0.75$$

The following table proves that a portfolio consisting of a long position on 0.75 units of stock and a short position on one call option will result in same value at the end of the next period regardless of whether the stock price increases or decreases.

Position	Value Today (H)	Value in Up State (H⁺)	Value in Down State (H⁻)
Long 0.75 stock	0.75 × 100 = $75	0.75 × 175 = 131.25	0.75 × 75 = 56.25
Short 1 call	–c	– (175 – 100) = –75	0
Overall	**75 – c**	**56.25**	**56.25**

From this example, you should be able to understand that for Portfolio H to be risk-free:

- H^+ should equal H^-
- $(nS^+ - c^+)$ should equal $(nS^- - c^-)$

Therefore (making n the subject):

$$n = \frac{c^+ - c^-}{S^+ - S^-}$$

We have already proved that Portfolio H is a risk-free portfolio (it will have the same value in the next period regardless of which way the stock price moves). This means that Portfolio H should grow in value at the risk-free rate. Therefore:

- $H^+ = H(1 + r)$
- $H^- = H(1 + r)$

Now we work with the following three expressions that we have already derived to solve for the value of the call option today, c.

$$S^- = Sd \qquad \text{... Equation 4}$$

$$n = \frac{c^+ - c^-}{S^+ - S^-} = \frac{c^+ - c^-}{(u-d)s} \qquad \text{... Equation 5}$$

$$H^- = H(1+r) \rightarrow ns - c = \frac{nS^- - c^-}{(1+r)} \qquad \text{... Equation 6}$$

You do NOT have to know this derivation for the exam. Just know Equations 7 and 8.

Inserting Equation 4 and Equation 5 in place of S^- and n in Equation 6:

$$\left(\frac{c^+ - c^-}{(u-d)\cancel{s}}\right)\cancel{s} - c = \frac{\left(\dfrac{c^+ - c^-}{(u-d)\cancel{s}}\right)(d\cancel{s}) - c^-}{1+r}$$

$$\left(\frac{c^+ - c^-}{u-d}\right) - \left[\frac{\left(\dfrac{c^+ - c^-}{u-d}\right)d - c^-}{(1+r)}\right] = c$$

$$\left(\frac{c^+ - c^-}{u-d}\right) - \frac{1}{(1+r)}\left[\left(\frac{c^+ - c^-}{u-d}\right)d - c^-\right] = c$$

$$\frac{1}{(1+r)}\left[\frac{(c^+ - c^-)(1+r)}{(u-d)} - \frac{(c^+ - c^-)d}{(u-d)} + c^-\right] = c$$

$$c = \frac{1}{(1+r)}\left[\frac{c^+ + c^+ r - c^- - c^- r - c^+ d + c^- d}{(u-d)} + c^-\right]$$

$$c = \frac{1}{(1+r)}\left[\frac{c^+(1+r-d) - c^-(1+r-d)}{(u-d)} + c^-\right]$$

Taking $\pi = \dfrac{(1+r-d)}{(u-d)}$ we get

$$c = \frac{1}{(1+r)}(\pi c^+ - \pi c^- + c^-)$$

$$c = \frac{1}{(1+r)}\left[\pi c^+ + (1-\pi)c^-\right]$$

Therefore:

$$c = \frac{\pi c^+ + (1-\pi)c^-}{(1+r)} \qquad \text{...Equation 7}$$

where:

$$\pi = \frac{(1+r-d)}{(u-d)} \qquad \text{...Equation 8}$$

Looking at Equation 7, the price of the call option can be viewed as the probability-weighted average of the two possible next-period call values (c^+ and c^-) discounted at the one-period risk-free rate. Do not confuse π and $1 - \pi$ with the actual probabilities of up and down movements (q and $1 - q$). One of the important takeaways here is that in this approach we do not need the actual probabilities of up and down movements to determine the value of the call. The approach that we have used to value the call is known as risk-neutral valuation, where the options are valued as though investors are risk-neutral, and they value assets by computing their expected future value and discounting it at the risk-free rate. The probabilities computed in the model, π and $1 - \pi$, are known as risk-neutral probabilities and they are just synthetic or pseudo probabilities. They produce a weighted average of the two possible call values in the next period, a type of expected future value, which is then discounted at the risk-free rate.

Also note that the volatility of the underlying is reflected in the difference between S^+ and S^- (which also drives the difference between c^+ and c^-). The greater the volatility of the underlying, the greater the difference between S^+ and S^-, and between c^+ and c^-. As S^+ increases, c^+ increases, but as S^- decreases, c^- remains at 0 (the option's value cannot fall below 0). The end result of greater volatility would be a higher option value (which confirms what we earlier said about the direct relationship between call option values and volatility of the underlying).

Example 6-1: One-Period Binomial Model

Pluto Inc.'s stock is currently trading at $40. Calculate the value of an at-the-money call option on the stock given that the stock can either go up by 60% or down by 37.5% over the next period. The risk-free rate equals 6%.

Solution:

We first compute the two possible values of the stock:

$S^+ = Su = 40 \times (1 + 0.6) = \$64$
$S^- = Sd = 40 \times (1 - 0.375) = \$25$

Then we calculate the intrinsic value of the call option at expiration in either scenario:

$c^+ = Max(0, S^+ - X) = Max(0, 64 - 40) = \$24$
$c^- = Max(0, S^- - X) = Max(0, 25 - 40) = \$0$

Next we compute the risk-neutral probabilities:

$$\pi = \frac{1 + 0.06 - 0.625}{1.6 - 0.625} = 0.4462$$

$$1 - \pi = 1 - 0.4462 = 0.5538$$

Now we can calculate the value of the call option today as:

$$c = \frac{(24 \times 0.4462) + (0 \times 0.5538)}{1.06} = \$10.10$$

Binomial Tree

```
                     ┌─────────────────────────┐
                     │ S⁺ = Su = $64           │
                     │ C⁺ = Max(0, S⁺ − X)     │
                     │ C⁺ = Max(0, 64 − 40)    │
  ┌──────────┐       └─────────────────────────┘
  │ S = $40  │
  │ c = ?    │       ┌─────────────────────────┐
  └──────────┘       │ S⁻ = sd = $25           │
                     │ C⁻ = Max(0, S⁻ − X)     │
                     │ C⁻ = Max(0, 25 − 40)    │
                     └─────────────────────────┘

      t = 0                   t = T
```

One-Period Binomial Arbitrage Opportunity

If the actual price of the call option is different from the value computed from the binomial model, there is an arbitrage opportunity.

- If the price of the option is *greater* than the value computed from the model, the option is overpriced. To exploit this opportunity we would sell the option and buy n units of the underlying stock for each option sold.

- If the price of the option is *lower* than the value computed from the model, the option is underpriced. To exploit this opportunity we would buy the option and sell n units of the underlying stock for each option purchased.

$$n = \frac{c^+ - c^-}{S^+ - S^-}$$

This value, n, is also known as the hedge ratio. It is also known as the option's delta, which we will study in great depth at Level II.

Example 6-2: One-Period Binomial Arbitrage Opportunity

Continuing from Example 6-1, suppose that the call option is actually selling for $11.50. Illustrate how an investor may exploit this arbitrage opportunity given that she trades 1,000 call options.

Solution:

Since the call option is selling for more than it is actual worth ($11.50 versus $10.10), it is overpriced. The investor should sell the option and buy n units of the underlying stock.

$$n = \frac{c^+ - c^-}{S^+ - S^-} = \frac{24 - 0}{64 - 25} = 0.6154$$

The investor should purchase 0.6154 units of the underlying stock for every option sold. Given that the investor trades 1,000 options, she should purchase approximately 615 shares (= 1,000 × 0.6154).

Her initial investment is calculated as:

Initial investment = (615 × $40) – (1,000 × $11.50) = $13,100

At the end of the period, the possible values of her portfolio can be calculated as:

$H^+ = nS^+ - c^+ = (615 \times \$64) - (1{,}000 \times \$24) = \$15{,}360$
$H^- = nS^- - c^- = (615 \times \$25) - (1{,}000 \times \$0) = \$15{,}375$

Since the investor initially invested $13,100 and ends up with $15,360, her total return is calculated as:

(15,360 / 13,100)−1 = 17.25%

This return is risk-free and is higher than the current risk-free rate of 6%. The pursuit of arbitrage profits will lead other investors to sell the call option on the stock as well, which will cause its price to decline until it reaches $10.10. The specific steps that investors will take to exploit the arbitrage opportunity are listed below:

Today:
- Borrow $13,100 for one year at 6%.
- Buy the hedged portfolio (purchase 615 shares of stock and write 1,000 calls) with an outlay of $13,100.

One year later:
- Sell the hedged portfolio for $15,360. The portfolio will be worth this amount regardless of the price of the underlying stock.
- Repay the borrowed funds along with interest. The total amount comes to $13,886 (= 13,100 × 1.06).
- The arbitrage profit equals $1,474 (= $15,360 – $13,886).

Binomial Put Option Pricing

To price a put option using the binomial model, we perform the same basic steps that we just described for a call, except that we use the put exercise rules instead of the call exercise rules to compute the intrinsic values of the option at expiration. The payoff of a put option equals:

$$\text{Put payoff} = \text{Max}\,(0, X - S_T)$$

Recall from Example 10 that the company's share is currently selling for $40. Further, since she is writing the call options, her initial investment is reduced by $11,500 (= 1,000 × $11.50).

Example 6-3: Valuing a Put Option

Atlas Inc.'s stock is currently trading at $50. Calculate the value of a European put option on the stock with an exercise price of $55 given that the stock can either go up by 40% or down by 25% over the next period. The risk-free rate equals 6%.

Solution:

We first compute the two possible values of the stock:

$S^+ = Su = 50 \times (1 + 0.4) = \$70$
$S^- = Sd = 50 \times (1 - 0.25) = \$37.50$

The values under the two scenarios should be the same. However, they differ slightly here because we rounded off the hedge ratio (n) to the nearest whole number. Going forward, we have used a portfolio value of $15,360 in the next period.

Then we calculate the intrinsic value of the put option at expiration in either scenario:

$p^+ = \text{Max}(0, X - S^+) = \text{Max}(0, 55 - 70) = \$0$
$p^- = \text{Max}(0, X - S^-) = \text{Max}(0, 55 - 37.50) = \$17.50$

Next we compute the risk-neutral probabilities:

$$\pi = \frac{1 + 0.06 - 0.75}{1.4 - 0.75} = 0.4769$$

$$1 - \pi = 1 - 0.4769 = 0.5231$$

Now we can calculate the value of the put option today as:

$$p = \frac{(0 \times 0.4769) + (17.50 \times 0.5231)}{1.06} = \$8.64$$

Binomial Put Option Pricing

$S = \$50$
$p = \$8.64$

$S^+ = Su = \$70$
$p^+ = Max\ (0, X - S^+)$
$p^+ = Max\ (0, \$55 - \$70) = \$0$

$S^- = Sd = \$37.50$
$p^- = Max\ (0, X - S^-)$
$c^- = Max\ (0, \$55 - \$37.5) = \$17.50$

$t = 0$ $t = T = 1$

LESSON 7: OPTION CONTRACTS PART 3: AMERICAN OPTION PRICING

LOS 57o: Explain under which circumstances the values of European and American options differ. Vol 6, pp 104–107

American Option Pricing

American options have every characteristic of European options, plus they come with the added flexibility that they can be exercised at any time prior to expiration. So as a starting point we can say that American call and put options must be worth at least as much as European call and put options respectively.

- $C_0 \geq c_0$
- $P_0 \geq p_0$

American options can be exercised at any time prior to, or at, expiration. The minimum value that any American option can take must be its exercise value because a payoff equal to the exercise value can be realized immediately by exercising it. If the American option were selling for less than its exercise value, whoever purchases it can immediately realize a payoff equal to its exercise value (by exercising it) and earn a risk-free arbitrage profit. Therefore, as a second step, we can say that American call and put options must be worth at least as much as their exercise values.

- Minimum value of an American call option = $Max\ [0, (S_0 - X)]$
- Minimum value of an American put option = $Max\ [0, (X - S_0)]$

Now notice that the minimum value of the American call option that we have determined (its exercise value, $Max\ [0, (S_0 - X)]$) is actually mathematically *lower* than the minimum value of the European call option that we determine in an earlier section, $Max\ [0, S_0 - X/(1+ RFR)^T]$. An American call option offers more flexibility, and theoretically should not trade for less than a European option with identical characteristics. Because the American call option must be worth at least as much as a European call, we revise its minimum value of the American call upward to the same level as the European call, $Max\ [0, S_0 - X/(1+ RFR)^T]$.

The minimum value of the American put, Max $[0, (X - S_0)]$, is greater than that of the European put, Max $[0, X/(1 + RFR)^T - S_0]$, so we do not need to make a similar upward adjustment to the minimum value of the American put. When it is in-the-money, the American put option can be exercised immediately for a payoff of $X - S_0$.

Therefore, we can now conclude that:

- Minimum value of an American call option = Max $[0, (S_0 - X/(1+ RFR)^T]$.
- Minimum value of an American put option = Max $[0, (X - S_0)]$.

Once you have digested all of the above, sit back and think about what we have really concluded. What we are saying about American calls is that they are always worth more in the market {Minimum value = Max $[0, (S_0 - X/(1+ RFR)^T]$} than their exercise value [Max $[0, (S_0 - X)]$. This implies that an American call option will never be exercised early, which probably seems counterintuitive.

Consider a deep in-the-money American call. You might think that if an investor does not expect the price of the underlying to rise any further, she should exercise the call and maximize (in her opinion) her payoff. But what we are saying is that she would be better off selling the call in the market, as the option's price would be higher than its exercise value. During the remaining term of the option, the underlying could increase in value (taking the option deeper-in-the money) or decrease in value (reducing the exercise value of the option). However, the investor's loss is limited on the downside (to the option premium) while there is no cap on the upside. The disadvantage of not exercising the option prior to expiration (possibility of the option moving out-of-the money) is outweighed by the advantage of not exercising the option prior to expiration (possibility of the option moving further in-the-money).

Having said all this, early exercise of an American call option may be warranted when the underlying asset makes payments during the life of the option. When a stock pays a dividend, its value falls by the amount of the dividend on the ex-dividend date. If the ex-dividend date is very close to the option's expiration date, and the dividend is significant enough that it reduces the price of the stock below the exercise price (and takes the call option out-of-the-money) after the ex-dividend date, early exercise of the American call option would be warranted. The investor would effectively capture the dividend and avoid the ex-dividend drop in the price of the underlying.

On the other hand, if there are significant costs of carry on the underlying, there is less of a reason to exercise the call option early. You would rather own an option on the underlying than the underlying itself, as the option position does not entail any costs of carry.

Now let's talk about American puts. It would be beneficial to exercise an American put prior to expiration when a company is in or nearing bankruptcy, and its stock price is close to zero. In such a situation, it is better for the put option holder to exercise the option immediately and realize a payoff equal to the exercise price (exercise value = $X - 0 = X$) as opposed to waiting for expiration to receive the same payoff. Because of the potential benefit when the possibility of bankruptcy exists, an American put is almost always worth more than a European put. Note that even if the price of the underlying does not go to 0, there is a point where the put is so deep in-the-money that early exercise would make sense. The potential upside on the put position on a distressed company is limited (the stock can only fall all the way to zero; it cannot go any lower), while the downside (assuming the put is already deep in-the-money) can be significant (if the underlying recovers). The same argument does not hold for American calls because they offer an unlimited upside.

Dividends and coupon interest discourage early exercise for puts. As a put holder, you would rather wait until right after the dividend or coupon is paid to exercise the put (as the price of the underlying would fall). Carrying costs on the underlying, which discourage exercise for calls, encourage exercise for puts.

READING 58: INTRODUCTION TO ALTERNATIVE INVESTMENTS

LESSON 1: THE BASICS OF ALTERNATIVE INVESTMENTS

Basic Forms and Categories of Alternative Investments

LOS 58a: Compare alternative investments with traditional investments. Vol 6, pp 124–128

Alternative versus Traditional Investments

Investments in shares of stock, bonds, and cash equivalents have historically been identified as being traditional in nature, mostly because they have traded in relatively highly liquid markets for more than a century. In today's markets, however, institutional investors and even high net worth individuals seek to enhance returns while diversifying by adding alternative investments as an asset class. Alternative investments include almost any asset that is not traditional in nature, from real estate and commodities to rare coins and artwork.

Alternative investments can be made directly or indirectly. For example, some investors purchase gold or specific real properties as direct investments, but most investors gain exposure by purchasing ownership in private equity funds, hedge funds, exchange-traded funds, or other special vehicles designed for active management styles. These investors seek either absolute returns throughout the economic cycle or relative returns against a benchmark by finding assets that have low correlations with traditional securities. Either way, these funds give managers flexibility to use derivatives and leverage, to make investments in illiquid assets, and to take short positions.

Investments in these special vehicles are generally characterized by:

- High fees.
- Large size of investments.
- Low diversification of managers and investments within the alternative investment portfolio.
- High use of leverage.
- Restrictions on redemptions.

Other characteristics that are common to many alternative investments include:

- Illiquidity of underlying investments.
- Narrow manager specialization.
- Low correlation with traditional investments.
- Low level of regulation and less transparency.
- Limited and potentially problematic historical risk and return data.
- Unique legal and tax considerations.

Despite the rapid growth in assets under management in alternative investments, they still make up a relatively small proportion of total investable assets. One potential explanation for this lack of popularity is that the correlations between alternative investments and traditional ones tend to converge during times of economic stress.

Example 1-1

Catherine Tills is a high net worth investor with a 50% allocation to traditional equities, a 40% allocation to traditional corporate and government bonds, and the remainder allocated to alternative investments. Tills's alternative investments consist solely of Hollywood movie memorabilia, including the original fedora worn by a famous archaeologist in a series of four movies, the sports car driven by a British secret agent, and the white suit worn by a disco dancer in a famous 1977 movie.

Identify two differences and two similarities between the two types of investments made by Tills.

Solution:

Similarities: Both traditional and alternative investments are made to satisfy the return objective outlined in the policy statement. Tills has most likely added the memorabilia to benefit from lower correlations and potentially higher returns. A second similarity would be that each investment is consistent with her long-term investment strategy. Tills is not likely to generate significant short-term realized returns on her memorabilia investment, which makes it similar to debt and equity investments in that they both have long-term horizons.

Differences: There is very likely to be a wide difference in the liquidity and even marketability of the memorabilia compared to debt and equity securities. In addition, there is typically complete historical data on debt and equity securities, but very limited return data on memorabilia.

LOS 58b: Describe categories of alternative investments. Vol 6, pp 128–129

Categories of Alternative Investments

Alternative investments may broadly be categorized as:

- *Hedge funds:* These are private investment vehicles that manage portfolios of securities and derivative positions using a variety of strategies (including taking long and short positions, and significant leverage). Their aim is to achieve positive absolute returns irrespective of the performance of the broad market.
- *Private equity funds:* These invest in (1) non–publicly traded companies, which may be either start-ups or established companies, and (2) public companies with the intention of taking them private. Private equity funds include:
    Leveraged buyout (LBO) funds: These funds borrow money to finance the acquisition of a company. They focus on acquiring established, profitable, cash-generating companies with solid customer bases and proven products.
    Venture capital (VC) funds: These funds specialize in providing financing to start-ups or young companies with high growth potential.
- *Real estate:* Real estate investments include investments in buildings and/or land, either directly or indirectly. They include:

Private commercial real estate equity (e.g., ownership of an office building).

Private commercial real estate debt (e.g., directly issued loans or mortgages on commercial property).

Public real estate equity (e.g., real estate investment trusts [REITs]).

Public commercial real estate debt (e.g., commercial mortgage-backed securities).

- *Commodities:* Investors can directly invest in physical commodity products or invest in businesses engaged in the production of physical commodities. Investors can also gain exposure to commodities through commodity futures contracts and funds benchmarked to commodity indexes.
- *Infrastructure:* Infrastructure assets are real, capital-intensive, long-lived assets that are intended for public use and provide essential services (e.g., roads, dams, and schools). Typically, infrastructure assets are financed, owned, and operated by governments, but of late the private sector has been increasingly investing in them. Most investment in infrastructure occurs indirectly through shares in infrastructure companies, private equity funds, listed funds, and unlisted mutual funds that invest in infrastructure.
- Other alternative investments include tangible assets (e.g., art, antique furniture, stamps, etc.) and intangible assets (e.g., patents).

Example 1-2

The Atlantic Endowment Fund (AEF) currently has zero allocation to alternative investments and wants exposure to grains and infrastructure. AEF is most likely to invest in:

- A. REITs and mortgage-backed securities.
- B. Hedge funds and leveraged buyout funds.
- C. Commodity futures contracts and private equity.

Solution:

The correct answer is C.

Corn or wheat futures contracts will provide exposure to the grain market, and private equity funds can invest in firms that will complete infrastructure projects.

LOS 58c: Describe potential benefits of alternative investments in the context of portfolio management. Vol 6, pp 132, 138–145

Benefits of Alternative Investments

Portfolio managers generally match their clients' risk and return objectives by investing in well-diversified portfolios that have assets with low or even negative correlations. This is not possible with many traditional assets but can be achieved with the addition of alternative investments into the portfolio.

Investors are usually attracted to alternative investments because of their diversification benefits. Historically, the returns on some categories of alternative investments have been found to have relatively low correlations with returns on traditional investments over long periods. As a result, the risk-return profile of a traditional investment portfolio can be improved by adding alternative investments to it. There are challenges, however, to forming such a portfolio. These include:

- Obtaining reliable measures of risk and return.
- Identifying the appropriate allocation.
- Selecting portfolio managers.

In addition, most categories of alternative investments have historically exhibited higher returns than traditional investments. These higher returns can be explained by:

- Tax advantages (e.g., for REITs).
- Portfolio managers' ability to exploit mispricings.
- Return premiums for illiquidity.
- Significant use of leverage.

Financial analysts, however, must consider the following when evaluating the historical record of alternative investments:

- Reported returns and standard deviations are averages, which may not be representative of returns and standard deviations for subperiods within the reported period, or for future periods.
- The volatility of returns of alternative investments, as well as the correlation of returns with those of traditional asset classes, may be underestimated. This results from the fact that returns on many alternative investments (e.g., direct real estate and private equity) are computed using estimated values rather than actual market prices.
- Hedge fund indexes may be inherently biased upward due to self-selection bias, backfill bias, and survivorship bias.
  Self-selection bias: Since disclosure of performance data to hedge fund indexes is voluntary, fund managers tend to reveal their performance only if it is impressive.
  Backfill bias: When a fund's performance is included in an index, its past performance is also included in the database. Therefore, only managers with consistently superior track records choose to disclose their performance and enter an index.
  Survivorship bias: This occurs due to the fact that unsuccessful funds tend to go out of business and only well-performing funds are willing to disclose their historical performance for inclusion in hedge fund indexes.
- Differences in weightings and constituents in index construction can have a significant impact on the indexes and their results and comparability.

Besides considering mean return and average standard deviation, portfolio managers also take into account other measures of performance, including historical downside frequencies and worst return in a month, for potential portfolio combinations.

Example 1-3

Christopher Franks, a high net worth investor with a USD 2.5 million equity portfolio, is considering the purchase of a building that is currently under lease to the U.S. federal government. The lease is transferable and expires in 15 years. The price of the building is USD 1.2 million, and the annual lease payments are USD 150,000 per year for the next 5 years, at which time the terms can be renegotiated, but the government has the option to cancel the lease after 5 years. Franks estimates the correlation coefficient between the building and his equity portfolio to be 0.14.

Identify two benefits that Franks can reasonably expect if he purchases this building and two issues that should concern him in the context of portfolio management.

Solution:

Clearly, Franks will benefit from the income generated by the property, at least for 5 years. The internal rate of return (IRR) of the investment is approximately 9% if the payments extend to the 15-year mark. Diversification also appears to be a key benefit with a correlation of only 0.14. The first concern Franks should have is with the accuracy of the correlation data on which his estimate was based. Although buildings leased to governments most likely have low correlations with equity securities, the precise diversification benefit is less easily measured. A second concern should be the manner in which this building fits into Franks' strategic asset allocation. The alternative investment allocation would be approximately 33%, and this is not likely to be optimal. The ability of the government to cancel the lease is another concern, but not one that would prevent Franks from making the investment.

LESSON 2: MAJOR TYPES OF ALTERNATIVE INVESTMENTS, PART I: HEDGE FUNDS

Hedge Funds

LOS 58d: Describe hedge funds, including, as applicable, strategies, subcategories, potential benefits and risks, fee structures, and due diligence. Vol 6, pp 133–145

General Characteristics of Hedge Funds

Hedge funds were created around the end of World War II to provide wealthier individual investors greater access to a wide variety of investment opportunities. Hedge funds are designed to give the hedge fund manager more choices than the traditional mutual fund manager has. Hedge funds have the ability to invest in any asset that can increase in value over time, as long as the asset involves legal activity and the hedge fund manager discloses the investment strategy.

Consider a list of critical points regarding hedge funds:

- Hedge funds are aggressively managed portfolios of investments. They undertake a wide range of investment strategies that may involve the use of leverage, derivative products, multiple asset classes, and/or short positions.
- They aim to generate high returns (either on an absolute basis or relative to a specified benchmark). Further, they are not constrained by any significant investment restrictions, so they enjoy more flexibility in decision making.
- They are set up as private investment partnerships, where the fund is the general partner (GP) and the investors are limited partners (LPs).

  The GP (management firm) receives a base fee (based on assets under management) and an incentive fee (based on performance).

  LPs own a fractional interest in the partnership based on amounts invested.

  There is a limit on the number of LPs that a fund can have. Further, LPs must be "qualified investors" in that they must possess adequate wealth, sufficient liquidity, and a certain degree of investment knowledge.

  Since fund investments are not offered to the general public, hedge funds are regulated to a much lower extent than are traditional investments.

- Hedge funds usually impose restrictions on redemptions. They also usually impose a lockup period during which investors are not allowed to make withdrawals or redeem shares from the fund. In addition, investors may be required to give prior notice of their intent to redeem. This notice period is typically between 30 and 90 days in length. Investors may also be charged a fee to redeem shares.

The increase in interest in hedge funds has led to the emergence of funds of funds. These are funds that invest in a number of hedge funds, hence diversifying across hedge fund strategies, investment regions, and management styles. Funds of funds allow smaller investors access to hedge funds in which they may not be able to invest directly. They possess expertise in conducting due diligence on hedge funds and may be able to negotiate better redemption terms. Funds of funds, however, have an extra layer of fees (i.e., the managers of funds of funds are paid an additional layer of fees on top of the fees paid to the underlying hedge fund managers).

Hedge Fund Strategies

Hedge Fund Research, Inc. (HFRI) identifies the following four broad categories of hedge fund strategies:

1. *Event-driven strategies:* These strategies take a bottom-up view (i.e., they begin with company analysis and then aggregate and analyze a larger group). They focus on short-term events that usually involve potential changes in corporate structure (e.g., acquisitions and restructurings) that are expected to affect individual companies. Hedge funds following these strategies may take long and short positions in common stock and preferred stock as well as debt securities and options. HFRI further subdivides this category into:

    Merger arbitrage: When a merger/acquisition is announced, there may be an expectation that the acquirer will overpay for the acquisition, and perhaps suffer from increased leverage. As a result, merger arbitrage managers buy the stock of the company being acquired and sell the stock of the acquiring company. Risks of this strategy include the possibility that (1) the merger/acquisition may not occur, and (2) the hedge fund may not be able to close its positions in time.

    Distressed/restructuring: These strategies focus on the securities of companies that are in financial distress, as they are typically available at deeply discounted prices. Fund managers take long positions in (undervalued) securities of companies that they believe will benefit from a successful restructuring.

    Activist: These strategies focus on the purchase of sufficient equity in a company to be able to influence its policies and strategic direction, with the eventual aim of increasing company value. Activist hedge funds differ from private equity funds in that they operate in the public equity market.

    Special situations: These strategies focus on companies that are engaged in restructuring activities other than merger/acquisition and bankruptcy. Examples of such activities include security issuance/repurchase, special capital distributions, and spin-offs.

2. *Relative value strategies:* These strategies seek to profit from pricing discrepancies (or short-term mispricings) between related securities. Examples of relative value strategies include the following:

    Fixed-income convertible arbitrage: These strategies seek to exploit a perceived mispricing between a convertible bond and its component parts (the straight bond and the embedded option on the stock). They typically involve purchasing convertible bonds and selling the same issuer's common stock.

    Fixed-income asset-backed: These strategies focus on price discrepancies between a variety of asset-backed securities (ABS) and mortgage-backed securities (MBS).

    Fixed-income general: These strategies seek to profit from differences in relative values of fixed-income securities, such as between two corporate issuers, between corporate and government issuers, between different parts of the same issuer's capital structure, or between different parts of an issuer's yield curve.

    Volatility: These strategies take positions on options to go long or short on market volatility, either in a specific asset class or across asset classes.

    Multistrategy: These strategies seek to profit from differences in relative values within or across several asset classes. They basically look for investment opportunities wherever they might exist.

3. *Macro strategies:* These strategies take a top-down view as they focus on the overall macroeconomic environment, taking long and short positions in broad markets (e.g., equity indexes, currencies, commodities, etc.) that are expected to benefit based on the manager's view regarding overall market direction.

4. *Equity hedge strategies:* These strategies take a bottom-up view and focus on public equity markets, taking long and short positions in equities and equity derivatives. Examples of such strategies include:

   Market neutral: These strategies use quantitative (technical) and/or fundamental analysis to identify under- and overvalued securities. They take long positions in undervalued equities and short positions in overvalued equities, while at the same time maintaining zero-beta exposure to overall market risk.

   Fundamental growth: These strategies use fundamental analysis to identify companies that are expected to achieve high growth. They take long positions in stocks of those companies to profit from capital appreciation.

   Fundamental value: These strategies use fundamental analysis to identify undervalued shares, and take long positions in them. Note that in this case it is the vehicle structure (not the type of assets invested in) that results in classification as an alternative investment.

   Quantitative directional: These strategies use technical analysis to identify under- and overvalued equities, and then take long positions in undervalued stocks and short positions in overvalued stocks. Their levels of net long or net short exposure, however, vary depending on their expectations of overall market direction (i.e., they do take on exposure to market risk).

   Short bias: These strategies use technical and/or fundamental analysis to primarily identify overvalued securities and take short positions in those securities. Their overall exposure to the market tends to be negative, even though they may take smaller long positions.

   Sector specific: These strategies use technical and fundamental analysis to identify opportunities in particular sectors that they specialize in.

Example 2-1

Eric Lynne is portfolio manager with Arctic Capital (AC), a hedge fund that uses many different types of strategies to enhance returns. He makes the following decisions:

1. Lynne takes a long position in Asia Financial (AF) while taking an opposite short position in AF's chief competitor, Bank of Pacific (BoP), believing that AF will dominate performance in the mortgage lending market in the coming months. Lynne also expects AC's beta for its financial services sector investment to be –0.06. Lynne further expects BoP's market share to decline in the corporate lending market.

2. Lynne expects the U.S. broad large-cap index to increase in value because of an anticipated surge in U.S. consumer spending. He also expects U.S. imports of Canadian lumber to be a large part of the spending increase as consumers ramp up construction of residential housing. Lynne takes a long position in the U.S. index and a short position in the USD to take advantage of his expectations.

> 3. Lynne purchases a convertible bond issued by Back Track Corp. (BTC) while simultaneously combining a short sale on BTC with a purchase of put options on the shares of BTC.
> 4. Lynne takes the long position in Midwest Energy (ME) because of a recently announced long-term share repurchase strategy announced by the executives at ME. Lynne believes ME's board will eventually repurchase more shares than originally announced.
>
> Identify each type of broad hedge fund strategy pursued by Lynne.
>
> **Solution:**
>
> 1. Market-neutral, equity hedge strategy.
> 2. Macro strategy.
> 3. Fixed-income convertible arbitrage, relative value strategy.
> 4. Special situations, event-driven strategy.

Potential Benefits of Hedge Funds

It would be inappropriate to make generalized statements regarding hedge fund performance, given the wide variety of hedge fund strategies. A specific strategy or fund may generate very high returns in some years, and then perform poorly in subsequent years. Studies that have analyzed data over long periods of time suggest that there is a less than perfect positive correlation between hedge fund returns and equity returns. This gives rise to diversification opportunities, which strengthen the case for investment in hedge funds. However, there have been (shorter) episodes during which there has been a strong positive correlation between the two. Further, the correlation between hedge fund returns and stock market performance tends to increase in times of financial crisis. Finally, as the hedge fund market has become more crowded, funds have begun to take on more risk to generate competitive returns.

Hedge Fund Risk Considerations

Hedge funds may use leverage to generate higher returns. While leverage has the potential to improve returns on investment, it could also magnify losses. Hedge funds may leverage their portfolios by borrowing capital and/or using derivatives.

- The smaller the margin requirements on these loans/derivative contracts, the greater the leverage that is available to the hedge fund.
- Margin calls can also magnify losses if the hedge fund is forced to liquidate or close certain positions. If the fund's position is relatively large, the liquidation (closing) of the position can have a significant adverse impact on price.
- Investor redemptions may also magnify losses for hedge funds. Redemptions usually occur when a hedge fund is performing poorly. They cause the hedge fund to liquidate certain positions quickly (which can adversely impact realized prices) and incur transaction costs.

Example 2-2

Cartwright Capital (CC) is a hedge fund that currently uses both option contracts and futures contracts to gain exposure to currencies, small-cap equities, and soft commodities. In addition, CC uses swap contracts to make volatility bets in both the commodities and the equity markets. CC's historical performance has placed it in the top 10% of similarly managed funds. In general, CC predominately uses market-neutral and macroeconomic strategies in both equity and fixed-income markets, but expects to increase its use of derivatives in the coming year.

The Hooper Foundation (HF) considers investing in CC. Describe the concerns HF should have before making this investment.

Solution:

HF should realize that the use of derivatives relies heavily on leveraged positions, and, although these positions have likely been successful for CC over the past few years, a main concern would be whether CC can remain successful in using options, futures, and swap contracts. Leverage can truly enhance returns when profits are realized, but it can significantly magnify losses if derivative prices move against CC. In addition, the daily margin requirements in the futures markets might pose a liquidity problem for CC if those investments have negative returns. Finally, HF should make certain the risk-return profile of its beneficiaries matches the strategic plan outlined by the hedge fund.

Due Diligence Issues

Investors should consider a number of issues when investing in hedge funds. Some of the key due diligence points to consider are listed here:

- Investment strategy.
- Investment process.
- Competitive advantage.
- Track record.
- Size and longevity.
- Management style.
- Key-person risk.
- Reputation.
- Investor relations.
- Plans for growth.
- Methodology used for return calculations.
- Systems for risk management.

Regulation of hedge funds is likely to increase in the future, which should help with the due diligence process.

Hedge Fund Fees

Hedge funds usually charge two types of fees: A management fee (also called base fee) is calculated on assets under management. An incentive fee (or performance fee) is based on realized profits. They may be calculated on profits net of management fees or on profits before management fees. Further, incentive fees may be subject to a hurdle rate, or a high-water mark provision:

- A *hurdle rate* defines the minimum return threshold that the fund must earn before any incentive fee is paid.

    A *hard hurdle* means that incentive fees are earned only on the return in excess of the hurdle rate.

    A *soft hurdle* means that incentive fees are earned on all profits, but only if the hurdle rate is met.

- A *high-water mark* refers to the highest value, net of fees, that the fund has reached.

If the hedge fund loses money over a period, the fund must recover those losses and reach a value above the high-water mark in order to receive the incentive fee. High-water mark provisions are put in place so that the hedge fund manager does not earn an incentive fee on the same dollar of investment return more than once.

Fee structures vary across hedge funds. A common fee structure among hedge funds is "2 and 20," which implies a 2% management fee and a 20% incentive fee. Funds of funds typically charge "1 plus 10." Fee structures may also vary across clients of the same hedge fund. Hedge funds may negotiate terms such as fees, lockup periods, and notice periods with potential investors. The effects of fee structures on returns to investors are illustrated in Example 2-3.

LOS 58e: Describe, calculate, and interpret management and incentive fees and net-of-fees returns to hedge funds. Vol 6, pp 139–145

Calculating Fees and Returns

Example 2-3

Bedlam Capital is a hedge fund with an initial investment capital of $100 million. In its first year, the fund earns a return of 40%. The fund charges a 2% management fee based on assets under management at the end of the year and a 25% incentive fee with a hurdle rate of 5% (applicable on the beginning capital position for the year). The ending value of the fund (before fees) for the first 3 years is as follows:

- 2014: $140 million
- 2015: $120 million
- 2016: $145 million

1. Given that the high-water mark provision applies, and that the incentive fee is based on returns in excess of the hurdle rate and is calculated net of management fee, calculate the total fees and investor's effective return for each of the 3 years.
2. Calculate the arithmetic and geometric mean annual returns over the 3-year period based on the fee structure specified in Question 1.
3. Calculate the capital gain to the investor and the total fee paid to the hedge fund over the 3-year period.

Solution:

1. 2014:

   Beginning capital position = $100 million
   Ending value of the fund (provided) = $140 million
   Management fee = 140 × 0.02 = $2.8 million
   Incentive fee = [140m − 100m − (100m × 0.05) − 2.8m] × 0.25 = $8.05m

Note that the incentive fee is based on returns in excess of the hurdle rate ($100m × 0.05) and on returns net of management fees ($2.8 million).

   Total fee = 2.8m + 8.05m = $10.85m
   Investor's effective return = (140m − $10.85m − 100m) / $100m = 29.15%

   2015:

   Beginning capital position = 140m − 10.85m = $129.15m
   Ending value of the fund (provided) = $120m
   Management fee = 120m × 0.02 = $2.4m

Since the fund has declined in value, no incentive fee will be paid.

   Therefore, total fee = $2.4m
   Investor's effective return = (120m − $2.4m − $129.15m) / $129.15m = −8.94%

   2016:

   Beginning capital position = 120m − $2.4m = $117.6m
   Ending value of the fund (provided) = $145m
   Management fee = 145m × 0.02 = $2.9m
   Incentive fee = [$145m − $129.15m − 2.9m − (0.05 × $117.6m)] × 0.25 = $1.7675m

Note that the incentive fee is based on returns in excess of the high-water mark ($129.15m) and on returns net of management fees ($2.9m) and the hurdle rate (0.05 × 145m = 7.25m).

   Total fee = 2.9m + 1.7675m = $4.6675m
   Investor's effective return = (145m − 4.6675m − 117.6m) / 117.6m = 19.33%
   Ending capital position = 145m − 4.6675m = $140.3325m

2. Arithmetic mean annual return = (29.15% − 8.94% + 19.33%) / 3 = 13.18%

   Geometric mean annual return = (140.3325m / 100m)1/3 − 1 = 11.96%

3. Capital gain to the investor = 140.3325m − 100m = $40.3325m

   Fee paid to the hedge fund = 10.85m + 2.4m + 4.6675m = $17.9175m

LOS 58f: Describe issues in valuing and calculating returns on hedge funds. Vol 6, pp 145–148

Hedge Fund Valuation Issues

Valuations are essential for calculating hedge fund performance and satisfying calls for redemption. Market values are used to value traded securities in hedge fund portfolios, but estimated values are used for non-traded securities.

When using market prices for valuing traded securities, it is common practice in the hedge fund industry to use the average of the bid and ask quote. However, it is theoretically more accurate to use the bid prices for long positions and ask prices for short positions, as they reflect the prices at which these positions can be closed.

For highly illiquid or non-traded investments, reliable market value data are unavailable, so values are estimated using statistical models.

Liquidity is a major concern in valuation, especially for strategies involving convertible bonds, collateralized debt obligations, distressed debt, and emerging market fixed-income securities. Even if quoted market prices are available, hedge funds may apply "haircuts" to quoted prices to reflect a liquidity discount. However, since this goes against most generally accepted accounting principles, some funds have started reporting two net asset values (NAVs): a trading NAV and a reporting NAV.

The trading NAV is based on the size of the position held relative to the total amount outstanding in the issue and its trading volume.

The reporting NAV is based on quoted market prices.

LESSON 3: MAJOR TYPES OF ALTERNATIVE INVESTMENTS, PART II: PRIVATE EQUITY

LOS 58d: Describe private equity, including, as applicable, strategies, subcategories, potential benefits and risks, fee structures, and due diligence. Vol 6, pp 148–158

LOS 58f: Describe issues in valuing and calculating returns on private equity. Vol 6, pp 145–148

Private Equity

Privately held firms are typically owned by the company's founders, their relatives, and an expanding group of friends and business associates, at least originally. Over time, however, privately held firms grow and need capital to support that growth. They turn to financial institutions for loans and perhaps other financial institutions like private equity firms that will provide necessary capital.

Private equity (PE) investment strategies include:

- Leveraged buyouts (LBOs).
- Venture capital (VC).
- Development capital.
- Distressed investing.

Private Equity Structure and Fees

Private equity funds are usually structured as partnerships, where outside investors are limited partners (LPs) and the private equity firm (which can manage a number of funds) is the general partner (GP). Most private equity firms charge both a management fee and an incentive fee.

- Management fees are usually calculated as a percentage (usually 1% to 3%) of committed capital, which refers to the amount of capital promised by LPs to the private equity fund. Private equity funds raise committed capital, and then draw down this amount over the next few years as they identify and make investments. Until committed capital is fully drawn down and invested, the management fee is based on committed capital and not on invested capital. Once the committed capital is fully invested, the fee is paid only on the funds remaining in the investment vehicle. Capital is paid back to investors as investments are exited. Therefore, no fee is paid on that portion of their investment.
- Incentive fees are usually earned by the GP only after the LPs have been paid back their initial investments. The GP typically receives 20% of the total profit of the fund as an incentive fee, while the LPs receive 80% of profits (in addition to the return of their initial investments). These distributions may be paid out either (1) as profits are earned over time, or (2) at exit from investments. If incentive fees are paid out as profits are earned over time, the GP may end up receiving more than 20% of the total profit by the time all investments are exited. This occurs when returns on portfolio companies are relatively high in the early years of the fund and decline later. PE partnership agreements usually incorporate clawback provisions to prevent this from happening. These provisions require the GP to return any incentive fees to the LPs until they have received their entire initial investment and the overall profit-sharing ratio conforms to the initially agreed-upon profit split.

In addition to the management and incentive fees, LBO firms may also charge:

- A fee for arranging the buyout of a company.
- A fee if a deal falls through.
- A fee for arranging divestitures of assets after the buyout is complete.

Private Equity Strategies

PE strategies may be categorized as LBOs or VC.

LBOs refer to acquisitions of public companies or established private companies, where debt is used to finance a significant proportion of the acquisition. Cash flows from the acquired company are the primary source of debt service payments while assets of the acquired company serve as collateral for the debt.

LBOs may be categorized as:

- *Management buyouts (MBOs)*, where the company's current management team acquires it.
- *Management buy-ins (MBIs)*, where the current management team is replaced by the acquiring team, which then runs the company.

Companies that are attractive targets for LBOs exhibit the following characteristics:

- Their stock prices are undervalued.
- Their management is willing to enter into a deal.
- They are currently inefficiently managed and have the potential to perform well if managed better.
- They have strong and sustainable cash flows, which is necessary to make interest payments on the increased debt load from the buyout.
- They have low leverage, which makes it easier to raise additional debt to finance a large portion of the purchase price.
- They have a significant amount of physical assets, which can be used as collateral for loans.

LBO managers aim to add value by improving company operations, growing revenue, and eventually increasing profits and cash flows.

It is important to note that returns on LBO transactions are largely dependent on the use of leverage. A typical LBO capital structure usually includes equity, bank debt (leveraged loans), and high-yield bonds, with bank debt providing a larger amount of capital than either equity or high-yield bonds. Mezzanine financing is also sometimes used as an alternative to high-yield bonds. Mezzanine financing refers to issuing debt or preferred shares that come with warrants (similar to options on common stock) or conversion (into common stock) options. Since they are subordinate to both senior and high-yield debt, these instruments usually carry a higher coupon rate. Further, they allow investors to participate in the upside of the company. Bank debt and high-yield bonds often carry covenants that place certain requirements (affirmative covenants) or restrictions (negative covenants) on the company. Bank debt is usually senior to high-yield bonds, so bonds issued to finance an LBO usually receive low quality ratings and must offer high coupon rates to attract investors. The optimal capital structure for an LBO transaction depends on a variety of factors, such as the company's projected cash flows, investor willingness to purchase different types of debt and accept different levels of leverage, the availability of equity, and the required rates of return for equity and different types of debt considering leverage. LBOs are less likely to occur if debt financing is unavailable or costly.

VC funds invest in private companies that have high growth potential. Investments are typically made in the form of equity, but may be in the form of convertible preferred shares or convertible debt. Once capital has been provided to the portfolio company, venture capitalists become actively involved in running the company, often sitting on the board of directors and assuming key management roles. Ultimate returns depend on the company's success in progressing from a start-up to a mature going concern.

VC investments are usually categorized based on the stage of development at which capital is provided to the portfolio company.

- The *formative stage* refers to investments made when the portfolio company is still in the process of being formed. This stage encompasses three financing steps:
  1. *Angel investing* refers to capital provided at the idea stage for the purpose of transforming that idea into a business plan and to evaluate market potential. This stage usually requires a small amount of financing, which is generally provided by individuals (friends and family), rather than by VC funds.
  2. *Seed-stage financing* refers to capital provided for supporting product development and/or marketing efforts. This stage is usually the first stage at which VC funds invest.
  3. *Early-stage financing* (early-stage VC) refers to capital provided to companies that are moving toward operation, but before commercial production and sales have started.

Formative-stage financing is generally done through ordinary or convertible preferred shares. Management retains control over the company.

- Later-stage financing (expansion VC) is provided after the company has commenced commercial production and sales, but before any initial public offering (IPO). Companies may use the funds to expand production facilities or stimulate sales via aggressive marketing and/or product improvements. Financing at this stage is usually provided through equity and debt, and management typically sells control of the company to the VC fund.
- *Mezzanine-stage financing* is provided to prepare the company to go public.

Other private equity strategies include:

- *Development capital* (or *minority equity investing*): This generally involves providing financing to more mature companies to help them expand, restructure operations, enter new markets, or finance major acquisitions. Although development capital is usually sought by private companies, public companies may also sometimes seek private equity capital. These investments are known as "private investment in public equities" (PIPEs).
- *Distressed investing* usually involves buying debt of mature companies that are in financial distress (bankrupt, in default, or likely to default). Distressed debt typically trades at a deep discount to par, and the idea is to benefit from an increase in the price of these securities as the company is turned around. The return on investment depends on the ability of the distressed investor to restructure the company operationally and financially. Distressed investors may assume an active role in trying to turn the company's fortunes around, or may take a more passive role.

Private Equity Exit Strategies

Private equity firms usually hold companies for an average period of 5 years, but holding periods can vary from 6 months to 10 years for individual companies. Determination of the appropriate exit strategy requires an evaluation of industry dynamics, overall economic cycles, interest rates, and company performance. Common exit strategies are the following:

- *Trade sale:* This occurs when a company is sold to a strategic buyer (e.g., a competitor), either through an auction or through a private negotiation.
- *Initial public offering (IPO):* This involves taking the private company public.
- *Recapitalization:* This is a very popular strategy when interest rates are low.

Basically, the private equity company issues debt to fund a dividend distribution to equity holders (including itself). Strictly speaking, this is not really an exit, but recapitalization is considered a prelude to a later exit.

- *Secondary sale:* This involves the sale of a company to another private equity firm or group of investors.
- *Write-off/liquidation:* This occurs if an investment does not perform well. The private equity firm liquidates the portfolio company to move on to other projects.

Example 2-2

Eagle Capital (EC) is a private equity firm specializing in investment in U.S. and Canadian golf courses. EC currently owns three courses:

1. Winter's Haven Golf Club in North Dakota. The course is 6 years old and EC provided the USD 8 million for design and construction costs. EC is 100% owner and is currently in plans to sell the course to a group of local golfers for USD 16 million.
2. Spring Haven Golf Club in Iowa. EC is expected to close on a sale to another private equity firm in which the internal rate of return on the investment is 21%.
3. Autumn Haven Golf Club in Massachusetts. This course has performed well below expectations, with a faulty irrigation system that regularly floods part of the course, local problems with environmental groups concerned about dying fish in the stream that flows around the property, and a significant drop in demand for golf in this part of the country. EC is hoping to find a buyer and will take a substantial loss.

Identify the exit strategy pursued by Eagle Capital in each case.

Solution:

1. Trade sale.
2. Secondary sale.
3. Liquidation.

Private Equity: Diversification Benefits, Performance, and Risk

Studies have shown that:

- Private equity funds have earned higher returns than equities over the past 20 years.
- Based on the standard deviation of historical annual returns, private equity investments (including VC) entail higher risk than equities.
- Private equity returns have less than perfect positive correlation with returns on traditional investments, so there are diversification benefits of including private equity investments in investment portfolios. Prior to reading too much into these results, however, it is important to bear in mind that (like hedge fund indexes) private equity returns indexes rely on self-reporting. They are therefore

subject to survivorship and backfill biases, both of which lead to overstated returns. In addition, in the absence of a liquidity event, private equity firms may not mark to market their investment portfolios on a regular basis, which leads to understatement of (1) measures of volatility and (2) correlations with other investments. Evidence also suggests that identifying skilled private equity fund managers is very important, as differences in returns between the top and bottom quartiles of PE funds are significant. Further, top-quartile funds tend to persistently perform better than others.

Portfolio Company Valuation

LOS 58f: Describe issues in valuing and calculating returns on private equity. Vol 6, pp 156–158

Investors typically use the following approaches to value companies in the private equity industry:

- *Market or comparables approach:* This is a relative valuation technique that uses equity multiples of different measures to value a company. Commonly used multiples include those based on earnings before interest, taxes, depreciation, and amortization (EBITDA), revenue, and net income. The value of these multiples is determined by looking at the value of similar publicly traded companies or transactions involving comparable businesses.
- *Discounted cash flow (DCF) approach:* This is an absolute valuation technique in which the value of a company is determined as the present value of its expected future cash flows.

  The value of the *company* is determined by discounting *free cash flow to the firm* at the *weighted average cost of capital*.

  The value of the company's *equity* is determined by discounting *free cash flow to equity* at the *cost of equity*.

Another (simpler) approach takes a measure such as income or cash flow, and divides it by a capitalization rate to estimate the value of the company.

- *Asset-based approach:* This approach values the equity of a company as the total value of its assets minus the value of its liabilities. Investors may use fair market values or liquidation values for assets. Liquidation values are lower, as they represent the amount that can be realized quickly if the company is in financial distress.

Private Equity: Investment Considerations and Due Diligence

Factors that must be considered when investing in private equity include:

- Current and anticipated economic conditions must be considered. Portfolio companies have a better chance of doing well if the economy is strong.
- Since private equity funds take on significant leverage, interest rates and capital availability expectations must also be considered.
- The quality of the GP is also very important. Investors should examine the following:

The GP's experience and knowledge (both financial and operating).

The valuation methodology used.

The alignment of the GP's incentives with the interests of the LPs.

The plan to draw on committed capital (since fees are charged on committed capital but returns come from capital drawn down and invested by the GP).

Planned exit strategies.

LESSON 4: MAJOR TYPES OF ALTERNATIVE INVESTMENTS, PART III: REAL ESTATE, INFRASTRUCTURE, AND COMMODITIES

LOS 58d: Describe real estate, commodities, infrastructure, and other alternative investments, including, as applicable, strategies, subcategories, potential benefits and risks, fee structures, and due diligence. Vol 6, pp 158–167

Real Estate

Real estate investments include direct and indirect ownership in real estate property (e.g., land and buildings) as well as lending against real estate property (e.g., providing a mortgage loan or purchasing mortgage-backed securities). Investors generally invest in real estate for the following reasons:

- It can offer competitive long-term total returns, driven by income generation and capital appreciation.
- Multiple-year leases with fixed rents for some property types provide stable cash flow that is relatively immune to economic shocks.
- It may offer diversification benefits due to its less than perfect positive correlation with other asset classes.
- It serves as an inflation hedge if rents can be adjusted quickly for inflation.

Forms of Real Estate Investment

Real estate investments can be classified into different forms on the basis of:

- Whether the investment is being made in the private or the public market. Investments in private markets can be made either directly or indirectly:
  - A direct investment can be made by investing in an asset (e.g., purchasing a house), or attaining a claim on an asset (e.g., through issuing a mortgage loan to the purchaser).
  - An indirect investment can be made through different investment vehicles (e.g., partnerships and commingled real estate funds [CREFs]).
    - Investments in public markets are usually made *indirectly* through ownership of securities that serve as claims on the underlying assets. Examples include investments in a real estate investment trust (REIT), a real estate operating company (REOC), or a mortgage-backed security (MBS).
    - Investments in REITs and REOCs are public equity investments in real estate.
    - Investments in MBS are public debt investments in real estate.

These securities are not considered alternative investments, but are classified as fixed-income securities.

- Whether the investment is structured as equity or debt:
  - An equity investor has an ownership interest in real estate or in securities of an entity that owns real estate. Equity investors have control over decisions such as whether to obtain a mortgage loan against the asset, who should be responsible for property management, and when to sell the real estate.
  - A debt investor is a lender who owns a mortgage loan or mortgage securities. Typically, the real estate serves as collateral for the loan, with the lender having a priority claim on the asset. The value of the equity investor's interest in the real estate is equal to the value of the real estate minus the amount owed to the lender.

See Table 4-1.

Table 4-1: Basic Forms of Real Estate

	Debt	Equity
Private	• Mortgages • Construction lending	• Direct ownership of real estate (sole ownership, joint ventures, real estate limited partnerships, or other commingled funds)
Public	• Mortgage-backed securities (residential and commercial) • Collateralized mortgage obligations	• Shares in real estate corporations • Shares in real estate investment trusts

Within these basic forms, the following variations exist:

- Direct ownership occurs when the title of the property is transferred to the owner and there is no financial lien (e.g., mortgage) on it.
- Leveraged ownership occurs when the property title is attained by the owner by investing her own funds combined with a mortgage loan.
- Financial institutions make debt investments in real estate by issuing mortgages.

Investments may be in the form of whole loans, which are based on specific properties (direct debt investments) or be made through investment in a pool of mortgage loans via publicly traded MBS (indirect debt investments).

Real Estate Investment Categories

- *Residential property:* Most individuals and families invest in a real estate residence with the intent to occupy it (i.e., they *purchase* a home), so real estate investment takes the form of a direct equity investment for them. Most buyers borrow funds to make the purchase. The funds are borrowed from financial institutions (originators), typically through mortgage loans. The originators of these loans make a direct debt investment in the home. Originators may hold mortgage loans on their balance sheets or securitize them to sell them as mortgage-backed securities (MBS) to investors. MBS are publicly traded securities and represent an indirect debt investment in real estate.

- *Commercial real estate:* Direct (equity and debt) investments in commercial real estate are generally considered appropriate for institutional funds and high net worth individuals due to the complexity of these investments, large investment amounts required, relative illiquidity of investments, and long investment horizons.
  - Direct equity investments also require active, experienced, professional management.
  - Direct debt investments require a thorough evaluation of the creditworthiness of the borrower and the ability of the property to generate enough cash to meet debt service payments.
  - REITs and commercial mortgage-backed securities (CMBS) offer individual investors the opportunity to make indirect equity and debt investments in real estate.
- *REIT investing:* REITs issue shares that are publicly traded. They invest in different types of real estate and provide retail investors access to a diversified real estate property portfolio that is professionally managed. REITs usually distribute all their taxable income to shareholders (in order to gain exemptions from paying income tax at the corporate/trust level). The risk and return characteristics of REIT investments usually depend on the types of investments they make:
  - Mortgage REITs are similar to fixed-income investments.
  - Equity REITs invest in commercial and residential properties and take on leverage, so they are similar to direct equity investments in leveraged real estate. They aim to maximize property occupancy rates and rents in order to maximize income and dividends.
- *Timberland and farmland:* These properties allow investors to generate income through sales of the produced commodity or by leasing the land to another entity.
  - Factors that drive returns for timberland include biological growth, commodity price changes, and land price changes.
  - The primary return drivers of return for farmland are harvest quantities, commodity prices, and land price changes.

Real Estate Performance and Diversification Benefits

The performance of real estate may be measured using three different types of indexes:

1. *Appraisal indexes* use estimates of value (based on comparable sales or DCF analysis) as inputs. Appraisals are performed periodically, often annually, but some properties included in the index may have been valued more than a year earlier. As a result, index returns are relatively smooth and tend to understate volatility.
2. *Repeat sales (transactions-based) indexes* are constructed using changes in prices of properties that have sold multiple times over the period. These indexes suffer from sample selection bias, as the sample of properties used may not be representative of the entire set of properties available. Further, the set of properties that have transacted multiple times may be biased toward properties that have seen changes in value (increases or decreases) depending on the economic environment. The greater the number of sales and the wider the array of properties transacted, the more reliable the index.
3. *REIT indexes* are constructed using prices of publicly traded shares of REITs. The reliability of these indexes increases with the frequency of trading. Studies have shown that real estate as an asset class enjoys less than perfect positive correlation with stocks and bonds, so there may be diversification benefits to adding real estate investments to a portfolio containing traditional investments. The correlation

between real estate and equities is higher than the correlation between real estate and bonds because real estate and equities are affected similarly by the business cycle. However, note that the low correlation between real estate and other asset classes may be the result of the methods of index construction, so actual diversification benefits may be less than expected.

LOS 58f: Describe issues in valuing and calculating returns on real estate, commodities, and infrastructure. Vol 6, pp

Real Estate Valuation

Real estate may be valued using the following approaches:

- *Comparable sales approach:* Under this approach the value of a property is estimated based on recent sales of comparable properties. Adjustments are made for differences between the subject and comparable properties with respect to size, age, location, and condition. Further, adjustments must be made for changes in market conditions between dates of sales.
- *Income approach:* Two income-based approaches to real estate valuation are the direct capitalization approach and the discounted cash flow (DCF) approach.

  The *direct capitalization approach* estimates the value of a property by dividing expected net operating income (NOI) generated by the property by a growth implicit capitalization rate (also referred to as the cap rate). Generally, when income and value are growing constantly at the same rate, the cap rate equals the discount rate minus the growth rate. The cap rate is based on cap rates on sales of comparable properties, general business conditions, property quality, and the quality of management.

  The *discounted cash flow approach* estimates the value of a property as the present value of its expected future cash flows over a specific investment horizon plus the present value of an estimated resale value (or reversion value) at the end of the holding period. This resale value is generally estimated using the direct capitalization approach.

- *Cost approach:* Under this approach the value of a property is estimated as its replacement cost, which equals the total cost that would be incurred to buy the land and construct a new, but similar, property on that site. This estimate of current replacement cost is adjusted for the location and condition of the subject property.

REIT Valuations

REITs may be valued using an income-based approach or an asset-based approach.

- Income-based approaches for valuing REITs are similar to the direct capitalization approach for valuing individual properties (described previously) in that a measure of income is capitalized into a value using an appropriate cap rate. Two common measures of income used are:

  Funds from operations (FFO): This is calculated as net income plus depreciation charges on real estate property (because it is a noncash charge and is often unrelated to the actual value of the property) less gains from sales of real estate property plus losses on sales of real estate property (as these are assumed to be non-recurring).

Adjusted funds from operations (AFFO): This is calculated by adjusting FFO for recurring capital expenditures (so it is similar to a measure of free cash flow).

- Asset-based approaches aim to determine a REIT's net asset value (NAV) by subtracting the value of its total liabilities from the estimated total market value of its assets.

Real Estate Investment Risks

Property values may fluctuate because of national and global economic conditions, local real estate conditions, and interest rate levels. Other risks for REIT investors include the ability of fund managers to select, finance, and manage the properties. These management issues affect the returns to both debt and equity investors. Changes in government regulations are another risk factor that must be considered.

Investments in distressed investments and property development entail even greater risks. Additional risk factors when it comes to property development include regulatory issues (e.g., failure to receive zoning, occupancy, and other approvals and permits), construction delays, and cost overruns. Further, if temporary financing is used to fund initial acquisition and development, there is a risk that long-term financing with acceptable terms may not be available when desired. Finally, many equity investment real estate funds use leverage to enhance potential returns. Investors must bear in mind that while it can improve returns, leverage also increases risk to equity as well as debt investors.

Example 4-1

A beachfront property located along the coast of northern Virginia consists of weekly rental units, a playground, a swimming pool, and a volleyball pit. The property operates at about 50% capacity during peak season. The owners are a local family looking to sell because it has been generating losses for several years and needs significant capital for upgrades. The building has structural damage, including bathrooms that have not been renovated for 20 years. The property is located in a prime area but has lost market share to newer buildings in its immediate vicinity. In addition, there is a turtle sanctuary on the south part of the property that is the breeding ground for sea turtles.

A private equity firm considers buying the property and believes the optimal strategic plan is to demolish the building and construct a new one.

Identify the relevant risks.

Solution:

1. The primary risk is the operating risk of demolition, new construction, and then operation of the new property. The private equity firm should prepare for cost overruns, construction delays, and weather issues. It should make certain it is properly insured for the demolition and protected against severe weather events.
2. There will be financial risk if any leverage is used at any stage of the process.
3. The private equity firm should perform due diligence to determine the regulations associated with demolition and reconstruction, especially since this is a distressed property.
4. There could be political risks that might include environmental groups making certain the turtle sanctuary is protected as well as the health and social cost of demolition. The private equity firm should hire a public relations firm to manage the political and social issues.

Infrastructure

The assets underlying infrastructure investments are real, capital-intensive, long-lived assets. They are intended for public use and provide essential services. Typically, infrastructure assets are financed, owned, and operated by governments.

The private sector is increasingly becoming more involved in infrastructure investments with an intention to (1) lease the assets back to the government, (2) sell newly constructed assets to the government, or (3) hold and operate the assets.

- Investors are tempted to hold and operate infrastructure assets when (1) there is relatively inelastic demand for the assets and services, and (2) the high costs of the assets create high barriers to entry, both of which result in a strong competitive position for the service provider.
- Investors expect these assets to generate stable cash flows, which adjust for economic growth and inflation.
- Investors may also expect capital appreciation, depending on the type of investment.

Benefits of Investing in Infrastructure

Investing in infrastructure may enable investors to:

- Add a steady income stream to their portfolios.
- Further diversify their portfolios, as infrastructure assets exhibit low correlation with other investments.
- Gain some inflation protection.

Since they typically entail investments in long-lived assets, infrastructure investments may also better match the longer-term liability structure of some institutional investors (e.g., pension funds and life insurance companies).

Infrastructure investments have become more popular over recent years due to increased interest by investors (demand side) and a greater desire by governments to privatize the provision of services and the underlying assets (supply side).

Categories of Infrastructure Investments

Infrastructure investments are frequently categorized based on underlying assets. They can be categorized (1) as economic or social infrastructure assets, (2) as brownfield or greenfield investments, and (3) by geographical location.

Economic versus Social Infrastructure Assets

- Economic infrastructure assets support economic activity. They include assets such as transportation and utility assets.
    - Transportation assets include roads, bridges, tunnels, airports, ports, and railway lines.
    - Utility assets include assets to transmit, store, and distribute gas, water, and electricity; generate power; treat waste; and broadcast and transmit information.

Note that assets that broadcast and transmit information may also be categorized separately as communication assets.

- Social infrastructure assets are directed toward human activities. They include assets such as education, healthcare, and correctional facilities.

Brownfield versus Greenfield Investments
These categories are based on the stage of development of the underlying assets.

- Brownfield investments refer to investments in existing investable infrastructure assets.

    These assets may be currently owned by a government that wants to (1) privatize the asset, (2) lease out the asset, or (3) sell and lease back the asset.

    Typically, some financial and operating history regarding the asset is available.

- Greenfield investments refer to investments in infrastructure assets that are to be constructed.

    The intent may be to (1) hold and operate the assets or (2) lease or sell the assets to the government after construction.

In addition to category, stage of development, and geographical location of the underlying assets, risks and expected returns on infrastructure investments also vary across forms of investment.

Example 4-2

Booker Capital (BC) is a private equity firm specializing in infrastructure investments. It has made or intends to make the following investments to generate a predictable income stream as well as gain some benefits of diversification:

1. The state of Pennsylvania has sold its turnpike system to a group of private investors that includes BC. BC is a minority owner and will have no management responsibility but has a claim on 18% of the operating cash flows from the tolls generated by the turnpike.
2. BC purchased a regional Arkansas prison facility that houses nonviolent state criminals. It owns 100% of the system and hired a reputable prison management firm to operate it.
3. The state of Delaware recently announced it intends to sell one of its bridges. BC expects to purchase the bridge for USD 50 million and then lease it back to the state.
4. The state of Maryland wants to build a bridge across the northern part of the Chesapeake Bay. BC hopes to be part of a consortium of private equity firms that manage the construction, operation, and maintenance of this new bridge.

Identify the types of infrastructure projects.

Solution:

1. Economic infrastructure.
2. Social infrastructure.
3. Brownfield investment.
4. Greenfield investment.

Direct versus Indirect Investments

Direct investments in infrastructure assets result in investors controlling the assets and having the opportunity to capture the entire value on offer. However, they entail a very large capital commitment, which gives rise to concentration and liquidity risk in investor portfolios. Further, investors then bear the responsibility of managing and operating the assets. Most investments in infrastructure are indirect.

Indirect investments include shares of (1) companies, (2) exchange-traded funds, (3) listed funds, (4) private equity funds, and (5) unlisted mutual funds that invest in infrastructure. Investors who are most concerned about liquidity may choose to invest through (1) publicly traded infrastructure securities and/or (2) master limited partnerships (MLPs). In addition to liquidity, publicly traded infrastructure securities provide reasonable fees, transparent governance, market prices, and the ability to diversify across underlying assets. Unfortunately, however, these securities represent a small segment of the infrastructure investment universe and tend to be relatively concentrated in categories of assets.

Master limited partnerships (MLPs) trade on exchanges and are pass-through entities similar to real estate investment trusts (REITs).

- Regulations regarding MLPs tend to vary across countries.
- Most of the free cash flow is passed on to investors. However, investors are liable for taxes on that income.
- Typically, a general partner manages the partnership, receives a fee, and holds a small partnership interest. Limited partners own the remaining partnership interest.

Risks and Returns Overview

Low-risk infrastructure investments have more stable cash flows and higher dividend payout ratios. They typically have less growth, however, and lower expected returns.

- An investment in an MLP with a brownfield investment in an asset that is being leased back to a government, such as a school, is a low-risk infrastructure investment.
- An investment in a private equity fund with a greenfield investment is a riskier investment.

Risks of investing in infrastructure include:

- Revenues not meeting expectations.
- Leverage, which may give rise to financing risk.
- Operational risk.
- Construction risk.
- Regulatory risk. Since infrastructure assets often provide services that are very important to society, governments typically regulate certain aspects, including the sale of the underlying assets, operations of the assets including service quality, and prices/profit margins.

Commodities

Investments in physical commodities entail costs for transportation and storage. As a result, most commodity investors prefer to trade commodity derivatives instead of actual physical commodities. However, it is still very important for investors to understand demand and supply dynamics in the market for physical commodities, as the prices of commodity derivatives are influenced to a large extent by underlying commodity prices. Commodity derivatives include futures and forward contracts, options contracts, and swaps contracts. Other commodity investment vehicles include:

- *Exchange-traded funds (ETFs):* These are suitable for investors who are limited to only investing in equities. ETFs may invest in commodities or commodity futures. Further, they may use leverage, and their expense ratios are typically lower than those for most mutual funds.
- *Common stock of companies exposed to a particular commodity:* For example, an investor who wants to gain exposure to oil may invest in an oil company like British Petroleum. Investors pursuing this strategy should bear in mind that the performance of their chosen stocks may not track the performance of the underlying commodity very closely.
- *Managed futures funds:* These are actively managed investment funds that may focus on specific commodity sectors or be broadly diversified. They are similar to hedge funds in that they charge management fees and incentive fees. Further, they may restrict sales to high net worth individuals and institutional investors (like hedge funds) or they may make shares available to the general public (like mutual funds). Investors usually prefer a structure similar to mutual funds, as they are more professionally managed, have low minimum investment requirements, and have relatively high liquidity.
- *Individual managed accounts:* These are managed by professional money managers on behalf of high net worth individuals or institutional investors.
- *Specialized funds:* These funds specialize in specific commodity sectors (e.g., oil and gas).

Commodity Performance and Diversification Benefits

Studies have shown that over the period from 1990 to 2010:

- Commodities earned a lower annual return than stocks and bonds.
- Commodity returns had a higher standard deviation (risk) than stocks and bonds.
- As a result, the Sharpe ratio for commodities as an asset class was much lower than for stocks and bonds.

On a positive note, commodities have a relatively low correlation with stocks and bonds, which suggests that there are diversification benefits from adding commodities to a portfolio consisting of traditional asset classes. Further, an argument can be made for commodities serving as a hedge against inflation. However, this is merely due to the fact that several commodities (e.g., energy and food) are heavily weighted in consumer price indexes. The volatility of commodity prices is much higher than the volatility of reported consumer inflation. Investors should be wary of commodity investments, especially when combined with leverage, as returns can exhibit high volatility. Such strategies have led to catastrophic losses for many investors.

Commodity Prices and Investments

Spot prices for commodities are a function of supply and demand, costs of production and storage, value to users, and global economic conditions.

- Demand for commodities depends on global manufacturing dynamics and economic growth. Investors anticipate demand changes by looking at economic events, government policy, inventory levels, and growth forecasts.
- Supply of many commodities is relatively inelastic in the short run as a result of the extended lead times required to increase production (e.g., to drill oil wells or to plant crops).
- As a result, commodity prices tend to fluctuate widely in response to changes in demand. Note that both demand and supply are affected by the actions of non-hedging investors (speculators).

Pricing of Commodity Futures Contracts

The price of a futures contract on a commodity may be calculated as follows:

$$\text{Futures price} = \text{Spot price} \times (1 + \text{Risk-free short-term rate}) + \text{Storage costs} - \text{Convenience yield}$$

Holders of commodities lose out on the interest that they would have earned had they held cash. Further, they incur storage costs on commodities. The long position in the futures contract gains possession of the commodity in the future without investing cash at present and avoids incurring storage costs. Therefore:

- The spot price is multiplied by $(1 + r)$ to account for the time value of money.
- Storage costs are added in computing the futures price.

On the other hand, the buyer of a futures contract gives up the convenience of having physical possession of the commodity and having it available for use immediately. Therefore, the futures price is adjusted for the loss of convenience. The convenience yield is subtracted to arrive at the futures price. The futures price may be higher or lower than the spot price of a commodity, depending on the convenience yield.

- When futures prices are higher than the spot price (when there is little or no convenience yield), prices are said to be in contango.
- When futures prices are lower than the spot price, prices are said to be in backwardation.

There are three sources of return on a commodity futures contract:

1. *Roll yield:* The difference between the spot price of a commodity and the futures price, or the difference between the futures prices of contracts expiring at different dates.
2. *Collateral yield:* The interest earned on the collateral (margin) deposited to enter into the futures contract.
3. *Spot prices:* These are influenced by current supply and demand.

Other Alternative Investments

Collectibles include antiques and fine art, fine wine, rare stamps and coins, jewelry and watches, and sports memorabilia.

- They do not provide current income, but have potential for long-term capital appreciation, can diversify a portfolio, and can also be a source of enjoyment for owners.
- They can fluctuate dramatically in value and can be relatively illiquid.
- Investors must have some degree of expertise to make wise investing decisions.
- Storage costs can be significant (e.g., for wine and art).

LESSON 5: RISK MANAGEMENT

LOS 58g: Describe risk management of alternative investments.
Vol 6, pp 176–179

Risk Management Issues

- Investments in certain types of alternative investments require long holding periods. For example, private equity funds and hedge funds have long lockup periods.
- Hedge funds and private equity funds are less transparent than other investments, as they may consider their investment strategies to be proprietary information.
- Investments in many alternative investments are relatively illiquid.

Risk Issues for Implementation

- Indexes are widely used to track the performance of several types of alternative investments. Historical returns on those indexes and the standard deviations of their returns may not really be representative of the risk-return characteristics of alternative investments.
- Reported correlations between alternative investments and traditional investments can be very different from actual correlations.
- There can be significant differences between the performance of an individual portfolio manager or fund and the performance of the overall investment class.
- Large investors can diversify across managers/funds, but small investors cannot.
- Hedge fund managers who have incurred large losses tend to liquidate their funds instead of trying to offset those losses.

Risk-Return Measures

Given the illiquid nature of most alternative investments, estimates of value (as opposed to actual transaction prices) may be used for valuation purposes. As a result, returns data may be smoothed and the standard deviation of returns may be understated. This makes the Sharpe ratio an inappropriate risk-return measure for alternative investments. In addition, the distribution of returns for most alternative investments is non-normal. Returns generally tend to be leptokurtic and negatively skewed (positive average returns but with higher than average risk of extreme losses). As a result, measures of downside risk are more useful. Downside risk measures focus on the left side of the returns distribution curve. They include:

- *Value at risk (VaR):* This estimates the minimum amount of loss expected over a given time period at a given probability.
- *Shortfall or safety-first measures:* These measure the probability that the value of the portfolio will fall below a minimum acceptable level over a given period. These measures use the standard deviation, so they underestimate risk for a negatively skewed distribution.
- *Sortino ratio:* This measure of downside risk uses downside deviation as opposed to standard deviation as a measure of risk.

It is very important to understand and evaluate tail events (low-probability, high-severity instances of stress) when it comes to certain types of alternative investments. Stress testing or scenario analysis is commonly performed to better understand potential losses.
See Table 5-1 for an overview of due diligence.

Example 5-1

Walter Burns, CFA, has a client with multiple alternative investments in her portfolio, including both physical bars of gold and gold futures contract positions, three real estate properties, shares in a hedge fund, and game jerseys from 10 Super Bowls, which she proudly displays in her residential entertainment room.

1. Discuss risk issues facing this client.
2. Describe two risk measures that would be appropriate to evaluate her portfolio.

Solution:

1. Investors seek alternative investments for diversification, and this client most likely has a diversified alternative investment portfolio with a range of different assets that are not likely correlated with each other and her larger portfolio. One concern is the ability to accurately measure this correlation. It is very likely there is enough data to compute correlation coefficients between and among gold, hedge fund returns, and estimates of the real estate properties. The investment in Super Bowl jerseys is more problematic, however, as there is not much data on these prices and this could lead to inaccurate correlation estimates. In addition, the estimated correlations might significantly differ from actual correlations, especially during times of economic stress.
2. Value at risk is a good tool for Walter to use as a downside measure of risk, as it will provide expected minimum losses at specific probabilities. For example, if the client's alternative portfolio is valued at USD 10 million, Walter might compute a value at risk of $175,000 at the 5% level. In addition, the Sortino ratio is appropriate to use because it considers only one side of the standard deviation to evaluate the risk-adjusted performance of an asset.

Table 5-1: Due Diligence Overview

Organization	• Experience and quality of management team, compensation, and staffing
	• Analysis of current and prior funds
	• Track record and alignment of interests
	• Reputation and quality of third-party service providers (lawyers, auditors, and prime brokers)
Portfolio Management	• Investment process
	• Target market and asset types and strategies
	• Sourcing of investments
	• Role of operating partners
	• Underwriting
	• Environmental and engineering review process
	• Integration of asset management, acquisitions, and dispositions
	• Disposition process, including how initiated and executed
Operation and Controls	• Reporting and accounting methodology
	• Audited financial statements and other internal controls
	• Frequency and approach to valuations
	• Insurance and contingency plans
Risk Management	• Fund policies and limits
	• Risk management policy
	• Portfolio risk and key risk factors
	• Leverage and currency risks, constraints, and hedging
Legal Review	• Fund structure
	• Registrations
	• Existing or prior litigation
Fund Terms	• Management and performance fees and expenses
	• Contractual terms
	• Investment period, fund term, and extensions
	• Carried interest
	• Distributions
	• Conflicts
	• Limited partners' rights
	• Key person and other termination procedures